The People's Gardener

Jim Buttress

The People's Gardener

A Marvellous Life
From the Royal Parks and RHS
to Britain in Bloom

SIDGWICK & JACKSON

First published 2016 by Sidgwick & Jackson
an imprint of Pan Macmillan
20 New Wharf Road, London N1 9RR
Associated companies throughout the world
www.panmacmillan.com

ISBN 978-0-283-07255-0

Picture Acknowledgements
All photographs are from the author's collection, with the exception of the following:
Page 10, top: © *The Times* / News Syndication
Page 13 and 14, top: courtesy of Tom Hart Dyke
Page 14, bottom: © *Gardeners' World Magazine* / Paul Debois
Page 15: © *Oldham Chronicle*

1 3 5 7 9 8 6 4 2

A CIP catalogue record for this book is available from the British Library.

Typeset by Ellipsis Digital Limited, Glasgow
Printed and bound by CPI Group (UK) Ltd, Croydon, CR0 4YY

Visit **www.panmacmillan.com** to read more about all our books
and to buy them. You will also find features, author interviews and
news of any author events, and you can sign up for e-newsletters
so that you're always first to hear about our new releases.

To Linda, for forgiving me for
forgetting her birthday
every year . . .

Contents

Foreword

Among all the gardeners I know, Jim Buttress is a one-off. Always affable, he is ever ready with a chat about the current state of the weather, the latest plant he has discovered, the state of the nation or the state of his vegetables. There is nothing unusual about that, I agree. But he also has a morbid fascination with Crystal Palace football club and a predilection for bowler hats, which he wears when judging at Royal Horticultural Society shows. He is, to my knowledge, the only man who still adopts this traditional headgear when considering the finer points of a trio of parsnips or a plate of tomatoes. The symbol of authority was abandoned by the aristocracy long ago, but Jim likes to keep the tradition going. He's funny like that.

He is, by all accounts, a stranger to modern technology, but that is in some ways an advantage, for his grasp of the other realities of life is clearly heightened by his refusal to get bogged down in the likes of Twitter and Facebook – one of the many things we have in common.

I can't remember when I first met him, but it is at least forty years ago and would have occurred at an RHS flower show. We still meet every year – and always at the Chelsea Flower Show – and share three post-nominal letters that delight and astonish us. We are both recipients of the RHS Victoria Medal of Honour (VMH), an accolade bestowed by the Society on no more than sixty-three people at any one time, one for each year of Queen Victoria's reign. We were both surprised to be so recognized and both, in Jim's words, 'chuffed to bits'.

His memoir is unlike many others I have read in that the voice of the writer leaps so clearly from the page. Can voices leap? I think so. Jim's style, character, opinions and prejudices shine through and make this a refreshing autobiography.

He is what P. G. Wodehouse would have called 'a good egg', though even 'Plum' would have had to use all his powers of invention to create Jim Buttress – a sort of hybrid between the pig-keeper George Cyril Wellbeloved and Lord Emsworth's head gardener, Angus McAllister.

Here is a man comfortable in his own skin, whose story will make you smile and sigh sympathetically by turns. He is a man comfortable with plants and companionable with people and that, I reckon, is as good a compliment as anyone could have.

ALAN TITCHMARSH
February 2016

1. Ten Floors Up

Now where do you think the life story of an old-fashioned gardener with a London accent is going to begin? Islington? The East End? Clapham? All right then, how about somewhere a little bit further out. Enfield, perhaps? And what sort of house do you reckon he lived in? Well, it's got to be somewhere with a nice big garden, right?

Wrong.

I've spent the vast majority of my life working with some of nature's most beautiful creations, and it has to be said in some pretty incredible settings; but in order to be able to tell you about all this we first have to go a few miles north of the border, and then about a hundred feet up in the air, because believe it or not I spent the first year or so of my life on the tenth floor of a tenement in the East End of Glasgow. Salubrious it was not. A garden? We didn't even have a window box. We were fifteen minutes from the nearest park or shop, and because there were no lifts, about fifteen minutes from the ground.

Fortunately for me I was far too young to realize just how depressing it all was, but my poor old mum wasn't. My word, how she suffered.

Yours truly, James Cuthbert Buttress, was born on 28 January 1945 in Dennistoun, Glasgow, the eldest child of Owen Cuthbert Buttress, who was born 9 March 1914, and Barbara Patience Buttress (née Raphael) who was born 21 November 1911.

Mum and Dad, or Pop as I usually refer to him, had met a couple of years before down in Worthing in Sussex, which is where Mum was from. She was working as a librarian at the time. The Connaught Theatre, a beautiful art deco building, was next door and whoever was appearing in Rep that month would come into the library to learn their scripts. It was warm, dry and, most importantly, quiet! Mum used to absolutely love this as she got to see many of her heroes and heroines in the flesh. She used to just sit there staring at them as they read.

My mum was a real giggler, and this got her into awful trouble one day with the captain of the local Home Guard, who, believe it or not, happened to be the local bank manager! She and one of her colleagues came walking out of the library one day when they saw the Home Guard putting sandbags between the columns outside the library and placing gas pipes in between the bags to look like guns. When Mum saw this she broke into fits of giggles and old Captain Bank Manager didn't like it.

'Madam!' he barked. 'May I remind you we're at war!'

Because of that whenever Mum watched an episode of *Dad's Army* she'd cry with laughter.

Pop meanwhile had been doing his bit for the Navy. He was a lieutenant gunnery officer while he served, first on a troop carrier called the *Nieuw Amsterdam*, which used to take the troops out to places like South Africa, and then, after complaining that he hadn't seen enough action, on the Atlantic convoys. These were targeted by the German U-boats of course and so he certainly got his wish. Like a lot of servicemen and women who served in the war he never liked talking about his experiences.

'What's the point in talking about it, boy,' he used to say. 'It's all gone now.'

When I was a boy, Remembrance Sunday was the only time I was reminded that he'd been involved in the conflict. We'd usually be down the allotment me and Pop, and just before 11 a.m. if I was close by he'd say, 'Go on, boy, off you go,' and I'd have to run off to the other end of the allotment. Once I was out of the way he'd stand up and observe the two minutes' silence. In hindsight it was quite sad watching him stand there, alone with his memories.

Towards the end of the war Pop was stationed in Worthing, which is how he met Mum. Now I don't know how many of you have been to Worthing, but the Gorbals it ain't. For a start it's by the seaside – something Glasgow has never claimed to be – and from memory there aren't that many large blocks of flats. Back then the Gorbals was quite a desperate area, full of poverty, deprivation and violence, and on top of this it had taken a hammering from the German bombers. Poor old Mum. She was eight months pregnant when Pop was sent up there and on top of being holed up on her own in a flaming rabbit hutch seven days a week, when she did manage to make it down the ten flights of stairs to something approaching civilization she couldn't understand a single bloody word anyone said. They hadn't been married a year at the time and so she must have been wondering why she'd bothered. Pop was old-school you see, and he took his job training the Navy cadets very seriously. This meant that if he wasn't kipping, he was working, and that was all that mattered. We were still at war too and so everyone was preoccupied with that. You were just expected to get on with it.

Worse was still to come though, because on top of being dragged from Worthing to Glasgow and then thrown into solitary confinement, Mum was about to give birth to me – the baby from hell – and during one of the worst winters on record.

The birth itself was long and quite difficult by all accounts, and when I did decide to put in an appearance I wasn't exactly what you'd call a cuddly baby. In fact, according to Mum, the moment I popped out I did four things: crapped, screamed, peed and belched – and sometimes in unison. I never slept either, or if I did it was the odd half hour here or there. I don't remember any of this of course but it obviously left a bit of a mark on Mum because she used to love telling me.

'You were a nightmare when you were a baby,' she'd often say after a couple of gins. 'Honestly, Jim, you could have grown a whole field of roses with what you produced in a day.'

In all seriousness, it must have been a living hell for the poor old girl and although Mum never said as much I'm sure she must have suffered from depression. Think about it: you're ten floors up with nowhere to go, it's minus ten outside and the only company you've got is a noisy little human fertilizer production unit who refuses to go to sleep. I'm surprised she lasted as long as she did.

I remember talking to Mum about all this one day and I asked her why she never told Pop how bad she was feeling.

'It would have made me feel like I'd failed at being a mother,' she said to me. Do you know, that broke my heart.

Fortunately some help did eventually arrive in the shape of an old sea captain who lived in the same block as us. He was caled Stanislaw Lubez, which is eastern European. I could be wrong but I have a feeling he was from Poland originally and had settled in Scotland after the First World War. Anyway, he'd obviously been keeping a close eye on Mum and after a couple of months of motherhood he could tell that she was at breaking point. You see the effect I have on people? Nothing's changed.

He was the only person she ever saw on a day-to-day basis apart from Pop, and one day while she was collecting the milk he stopped her. Mum remembered the entire conversation.

'You look absolutely terrible,' he said, which obviously must have made her feel better.

'Look, why don't you leave the baby with me? You need a rest.'

'I can't do that,' said Mum. 'He'll just scream. You must have heard him? That's all he does.'

Heard me? Unless he was deaf or had soundproofing he'd have had no choice.

'Yes, once or twice,' he replied. 'But it's no problem. Look, I promise I'll take good care of him. You have to look after yourself too, my dear. Now why don't you go and get your hair done or something. I know it's not much of a place but there are plenty of hairdressers.'

Under normal circumstances Mum would obviously have thought twice about leaving her newborn baby with somebody she hardly knew, but at the time she was desperate. Talk about a shot in the arm, though. Once he'd talked her into it she had me wrapped up, packed up, and into his flat before you could say shampoo and set. She was certain it was going to be a once in a lifetime offer, on account of me probably making his life as miserable as hers, and so she rushed off to make the most of it. It was exactly what she needed. But what do you think greeted her when she got back? A sleeping baby Buttress, something she'd hardly ever seen before. Mum couldn't believe her eyes.

'How did you do it?' she asked him.

'Oh, it's just a knack, my dear. Honestly, he's been as good as gold.'

A few months later when they'd got to know each other better she pressed him again on his sleep trick and Stanislaw admitted to Mum that he'd put a drop of Scotch into my milk.

'I used to do the same with my nieces and nephews when they were young,' he'd said to her. 'It was the only way to shut them up!'

Although it probably doesn't happen these days I know lots of mums and dads who, back in the day, rubbed a little bit of whisky on the gums of their young 'uns, especially if he or she was teething. But pouring it into their milk? No wonder I slept! I must have been one of the first babies ever to wake up at the age of two months with a bloody hangover. All I can say is, thank God it wasn't real ale, otherwise I'd never have made it past infancy.

Do you know what, though, that relationship he had with Mum worked both ways because although the old sea captain had some family back in Poland or wherever, he had absolutely nobody in Scotland, not to mention bugger all to do, and so having me to look after gave him a purpose in life. Sure, I might have been a whinging little pain in the arse, but for the time I was in his care I was *his* whinging little pain in the arse, and that obviously brought a bit of meaning and responsibility into what was probably quite a humdrum existence. Mum got out, he got me, and I got pissed. Marvellous!

Because Pop wanted to have me baptized (he was a devout Catholic and Mum a Protestant), old Stanislaw ended up becoming my one and only godparent. He was the only person they knew up in Glasgow and as Stanislaw was also Catholic – not to mention a seafaring gentleman – Pop came to look on him like an uncle, and so when it came to recruiting a poor unfortunate to take on yours truly he was happy to be welcomed on board. He told Mum that becoming my guardian was one of the proudest moments of his life. How about that?

Now before I move on, let me just tell you what happened to Stanislaw, because although we moved from Glasgow soon after Pop was demobbed – much to Mum's relief, of course – we obviously kept in touch with the old captain and, let me tell you, he took his duties as a godfather very seriously indeed.

I'm sure some of you will remember this, but when I was a kid there used to be these removal companies that did all the parcel deliveries for the Royal Mail, and every birthday and Christmas one of the removal vans would arrive at our house. I remember it as if it were yesterday. Out would hop a man wearing a brown coat, he'd hand Mum a parcel, which was addressed to me, and I'd start jumping up and down with excitement. I used to sit there for days on end waiting for these blokes to arrive and when they did I could have exploded. Inside the parcel would be a lovely card with something like a racing car or an aeroplane on the front and a nice message inside, a letter for Mum and Pop letting them know what was happening, and then a present for me. Let's be honest, that was what I was waiting for. How many kids do you know who open the card first, unless they're told to? No chance! The moment that brown paper was off I knew exactly what to do, and my word did he spoil me. I got the lot: Monopoly, Escalado, Cluedo, Carpet Bowls – you name it, he sent it, and I remember every single game was made by Waddingtons, who were the Rolls-Royce of toy manufacturers. Seriously, if you got something made by Waddingtons when I was a boy, you were chuffed to flaming bits. The only downside to all these presents came at Christmas, or to be exact Boxing Day, because as soon as I'd had my breakfast Mum would sit me down with a pad of paper, a pencil and a load of envelopes and she'd say, 'Right then, Jim, thank you letters.'

I hated it.

Not because I wasn't grateful to the people who'd sent me presents, I was over the bloody moon! I just couldn't stand writing letters. It would have been all right if mum had let me just write: Dear so and so, Thank you ever so much for my present. It's terrific. Best wishes, Jim – but, oh no, I had to put chapter and verse in there. I had to say how I was doing at school and tell them which sports I was in to. It used to take me hours. And God forbid I spelt any words incorrectly.

'That's wrong,' she'd bark. 'Start again!'

You know what kids are like. They want to be out there playing with everything.

When it got to my ninth birthday nothing arrived from the old boy and I remember Pop looking at me and saying, 'I think he's gone, Jim. You know what he's like, he never misses. I'll get your mother to write him a letter just in case he's ill or something.' He didn't have a phone so that was the only way we could check.

Before Mum could even pick up a pen and paper a letter arrived from a solicitor informing them that Stanislaw had indeed passed away, but that he'd left me £500 in his will. He was a good age, by the way, at least eighty-five. Five hundred quid, though. Do you know that's the equivalent of about £10,000 today? Ten grand!

Seriously, what a wonderful old boy he was. The presents and the money were marvellous of course, but the best thing old Stanislaw ever did for us was to befriend my mum, because if he hadn't offered to take baby Buttress off her hands every now and then, God only knows what might have happened. One thing's for sure, I'd have had fewer hangovers!

2. Granddad's Smallholding

The place we ended up moving to after Pop had been demobbed was Haywards Heath down in Sussex, which is about fifteen miles north of Brighton. I'm not sure exactly why they chose Haywards Heath but I'd say it probably had a lot to do with it being close to Mum's family, and so it was here that I started to get to know them all a bit better. Pop's too. We never saw hide or hair of anybody while we were up in Glasgow, not that I would have remembered, and so it was only when I was about a year old that all my grandparents and aunties and uncles got a look at me. Lucky old them, eh!

While we're here let me just give you a quick description of Mum and Pop. Mum was a very upright lady in the way she carried herself. She had brown hair and was quite slim. I suppose there was a touch of the Hyacinth Bucket about her. Only in looks though! Pop also had brown hair and because of his Navy background was also very upright and always walked with a straight back. When it comes to character they were polar opposites really. She was disorganized and never, ever knew where anything was, and he was like me (or me like him) and had everything in little neat piles. She always carried an enormous handbag and it was always stuffed with all kinds of everything. Chaos! Mum was also a bit of a social animal and she loved nothing more than going out for dinner or to a dance, whereas Pop used to prefer smaller gatherings.

Because he liked to be organized, whenever they did go to a dance Pop would always insist that they set off about two hours before and so they always arrived just as they were laying out the tables!

Perhaps because she was a librarian I've never known anybody read a book as quickly as my mum. She was a speed reader, and no mistake, and could get through them as fast as you could pass them to her.

Theirs was an old-fashioned kind of marriage. They weren't necessarily the perfect match, and if they'd been around today they might not have stayed together, but back then things were different and you just got on with it. They were most certainly devoted to each other though.

When it comes to gardening I can tell you exactly where my passion came from: old Pop – and he got it from his dad. Everyone called Pop Cuddy, by the way, which is an abbreviation of his middle name, Cuthbert. He was an only child and grew up in Forty Hill, which is a suburb of Enfield, and right on the edge of Forty Hill is a place called Myddelton House, which is the ancestral home of E. A. Bowles. These days it's home to one of the finest gardens you'll ever see anywhere in the country, not to mention one of the largest collections of bulbs, and this is all down to E. A. Bowles – or, as his friends used to call him, Gussie. Now Gussie Bowles was and still is an absolute legend within British horticulture, and as well as spending many years on the RHS Council he was also awarded, way back in 1916, the Victoria Medal of Honour (which I was awarded in 2006) and served as Vice President of the Society from 1926 until his death in 1954. Seriously, if you've never heard of Gussie Bowles, look him up, and if you've never been to Myddelton House, go!

Anyway, not only was Gussie Bowles a very dedicated and well-respected horticulturist, he was also a talent-spotter of young gardeners – not to mention mentor to dozens of other well-known gardeners – and it was this side of the old boy's character that very nearly landed Pop his dream job. This story makes me want to weep.

When he was just a nipper, Pop used to sit on a wall at the edge of his garden and when Gussie Bowles rode past in his pony and trap Pop would always give him a wave. I suppose it was like something out of *The Railway Children*. Anyway, one day, instead of waving back like he normally did, Gussie pulled up and started talking to Pop, and of course the first thing he asked him was whether he liked gardening.

'So, young sir. Do your parents have a garden?'

'Yes, they do, Mr Bowles.'

'And do you take any interest in said garden?'

'Yes, Mr Bowles. It's my hobby.'

Well, this was manna from heaven to old Bowlesy.

'Is it really, young man?' he said. 'In that case, how would you and your mother like to come up to Myddelton House for some tea?'

'I'm sure we'd be delighted, Mr Bowles.'

'Excellent! Tuesday next at 4 p.m., all right?'

Pop couldn't have been more than about seven or eight years of age at the time, but from then on he and Gussie Bowles became great pals. I mean, what an introduction!

So once a week Pop and his mum would go up to Myddelton House for tea, and then when he wasn't at school he would go up there again and help Gussie in the garden. He spent every minute of every holiday there, according to Pop. Not a bad apprenticeship, was it? It's like being taught football by Bobby Charlton.

The only problem with this arrangement was Pop's hay fever. He suffered terribly with it when he was a boy, and because there was no medication at the time he'd have to sit in a darkened room on his own for hours on end. Not much use to a gardener, eh?

Over the coming years Pop learned a lot from old Gussie and Myddelton House became like his second home. Well, as you can imagine, by the time he was ready to leave school there was only one thing Pop wanted to do with his life, and that was to get his hands dirty.

'I'll tell you what, Owen,' said Gussie. 'Why don't you come and work for me? I can't afford to pay you much but I can train you up and then help you become a student at RHS Wisley. How does that sound?'

What an opportunity! Pop had dreamed about going to Wisley, and with Gussie being a member of the RHS Council, not to mention one of the most respected horticulturalists in the country, providing he worked hard and kept his nose clean he would have been a shoe-in. No doubt about it.

This doesn't have a happy ending, I'm afraid. You see when Pop went home to tell his dad the good news the poor boy got the shock of his life. Instead of jumping for joy his dad just looked at him, and said:

'I haven't wasted my money on a good education so you can become a gardener. Go and tell Mr Bowles that you're grateful for his offer but that you'll have to turn it down.'

And that was that.

He was absolutely devastated, and who can blame him? Do you know, Pop ended up spending his entire adult life working in the insurance industry, and all because his dad told him to. Sad, isn't it? I've got nothing against insurance people of course, and I think he even ended up enjoying it, but gardening wasn't just a course or a job Pop was forced to turn down, it was a vocation. All his old man could see was money, and because he'd educated his boy privately at

Ignatius College in Enfield, which back then was a very expensive Catholic school, a job in horticulture wasn't going to offer a good enough return on his investment.

Fortunately for me, my dad never lost his passion for gardening and as I became more and more interested in it he did nothing but encourage me. Apart from that first year in Glasgow we always had a garden where we lived, and Pop and I always had allotments. Well, he did. I was just his little helper.

As you might already have gathered, Pop's old man, Owen Buttress Snr, was as hard as bloody nails. He came from a long line of fruit and veg traders but was actually a master tailor by trade, and even had his own shop in Cambridge. It was profitable too – apparently he used to specialize in making gowns for all the masters and students. Granddad also had a business partner and one day, not long after Pop had started his life sentence in insurance, he decided that he was fed up with making clothes for other people and so sold his half of the business to his partner. Soon after that he and my grandma moved from Forty Hill to a place called Wickford in Essex, where they bought a lovely little smallholding. It's like an episode of *The Good Life*, isn't it? Seriously, that place was like paradise. Do you remember *The Darling Buds of May* by H. E. Bates? Well, it doesn't matter whether you've read the book or watched the TV series; this place was exactly the same. They grew everything there: strawberries, raspberries, gooseberries and blackberries. They had apple trees, pear trees and plum trees – and as for the veg? Well, it was never-ending. Lettuce, tomatoes, leeks, spuds, carrots, caulis, swede, courgettes: you name it, they grew it. Do you know the old boy even grew his own tobacco? He did. He used to cure it and then either roll his own or put it in a pipe. Golden Virginia it was not! It smelt more like cow dung. They had livestock too, and I remember there were pigs and goats running all over the place. I loved it.

This smallholding of theirs was right in the middle of nowhere, with no direct supply of electricity. To preserve the produce everything had to be pickled: the tomatoes, the cucumber, the eggs – everything. They were totally self-sufficient. There was no running hot water either, which meant that if you wanted to have a bath or wanted to wash some clothes you had to heat up the water on the Aga. I remember watching Grandma lifting out all these great big sheets and then running them through a huge mangle in the boiler shed. Talk about hard labour. As for the plumbing, though. Bloody hell! Unless you needed a number two it was always safer to go in the bushes.

Do you know, I must have been the only member of my entire family who got on with Granddad, and that includes his wife, Maud! I promise you, he was like a deterrent. How they had my dad I'll never know. For a start he was deeply religious. Now don't get me wrong, I've got nothing against people with a faith, regardless of which god they follow, but he was the kind of hard-liner who not only tried to ram it down people's throats, but also had no time whatsoever for anyone with a different opinion, and so people used to avoid him like the bloody plague. My mum in particular couldn't stand him. As I've mentioned, she was a Protestant, and so he did his best to make her life a misery. Do you know, by the time the old boy died she was a bigger atheist than he ever was a Catholic. Pop, although not nearly as fervent as Granddad, was also quite a religious man and this used to annoy Mum even more.

'You get it from him, don't you?' she'd bark.

Whenever I went to visit Granddad and Grandma I was immediately transported into what I considered to be heaven on earth, and so I was quite happy listening to all his religious ramblings. It just washed over my head. As far as I was concerned it was a small price to pay.

I haven't mentioned my brother and sister yet, have I? Well I'm the oldest of three. There's Caroline, who is four years younger than me, and Patrick, who is six years younger. You couldn't wish for a better brother or sister.

Well, unfortunately, little Caroline and Patrick used to absolutely hate going to Granddad's. They couldn't stand it. While I was out picking fruit, tethering goats and cleaning out the dog's kennel they'd be sitting in the air-raid shelter crying their eyes out. They wanted to be home with Mum, you see, reading a book or listening to *Children's Hour*; not chasing pigs and being berated by a religious geriatric. I, on the other hand, didn't mind one bit and so instead of running and hiding from the old rascal I used to follow him around. Consequently we became very close. God only knows what he thought of me.

They had a very strange bunch of neighbours down in Wickford. To the left of them was a chicken farmer and to the right of them a High Court judge. My God, he was eccentric. Wilberforce was his name, and I remember he used to have his own plane which he flew absolutely everywhere. He didn't have a licence or anything, just a plane, a big field behind his house and obviously a lot of confidence! We used to go picking mushrooms in that field of his and I was fascinated by the fact that they would just pop up overnight.

Despite being one of God's own Rottweilers Granddad used to absolutely love his sport, and he ended up taking me to my first ever football match. OK, I know that some of you might not be interested in the beautiful game, but it is relevant. You see, in addition to gardening, real ale and rabbiting on, the one big passion I have in life is sport – especially football – and so this was the start of something big for me. I promise I'll keep the footy chat to a minimum, by the way, but for the time being just humour me.

Now whatever he did in life, whether it was going to church or digging up spuds, Granddad always insisted on wearing a smart tweed suit, and I remember that he was wearing a suit like this when he picked me up and lifted me onto a double decker bus to go and watch Chelmsford City, his nearest club. Well, I absolutely loved it. I was only about six or seven years old at the time and it was the first live sporting event I ever went to. There were probably no more than five hundred in the stadium that afternoon but to me it felt more like a million. There were people chatting, cheering and shouting. It was incredible. My first 'atmosphere', if you like. I'd never experienced anything like it. I remember getting back on that bus after the game and, let me tell you, I was full of it.

'When can we go again, Granddad?'

'Who was it that scored the first goal?'

'Will he be playing next time?'

You couldn't shut me up.

About ten minutes into the journey back it all became too much for me and I flaked out on Granddad's knee. What a great day that was, and what a life-changer. About a year later, when I was eight, Pop took me to see Crystal Palace, who were our local team, and I've been following them ever since. No glory supporters in our house, thank you very much! I remember coming out and saying, 'That was great, Dad. When can I come again?' And he said, 'When you've saved up enough money!'

The big treat during a weekend visit to Granddad and Grandma's was Sunday tea. My word, what a spread. Grandma's sister and her husband used to come round and we'd all sit around the kitchen table. There in the middle would be a big old ham and next to it a huge loaf of home-made bread. Now the smell of that bread is something that has stayed with me from those days to this, and even now whenever I pass a bakery I'm immediately transported back to that kitchen. Surrounding the bread and the ham would be beetroot, tomatoes, boiled potatoes, spring onions, cheeses, pickles; and as I said, it was all home grown. I loved it!

God, he could be a miserable old bugger though. How my grandma never ended up throttling him I'll never know. She used to do everything she could to avoid him! He got worse as he got older. When Maud died he had to move into an old people's home in Westcliff-on-Sea and once a week Pop would go down and see him after work. The journey there and back used to take him hours and quite often he didn't get home until gone 11 p.m. Mum used to go bananas! Not that the old rascal ever thanked him. He would just pick holes in everything. 'You've brought me the wrong kind of tobacco,' or whatever. He was the original curmudgeon, my granddad.

Being at his smallholding made me fall head over heels in love with the outdoor life, and from the moment I first set foot on that place I think I knew that whatever I'd end up doing in life, it wasn't going to be under cover. It didn't matter if it was raining, snowing, hailing or blowing a gale – if I was out, I was happy.

Do you know, many years later I even considered taking up farming, because of Granddad and his smallholding. That is until Pop put me right.

'You don't have the brains, boy, and I don't have the money, so if I were you I'd stick to horticulture.'

How right he was.

3. Down the Allotment

As I said earlier on, since moving down from Glasgow we always had a big garden at the family home, and Pop's own obsession for growing had started rubbing off on me as early as the age of four. The words I always longed to hear him say were 'Are we off down the allotment, boy?'

I didn't need asking twice. It was like being told it was Christmas.

'Yes, Dad!' I'd shout, and in about five seconds flat I'd be standing by the front door with my wellies on.

'Don't forget your coat, otherwise your mother will kill me.'

It didn't matter what I was doing or what time of day or night it was, if Pop said, 'We're off,' that was it, I'd be up and at 'em.

I suppose I was spoiled for choice in a way because not only did we have the allotment – not to mention Granddad's smallholding – but we had a garden that must have been half the size of a football field. All right, I might be exaggerating there a bit but that's how I remember it. It was massive. Pop was also a dab hand when it came to things like carpentry and he taught me how to build garden sheds and chicken houses – the lot. As I said, I was his little helper.

I remember the chicken house we had at home. It was like a wooden village and he must have had about a hundred chickens in there. Once, when I was about five years old, Pop came into the house one Sunday afternoon with his hat in his hand.

'Come and see what I've got here, boy,' he said, and when I went over to look I couldn't believe it. As he took his hand away there in his hat were eight or nine chicks.

'I thought that fat one was getting broody. What do you think, boy?'

'I think they're marvellous, Dad. Can I name them?'

'No you can't!'

But Pop understood that I'd caught the bug, and from the moment I took an interest in gardening and the outdoor life he did nothing but encourage me. A year or two after I started getting involved he began taking me to all the gardening and flower and produce shows and of course that opened up a whole new world to me. We did a Chelsea or two together and we did local shows. He even took me up to places like Olympia for the big farming exhibitions. I may have been only five or six years of age but thanks to Pop I was already turning into quite a competent little gardener.

The first time I ever entered anything into a show was at Haywards Heath when I was about six. The local horticultural society used to have an annual Fruit, Veg and Flower Show on the village green. They had all the usual classes: flowers, veg, preserves, cakes. Things are pretty much the same to this day, all round the country. Nothing's changed really and why would we want it to?

Just to prove how old I am, I remember that the Civil Defence Volunteers, or the Home Guard as they were also known, used to put on a display. That'll take some of you back. It was fantastic. They'd pretend to set fire to a building or something and then rush in to rescue whoever was in there. Well, when they stretchered these poor buggers out they were all covered in tomato sauce. Pop used to stand there and laugh his head off but to me this was pure drama – the height of excitement.

After that they'd put on some showjumping, which used to keep the little girls happy, and then after that the judging would start. Well, as I'm sure you can imagine, from the moment they opened the gates to that show until the moment they closed them I was in the flower and produce tents gawping at all the entries. I'd go round each one time and time again with my pretend clipboard (no bowler in those days, though), and after a few hours I would have decided who my winners were, and, believe me, they were never that far away from the choice of the judges themselves.

One day, after a couple of years of playing judge at the Haywards Heath show, Pop had a word with me.

'I think it's about time you entered something, boy. What do you think?'

What did I think? I'd never been as terrified or excited about anything in my entire life.

When I was about six years old Pop had given me my own little patch at the end of our garden, and although it was under a tree and the soil wasn't brilliant I still managed to grow a few spuds there. In fact that was probably what locked me into gardening. Planting something yourself is a game changer and the day I picked my own produce for the first time is still one of the biggest thrills I've ever experienced. Sure, they weren't the best spuds the world had ever seen, but they were mine, and what's more I'd grown them!

Anyway, once Pop's suggestion had sunk in I set to work and by the time the Haywards Heath show came around I had in my possession a few pounds of fairly decent potatoes.

'They'll do, boy,' said Pop.

Come the day of the show, off we popped, and I presented my entry to the show secretary.

'My word, these do look good, young man. Where did you grow them?'

'I've got my own allotment.'

'Really?'

'Yes. It's at the bottom of our garden.'

Obviously the potatoes weren't placed but I got a certificate that said 'Well Done' on it, and best of all I got – wait for it – a rosette! Well, if I could have retired there and then I would have. I was absolutely over the moon. I felt like a proper gardener.

Later on that day after everyone had gone home, Pop and I went back to the village green – him with a big wheelbarrow and me with a small one – and we shovelled up all the horse manure. We weren't daft! I remember Mum went berserk.

'Cuddy, it's embarrassing. What if somebody sees you?'

'So what if they do? I'd have to pay for this normally.'

Once we got it all home (it took about five trips), Dad slipped me a shilling.

'Good job, boy,' he said.

I'll tell you, what a day!

When Pop was forced to actually purchase things for our allotment or garden he more often than not went to a local hardware shop called – I think – Grimsticks. It was around the corner from my first primary school, which I'll come on to in a bit, and like Granddad's smallholding it evokes all kinds of wonderful memories for me. They sold the lot there: pots, lime, fertilizer, compost, pea sticks, runner bean poles, tarred string and every kind of vegetable seed or bulb you can imagine. Things like lime and fertilizer – not to mention a lot of the seeds and bulbs – were all sold loose back in those days and this was the thing I enjoyed most. Once you'd told him what you wanted, let's say broad bean seeds, the old boy behind the counter would take a small brown paper bag and a scoop and then head off to the relevant tub. I'd always follow him, by the way. After he'd scooped the seeds in he'd then walk back behind the counter and seal up the bag using a label bearing both the Latin name – in this case *Vicia faba* – and underneath the English name. Now I know it's only a bloke in a brown coat putting some seeds in a bag, but if you add in the smell of the place (that was the tarred string), it was just amazing.

Do you know what my Christmas presents were in those days? Well, from the age of about four until I left home I'd get things like watering cans, trowels, wellington boots, spades, hoes or seeds. About November time I'd get a deluge of questions. 'What do you need, Jim? Are your wellies still holding up? How about a nice new fork?'

Apart from the toys my godfather used to send me I only ever received two non-gardening presents, and that was because I requested them. I used to ask for a *Thomas the Tank Engine* book and – best of all – a *Boy's Own* diary. I was a mad keen diarist right up until my early twenties. Back then I used to fill it with gardening stuff:

FRIDAY: Went to the allotment with Dad when he got home and we planted some leeks. Dad says if they're good enough we might enter them in the show.

SATURDAY: Helped Dad mend the chicken shed and then weeded the front garden. Still don't like weeding!

You know the sort of thing. Little notes on what Pop and I had been doing and what we hoped to achieve with what we'd planted.

By far my favourite Christmas or birthday present, which I started to get when I was a little bit older, was a voucher to buy seeds. This used to send me into a right state – and why? Because it meant I had to get myself a seed catalogue, and let's face it, you'd be hard pushed to find an adult anywhere in the country who as a child didn't like gazing at hundreds of colourful photos of whatever it was they were interested in. Some probably liked looking at bikes and some at dolls and things, but for me it was packets of seeds and what they grew into. I actually became obsessed by seed catalogues for a time. They were free, you see. Pop used to get a magazine each month called *Amateur Gardening*, which is still going to this day, and they used to carry adverts in the back for these seed companies who, if you asked them nicely, would send you a shiny new catalogue. I used to send off for about two or three every single month and have actually kept one or two. It was as much about getting your own post as anything else. It made me feel like a grown-up.

The one catalogue I remember most was from a company called Dobbies, who are also still going and are based up in Edinburgh. I'd sit there hour after hour after hour trying to decide which seeds I'd buy; in fact I don't think I ever actually wanted to decide, because when I did that was it, I was done. Looking at catalogues and wishing that you could buy something is one thing, but when you've got a voucher in your hand and can actually put in an order that's a different kettle of fish. It was the highlight of my year when I was a boy, and it would quite literally go on for weeks. The first thrill was getting the voucher of course, and then after that choosing my seeds. But filling in the order form? Well, that was something else. I loved writing every letter. After that I'd send it off and then wait nervously every morning for the postman to arrive. When eventually the envelope arrived – adorned with the words 'Dobbies of Edinburgh' on the front – I would nearly collapse with anticipation. There'd be something like fifteen or twenty packets in there and after getting them out of the envelope I'd line them all up in two rows and just look at them. How daft is that?

Eventually I'd get round to planting all these seeds, either in my patch in the garden or the little bit Pop had given me at the allotment, but to be honest I don't remember ever producing a great deal from them. That didn't matter though, at least when I was young. It was the process that mattered. Some of you will probably think it's all a little bit strange, but that's what floated my boat. I was the seed-king of Haywards Heath!

The best allotment we ever had was the one Pop got when we moved to Purley in Surrey, which is in the borough of Croydon. He'd got a promotion at the Norwich Union, I think, and so we were able to move a bit closer to London. There were also one or two good Catholic schools in Purley and so I'm sure that too would have had a bearing. That would have been in the early 1950s and it was yet another little demi-paradise which yours truly would quite happily have never, ever left. It was on something called the Round-shaw Park which was on the Roundshaw Estate near the Purley Way and it was situated right at the end of the runway of the old Croydon Airport. That closed down years ago, of course, but back then it did most of the Jersey and Guernsey flights for London and it was also where the early morning cut-flowers arrived, destined for places like Covent Garden Market. I remember watching dozens of lorries pull in to collect them all. It was a hive of activity.

Now in those days we still had things like smog, which, if you were flying a plane, could be more than a little bit dangerous. There were no electric landing lights then, and so the Fire Brigade would turn up, line the sides of the runway with barrels of oil, and then set fire to the bloody lot. Health and safety? Not on your nelly. It didn't exist back in those days. Me and my brother Pat would sit there and watch all this going on, and then later on, if it was a Saturday, we'd shift round a bit and start watching a football match on one of the football fields next door, or if it was a Sunday, cricket. Seriously, what a life.

I remember when we first got the allotment. What a mess that was. It was all nettles. It took us days to clear it and even when we'd finished it was still a mess. I asked Dad what we were going to do with it.

'We'll put spuds in first, boy. That'll help clear the ground.'

I actually remember the first bucket of spuds we dug up there. 'I think we've cracked it, boy,' Pop said to me. 'It should be good from now on.'

And it was.

The house in Purley was quite a big semi-detached but it had an enormous garden. It had to if Pop was going to buy it. As with Haywards Heath, Pop made sure I had my own patch, and because I was a little bit older I decided to go to town a bit. First I wanted a pond.

'You want a what?' said Pop. 'But you're just a nipper. What on earth do you want a pond for?'

I wanted to turn that little patch of land into *my* garden – a garden within a garden, so to speak – and in my mind any garden proprietor worth his salt would have to insist on a pond. In the end I sank an old kitchen sink in there, lined it and then blocked up the plughole. Once that was in I sent off for a few plants to put round it. They were as cheap as you like and were all pernicious weeds most probably, but they were guaranteed to grow.

Anyway, not long after that I decided I wanted a green-house.

'That makes a bit more sense than a pond,' said Pop. 'How are you going to pay for it, though?'

'I haven't got any money, Dad.'

'I thought as much. Hang on,' he said. 'I've got an idea.'

Pop had his own greenhouse, of course, and on the side of that he put up a little lean-to for me and then he lined it with some glass. He kept his boiler in there too, which meant everything was always nice and warm – if occasionally covered in ash! It was crude but it was mine. I was as pleased as Punch. I'd arrived!

Incidentally, old Pop was without doubt one of the world's greatest ever boiler starter-uppers. I'll explain. We had a wood-burning stove in our hallway and during the winter Pop would get up, and the first thing he'd do is light it. Then he'd move into the sitting room and he'd lay the open fire. Mum was no good with fires and as she was also no good at getting out of bed in the morning, Pop had no choice. After that he'd have to light the hot-water boiler followed by the one in his greenhouse. It doesn't stop there though. You see, once his boiler-athon was finished he'd start on making breakfast, but he wouldn't just make breakfast for himself. Oh no. He'd make mine, Pat's and Caroline's, and then he'd start on the sandwiches. Four rounds of sandwiches! How he managed all that day in, day out I'll never know. Different generation. It's funny, but Mum would always appear at the bottom of the stairs just as he'd finished cutting them.

A few years later I managed to get myself a proper greenhouse and the first things I grew in it were cucumbers. Well, you can imagine what it was like when they were ready for picking. I just smiled for weeks on end. I grew some tomatoes after that and they too turned out OK. This is the life, I thought. This is why we do it.

On one side of the greenhouse I had a bench, and on there I grew some beautiful house plants called cineraria. You rarely see them these days but back then they were very fashionable. I remember watching those plants come through and, my word, they were stunning. They bore the most beautiful shades of purple and blue I'd ever seen in my life. Anyway, a few days before I was going to take them out I came down to find that they'd all turned as black as the devil's waistcoat. There'd been a frost overnight and because I hadn't a heater it had killed them. I was absolutely inconsolable. I'd never experienced anything like this before. Sure, not everything I planted grew or grew like it should, but I'd never had something as devastating as that happen to me. It was like suffering a bereavement.

'That's gardening, boy,' said Pop. 'We'll have to get you a heater.'

I remember saying to him, 'It's a bit late now, Dad!'

A few days later he got me a little paraffin heater and so after that everything was OK.

Do you know, I can still see those flowers to this day? It makes me shiver!

4. The Worst Pupil in Purley

There's one part of my childhood I haven't told you about yet, and to be honest I've been absolutely dreading it. I am of course talking about – school. Even the word makes me want to run and hide. I'm afraid I was to learning what bindweed is to successful gardening, and if the nuns who originally taught me had had their way I'd have been dealt with in exactly the same manner.

My earliest recollection of being at primary school is of sitting in the classroom and looking at these nuns, thinking, what on earth am I doing here? What I should have done is got up and walked straight out, because they turned out to be the nastiest bunch of 'you know whats' I've ever had the displeasure of knowing. Sisters of Mercy? They were more like the Spinsters of Misery. What's more they seemed to revel in dishing it out. The only upside I seem to remember from that first year was a pretty little blonde girl who I used to sit next to; or at least I used to try and sit next to her. Every time I sat down at her desk I got the same thing.

'James! What are you doing bothering her? She's a good little girl. Now come up here where I can see you.'

I absolutely hated it, and what's more I hated them. Eventually I got so peeved off with the Spinsters of Misery that I just became disruptive, and, do you know what, it was a masterstroke, because whenever I got too much for them they'd take me out to the walled garden and then lock the door. Once I was out there I'd do a bit of work in the gardens, so really I couldn't have been happier. Occasionally they'd lock me in a cupboard under the stairs if I was being particularly obnoxious but more often than not I'd go outside. Can you imagine that these days? They'd get arrested.

My absolute worst memory of life at Stalag Luft St Joseph's is milk time. Do you remember those little bottles of milk we used to get? Well, some of you will. We used to have to drink them every day we were there, and for somebody who wasn't too keen on milk it was a recurring nightmare! During the winter the milk would often turn up frozen, so the nuns used to open the bottles, throw it all into a cauldron and then put it over a paraffin heater. Now in my mind there's only one thing worse than a cup of lukewarm milk and that's a cup of lukewarm milk with skin running down the side of it. They would line us all up like something out of *Oliver Twist*, except I wasn't asking for more. I used to try anything not to have to drink that milk. I tried biting them, I tried punching them and I tried kicking them, but none of it seemed to work. They just held my head back, forced my mouth open, pinched my nose and poured it in. Do you know, from that day to this I've never drunk a drop of milk except in tea or coffee, and whenever I see a nun I get palpitations!

There are two other things I remember from primary school that involve neither nuns, milk, or mild forms of violence, and that's King George VI's funeral and Queen Elizabeth II's coronation. They brought a television into school so we could watch those two events and I can remember them as clear as day. During old George's funeral we were told by the nuns to be solemn as it was a sad occasion, and then during the coronation we were told to be happy.

Like most families back then we never had a television at home, we just had a radio, and as many of you will remember they weren't like the ones you have today; in fact ours was the size of a small garden shed. I'm not kidding! Pop and I could have kept half our gardening gear in there. It was a great big wooden thing with a couple of knobs on the front of it, and when you turned one of them a light came on – eventually! Seriously, I've seen brass monkeys warm up quicker than our old wireless did.

Anyway, that was my introduction to television – the old king's funeral and the new queen's coronation. Who'd have thought that some thirty years later I'd be in charge of some of the Royal Parks? Well, certainly not those nuns. They probably thought I'd be going to hell in either a handcart or a Black Maria when I left school, but I had other ideas.

You see back in the 1950s there were three professions little boys aspired to: they wanted to be either a policeman, a soldier or an actor. All standard stuff really. Not me though. Oh no. You see when I was a nipper I always wanted to be a market gardener. That's right. From the age of five or six that's all I ever wanted to be. My pals at school all thought I was crazy, and so did the nuns to be honest, but for slightly different reasons. But when it came to the crunch, who was the one living the dream? Well, it wasn't them, was it? You see, because of what I did with Pop in the garden and up at the allotment, I could virtually touch what I wanted to become, and that kind of attainability made it all the more exciting. It wasn't a dream, it was real.

Then there were the idols of course: the footballers and the film stars, etc. I mean everyone had one or two of them when they were young. All my pals used to idolize people like Stanley Matthews, Len Hutton or David Niven, and who can blame them? And who do you think I idolized? Well, have a guess. Montgomery Clift? Nowhere near. Boris Karloff? He would have been the nun's favourite. OK, how about Billy Wright? Sorry, not even close.

When it came to heroes in the Buttress household circa 1950 whatever-it-was, there was only one contender and that was Percy Thrower. Seriously! Old Percy was like a god to me. He was my first hero.

This was when we eventually got a telly of course – about 1959 – and I remember he used to come on every Friday night at about 7 p.m. He was the Laurence Olivier of the flower beds in a way. He was Mr Gardening. He used to wear a lovely old trilby hat and he had a wonderful brogue about him. Do you know, his voice was like spun gold to me and even now I could quite happily listen to it for days on end.

At the start of the show he used to walk into what I believed was his own greenhouse, when in actual fact it was probably an old studio at Television Centre on Wood Lane. That didn't matter though at the time, because I was in Percyland, and whatever he said or suggested was gospel. Well, it was to me. After closing the door of his greenhouse behind him (OK, just humour me a bit), Percy would hang up his coat on a nail on the door and then say something like:

'Good evening. Tonight we're going to do some potting on.'

Pop would be sitting in his chair chuckling away, and I'd be in front of him lying by the fire. This was my *Ready Steady Go* and he was my Beatles; or, I suppose in those days, Mantovani!

Now I don't want to insult anybody's intelligence here, but just in case there are one or two younger ones reading this book – or should I say anybody under sixty – let me tell you a bit about Percy.

Well, Percy Thrower was Britain's first ever celebrity gardener, so in a way he helped to popularize gardening and bring it to the masses, just like Pavarotti did with opera. Now you could say gardening was already with the masses to a certain extent, on account of the number of people who practised it, but Percy took it to a new level and the effect he had was double-edged. You see if you were already a gardener Percy would help you refine what you did and that kept you interested, and if you weren't a gardener Percy made you want to start. He broadened the appeal of gardening so much that by the early 1950s it was more of a craze than a pastime.

When it came to credentials, Percy was gardening through and through. His old man had been a gardener at Bawdsey Manor in Suffolk before becoming the head gardener at Horwood House, which is near Bletchley. Like me Percy got into gardening young. Well, when your dad's into it that's what usually happens. After leaving school Percy did his apprenticeship under his dad at Bawdsey and after that became what was then known as a journeyman gardener. That's a term that's not used much these days but back in the day it meant that you'd completed your apprenticeship but were not yet considered a master or an artisan. On leaving Bawdsey, Percy had stints at places like Windsor Castle and Leeds Parks Department and then during the war he became a big noise in the Dig for Victory campaign. Now if you don't know who Percy Thrower is you almost certainly won't know what Dig for Victory was, so if you're stuck go and ask somebody senior. Anyway, a few years after the war had finished, Percy broke into radio and television, and the rest, as they say, is history. He also wrote a lot of books too. In fact I do believe Alan Titchmarsh became Percy's editor towards the end of his career. Percy's career that is, not Alan's! He had the same effect on all of us really. What can I say; the man was an absolute legend.

You remember I told you I used to get a diary every Christmas? Well, when Percy became a celebrity he started putting his name to a few things and a diary was one of them. Anything Percy brought out I wanted to have.

I'll let you into a little secret . . . I used to pretend to be Percy Thrower. It's daft when I think about it now but what I used to do was put on a coat, walk into Pop's greenhouse, take the hat off, hang it on the back of the door and then proceed to give a demonstration. All the time I'd be talking into an imaginary television camera.

'Good evening, everyone. Tonight I'm going to show you how to take cuttings. First, you need to . . .'

I'd stand there for hours on end yapping away to myself. I wonder what Percy would have made of it? He'd probably have thought I was barmy.

From an educational point of view Mum and Pop thought things might improve once I went to secondary school. They probably thought I was a slow starter. No such luck! In fact the only exam or test I ever passed at either of my schools was my cycling proficiency test, and I very nearly flunked that. The police used to do a sweep at the local schools looking for bikes that didn't have things like lights or reflectors. Well, apart from a frame, two wheels, a chain, some pedals and a saddle, my bike didn't have a single bloody thing on it, and so when the police turned up it was the first one to be thrown in the compound. This was the day before my cycling proficiency test was due to take place and so in the end I had to borrow a bike from a mate. You had to get sixty per cent to get the badge, and what did I get? Sixty-one! Just you wait until I tell you about my time as a student at RHS Wisley. It doesn't get any better, I'm afraid.

The secondary school I went to was the John Fisher School in Purley, and of course it was Catholic. Mum wasn't happy about me going to another Catholic school – especially after my experiences with the nuns – but I think she gave in to Pop just for a quiet life. I can't repeat what Mum thought of all the nuns and priests but suffice to say it wasn't too complimentary.

As with primary school I'm afraid my relationship with the poor priests charged with trying to educate me at John Fisher left a lot to be desired, and so I ended up spending more time in the corridor than I did in the classrooms. The person you had to watch out for in these situations was Father MacLean, because if he saw you standing in the corridor he knew you'd been a naughty boy, and he didn't take any nonsense from anyone, least of all a little tearaway like me. I had this trick though. You see, if ever I saw him coming I'd pretend I was just that moment walking out of the classroom.

'Where are you off to, Buttress?'

'Toilet, sir.'

'Hurry along then, hurry along.'

It didn't always work out though. I remember once the teacher saw me strolling off down the corridor. Well, I had to make it look like I really was going to the toilet.

'Where are you going, Buttress? I thought I told you to stand in the corridor.'

Bugger it! Caught red-handed. Needless to say Father MacLean wasn't amused.

My problem was my big mouth, I'm afraid. I never knew when to shut up and when it came to cheeking my elders I was the best in show. Sport though. Now that I *was* keen on and when I wasn't pretending to go to the toilet or making the priests' lives a misery I'd be playing football in the schoolyard. But what I really enjoyed doing during lunchtime was helping out old Fred Earl, the school gardener. He was a Scouser was Fred and every lunchtime I'd pop into his shed, he'd make us both a nice cup of tea, and then he'd give me a slice of cake. After that he'd take out a packet of Player's Weights.

'Would you like a fag, Jim? Here, go on, nobody's looking.'

So while the rest of the kids were in the canteen having fish and chips and what have you and being good little boys, I'd be in the gardener's hut drinking tea, having a fag and talking about gardening. I was only about thirteen at the time. After that Fred and I would walk round the school grounds and check the flower beds. I'd just bombard him with questions of course, and he'd happily answer all of them.

Now there was one priest at John Fisher who I absolutely hated. His name was Father Hatchard and he taught French. What a miserable old swine he was. One day he asked me and my mate Paul if we'd help him out with a job. This was out of school time, by the way.

'I'll make sure you get a few shillings,' he promised.

What it was: during the war the school had built an underground air-raid shelter and all the flint they'd brought up when they dug the shelter out had to be moved to make a parking space for Father Hatchard's car. Well, Paul and I spent an entire summer holiday shifting that stone – by hand, I might add – and do you know what he gave us when we'd finished? Not a single bloody penny. In fact we didn't even get a thank you.

I remember going home on a Sunday afternoon and telling Pop what had happened. He wasn't happy.

'You what?' he said. 'That's exploitation. I'm not having that.'

Now for my dad to say or do anything against the Catholic Church was, until then, unheard of, but this riled the old boy like you wouldn't believe. He went straight round to the school, sought old Hatchard out and then he gave him a right roasting.

Hatchard apologized and coughed up straight away. Ten shillings each we got in the end. You should have seen the look on the old priest's face. Talk about looking embarrassed. He was crimson by the time Pop had finished with him.

Ironically enough, the teacher who I actually got on best with at John Fisher was the headmaster, Canon Byrne; or Monsignor Charles Byrne as he was also known. I adored the old boy. He could be hard when he had to be but the majority of the time he was just a kind and gentle eccentric really. He had a cat that was an absolute lunatic that would attack anything that moved, and he had an old Irish red setter called Malachy, which was named after a saint from way back. He used to walk for miles and miles with that old dog and he always carried a prayer book. He used to talk to anyone and everyone. It didn't matter whether you knew him or not, he'd still stop and ask you how you were.

Every summer he used to have a big reunion of all the priests he'd studied with. First they'd have a Mass, which Paul and I would serve for them, and then they'd have a lunch, and it was a proper lunch! After the Mass he'd call Paul and me over and slip us a few shillings and a bar of chocolate each.

The first time I ever met Canon Byrne was at my interview. You see I'm not sure about today, but when I went John Fisher was a fee-paying school and so you had to go for a test and an interview before you could be accepted.

I remember first walking into his office with Pop. For a start, the old boy used to chain-smoke a pipe which meant I could hardly see a thing, but then once the air had cleared a bit I realized that we were completely surrounded by clutter. It was everywhere: books, papers, religious pictures. And there at his desk sitting behind all this paraphernalia was old Canon Byrne. Malachy was there next to him, scratching himself, and as the canon asked us both to take a seat Pop ended up sitting on his mad cat. Well, that was it. There was scratching and there was screeching. Poor old Pop almost died, first from injuries sustained by that bloody cat and then from embarrassment.

'I'm terribly sorry, Mr Buttress. He doesn't mean any harm.'

Doesn't mean any harm? That cat would have eaten Pop alive if Canon Byrne hadn't extracted him claw by claw.

Anyway, after the canon and Pop had done with all the religious chat the monsignor looked over at me.

'James, what are five eights?'

'Forty.'

God, I was proud. You see, I was rubbish at maths.

'And now what are eight fives?'

Silence.

I was stumped.

'I don't know, sir.'

Canon Byrne smiled at me. 'My word,' he said. 'We have got a bit of work to do, haven't we, James? Anyway, see you at the start of term.'

And that was it. That was my test!

Just as we were leaving, the canon called Pop back.

'I hope you don't mind me asking, Mr Buttress, but could you pay cash?'

That was typical of back then.

In the end poor old Pop should have kept his money really, because apart from sport and socializing with the gardener, the only thing I took away from the school was about ten words of Latin; which, given what I do for a living, has obviously come in quite useful.

It wasn't that I didn't have any interest in things like English, history and geography; I just had a lot more interest in the gardening. Mum used to try and help me with the homework and I used to drive her potty.

'For God's sake, will you please pay attention, Jim!'

'Sorry, Mum.'

The funny thing is that, despite me being totally hopeless academically, the majority of the teachers, barring old Hatchard, used to absolutely love me – and I them. I'd have a go at anything you see, as long as it was practical and I didn't have to think, and I reckon they admired that to a certain extent. If the school held a fair, I'd first help build all the stalls with Dad and then run them, and I did the same at the church fête. I was into everything.

I probably shouldn't be telling you this, but when I was about fifteen years of age I started drinking in our local pub, and at least three times a week I'd play Bar Billiards against some of my lay teachers. We used to have a right laugh. The funny thing was that just a few hours previously they'd have been kicking me up the arse for misbehaving and now we were having a beer together!

Now there was only one thing I hated more than academia when I was a kid and that was going to church. From the age of nine until I left school at sixteen, I served Mass every single morning. I used to get up at about 6.30 a.m. and then cycle to the school chapel or local church, which was about a mile away. There was only ever me and a priest there. Then, once I'd served Mass I had to dart home, wolf down a bit of breakfast and then cycle back to school again. As I got older the two occasions I dreaded most were Easter and Christmas. It was Mass after Mass after Mass, and Pop used to drag me to the lot. I'll tell you, the moment I left home that was it – never again. Pat and Caroline are both church-goers so it obviously rubbed off on them exactly as Pop would have hoped. Not me though. I must have spent the equivalent of a couple of years being bored to death in churches. What a waste.

When I told Pop that I wouldn't be carrying on he was disappointed but remained philosophical.

'Oh well, boy,' he said. 'You can't win them all. At least you know the difference between right and wrong.'

I did too, but that wasn't thanks to the Church. It was all in bloody Latin!

5. Beer with Mrs Boston

Now I don't know about you but back in my day when it came to things like pocket money you had to work for it, and you had to work hard. Pop would give me job after job, and then every so often, when I wasn't expecting it, he'd hand me a couple of shillings.

'There you go, boy,' he'd say. 'You deserve that.'

That felt better than just being handed it on a plate.

My least favourite job, as is often the way, was the one I had to do most often and it was called the firewood run. When we lived in Purley our house was on the top of a big steep hill and every Saturday I'd take this cart that Pop had made for me and I'd wheel it all the way down to the local greengrocer's in the town. Once there I'd fill it up with orange crates, tomato boxes and the like. You remember the ones. They were all wooden back then and about six or seven inches high. Well, they were no use to the greengrocer anymore so I'd save him the trouble of getting rid of them.

Once I'd got as many on as I could manage, the old boy who owned the place would give me some string to tie them down and then I'd push the cart all the way back up the hill. Tired? I could hardly move by the time I got back. It didn't stop there though, because as soon as I'd got it all back I had to untie them and then chop it all up for firewood. Even at that age I had calves the size of melons and forearms like bloody marrows.

Later on, though, when I was a bit older, the shillings stopped coming.

'Things have changed now, boy,' barked Pop. 'You've got to earn your keep and the jobs you do for me just about cover it. If you want your own money you're going to have to go out and work for it.'

Well, I had no issue with work, as you well know. The question was: what was I going to do?

Pop had a suggestion.

'Why don't you go and do people's gardens for them? There are plenty of pensioners and posh folk around here, and they've all got a bob or two. You go and knock on some doors and I'll have a word with a friend or two.'

Perfect!

Getting paid for doing something you love has to be the ambition of every man, woman, boy or girl who's ever lived, and I was no different. All I had to do now was find a few gardens in need of attention, and preferably with rich owners.

I was lucky I suppose, because within just a week or two of looking I had three decent jobs on the go.

The first person ever to employ me as a gardener was a Mrs Helen Boston. She lived close to my school and the caretaker there, who knew Mrs Boston well, told me she was looking for a gardener. She was big, she was loud and she was as hard as bloody nails. Do you remember the deputy headmistress from that old show *Please Sir!*? The battle-axe who used to bark at everyone? Joan Sanderson, I think the actress's name was. Well she was just like her – but about twice the size.

Her husband had passed away a few years before from injuries he'd sustained in World War Two. He was a major in the army I think, and he'd got involved in everything. There was no standing behind the Tommies with him. He led from the front according to her.

Anyway, she was no different really, except that instead of frightening the bloody Germans half to death she used to terrify the population of Purley.

I remember the first time I knocked on her door. She was quite a tall lady and so that in addition to the voice made for quite an intimidating experience.

'Yes? What do you want?'

'The caretaker at my school says you're looking for a gardener?'

Then she gave me a right stare.

'Mmm. You look like quite a strong young lad. Come back Saturday morning and I'll give you a trial. I warn you though, it'll be hard work!'

She wasn't wrong. Now because her old boy had died after the war she got hardly anything when it came to a widow's pension and so to make ends meet she split her house in two: she moved up into the first floor and then rented out the ground floor as a flat. It was a big old place so she still had plenty of room, but the garden? Well, that was absolutely enormous, and to all intents and purposes it was all mine.

I absolutely adored Mrs Boston. She liked a drink, spoke her mind and was completely old-school.

I used to turn up at hers about ten in the morning on a weekend and I remember the first time I saw the garden. What a bloody mess! There was a flattish area near the house that was supposed to be a lawn and that had two rose beds running either side of it. Then behind that there was a bank, and that went down to what eventually became a kind of allotment area. It took some doing but by the time I'd finished with it that garden looked fabulous, and as for the area at the bottom – well, she was almost self-sufficient.

Honestly, we grew the lot, me and Mrs Boston. We had radishes, onions, beetroot, spuds, lettuce, spring onions and carrots. Put that together with the three or four apple and pear trees she had up there and you had the makings of a pretty decent plot. We could have fed a small army with what we produced.

Saturday was my favourite day for working there because after I'd finished work I'd collect my two shillings or whatever it was, have a wash, get changed, bomb over to my mate Paul's house and then we'd go and watch Crystal Palace. How about that then? I had gardening in the morning, football in the afternoon and then after that we'd have egg on toast and a cup of tea in the local cafe. Perfect. Honestly, life couldn't have been much better.

When I got to Paul's house his dad always used to hand him ten shillings, which, in addition to my two shillings – and whatever else I could scrape together – was more than enough to see us through the day. Paul and I didn't worry about things like who paid for what. If I was flush then I'd pay and if he was flush then he'd pay. It was a perfect arrangement.

Once we got to Selhurst Park we'd get a programme each, which were about four pence, have a go on Spot the Ball and then take our place on what was called the hill. Back then Selhurst Park was what you might call 'underdeveloped', and at one end of the ground, instead of having a stand or even a terrace, there was just a hill! It's a bit different nowadays of course, but not much.

After the game, win, lose or draw, we'd go straight round to the players' exit and get ourselves a few autographs. That was an obsession of mine for a while. I used to collect autographs like Monty Don and Alan Titchmarsh collect female admirers and at one time I had literally hundreds of them.

Honestly, I had the lot. I had the Palace squad's of course, not to mention every player of every team who ever visited. I had cricketers too, loads of them. I used to write to every football and cricket club in the country asking for autographs and more often than not they'd oblige. One or two used to send out facsimiles of players' signatures, which didn't go down well. They went straight in the bin!

When I left home a few years later Mum badgered me to clear my room out but I kept putting it off. And what do you think happened? She got tired of waiting and so threw everything out: my programmes, my autographs – the lot. It was my own bloody fault. I had Denis Compton, Len Hutton, Billy Wright, Stanley Matthews, Brian Close, Godfrey Evans – every bloody sporting hero you can imagine.

Paul and I are still good mates to this day, and although he too was a mad keen gardener he had in his possession something I never had – brains – and so decided to become a dentist. He's done well for himself has Paul and I'm dead proud of him.

Anyway, let's get back to Mrs Boston.

Believe it or not, the only part of the garden I had any trouble with was the lawn. You see growing fruit and veg was like falling off a log to me, as was tending to things like rose beds, and it would have been the same with the lawn if it hadn't been for Mrs Boston's bloody lawnmower. That thing became my nemesis. It was what I would now call a reluctant lawnmower, on account of the fact that it seemed to be allergic to cutting grass, and I'll tell you what, it made my life a flaming misery. The worst part was cutting the bank that led to the allotment area. I didn't have the strength to run it down the side and so instead I used to have to put the mower at the bottom of the bank facing up, take a big run-up and then push it as hard as I could. By the time I'd finished cutting the grass at Mrs Boston's I was fit for absolutely nothing. The old girl used to love watching me do this. In fact I can see her now, standing at her window, whisky in hand, chuckling away to herself as I went to war with her old Suffolk Punch. After a while she'd take pity on me and bring me down something to eat and drink. She had a lovely old conservatory where she used to grow her seeds and once she'd made the sandwiches she'd call me in there.

'Come along, my boy. Game, set and match to the lawnmower, I think!'

Now Mrs Boston was a marvellous cook and in the winter, as opposed to having sandwiches, she'd always make me a hot meal. My favourite was hot gammon ham, beetroot, stuffed marrow and white sauce. She only ever made proper food, Mrs Boston, and this was the best. Just thinking about it honestly makes my mouth water! Between you and me she always gave me a nice beer to wash it down with.

'For heaven's sake don't tell your parents, Jim, otherwise they'll have me arrested.'

What a great character.

I remember sitting in the conservatory one day. Mrs Boston had gone out to do some shopping, I think, when all of a sudden I spotted some used Norwich Union envelopes. She was using them to keep all her seeds in and when I took a closer look I saw that they were all addressed to her husband. That's funny, I thought, Dad works for the Norwich Union. Anyway, when I got home I told Pop about the letters and when I gave him Mr Boston's full name he pulled up.

'You're joking me, boy, really? Old Mr Boston employed me, and let me tell you, he was an absolute sod.'

Dad never usually swore in front of the kids so I'd obviously touched a nerve.

'Do you know what he used to do?' said Pop. 'He used to

get into the office at about ten in the morning and just bark at us. Then, at about eleven he'd be called out on what he always called "urgent business" and would just disappear for about four hours. We later found out that all he did was go to his club and get pissed every day, but then after that he'd come back to the office and start terrorizing everyone again. I honestly never saw him do a scrap of work. And he was old Mrs Boston's other half? The poor cow.'

What a small world, eh?

So much for Major Boston leading from the front.

As I said, Mrs Boston only paid me a couple of shillings a week, which for the amount of work I was doing was next to nothing, but I'll tell you what, hand on heart I honestly couldn't have cared less. In fact I'd have done it for nothing. You see, not only did I enjoy every second (apart from mowing, of course), but I was also learning my trade and at the same time doing the old girl a good turn. I mean, come on, what's wrong with that? It was enough for me.

I had five wonderful years with Mrs Boston, from when I was ten until I was fifteen, and it probably won't surprise you to learn that I was still doing jobs for her right into my twenties. I used to do her shopping every week. She'd ring me up with her list.

'One bottle of whisky. Actually make that two. Three loaves of bread, a pound of butter . . .'

Then, when I dropped it round to her house, she'd start complaining about the price.

'You paid how much?! Oh no, no, no.'

I never once left with the full amount! It was just the way she was. Honestly, I loved that woman to bits.

The second job I managed to get was up at the John Fisher School. Me and my mate Paul used to help out the caretaker there during the holidays – you know, painting classrooms and the like – and it won't surprise you to learn that I did more work there out of term than I ever did during. We were there every day during every holiday – including Christmas. We even built the new cricket nets one year.

Do you know, I even had a job when we went on holiday? We used to go to Worthing sometimes to stay with Mum's family and while Caroline and Patrick would stay with Mum and Pop like normal children, I'd go off and help the milk-man on his horse and cart. I'm not kidding. The first year we went there I watched him deliver to the street we were stay-ing on, decided I wanted to help, and so I asked him.

'Yeah, of course you can, so long as it's all right with your mum and dad.'

Well, you wouldn't be able to do it these days of course, but back then people thought differently.

After that there was no stopping me and from then on I spent every morning of every holiday we ever had at Worth-ing helping the milkman.

'Two white ones at number six, a gold one at number eight, and a dozen eggs and a white one for the old girl at number ten, all right? Off you go.'

Playing on the beach and riding donkeys was the last thing on my mind when we went on holiday. The bit I looked forward to was work.

I remember one year we went to Sheringham up in Nor-folk for about a week and I ended up selling ice creams. I got talking to the bloke who ran the ice cream stall and before I knew it I had a white coat on and I was selling cornets and ice lollies. It wasn't that I didn't love my family or anything; in fact nothing could be further from the truth. I was just fascinated by life, I suppose, and wanted to be involved in as much of it as possible. It was always working people who I gravitated towards, and the harder they worked the more fascinated I was.

One year, when I was very young, we went to Swanage on the Dorset coast. We had a beach hut there and one morning I went missing. Poor old Mum went spare.

'For heaven's sake, Cuddy, where's he gone now? I only brought him back ten minutes ago.'

Fortunately they didn't have to look far. In a hut just a few down from ours sat two big old women. Honestly, according to Mum it was like something out of a Les Dawson or Norman Evans sketch. These old dears had bosoms like barrage balloons and they were sitting there with fags hanging out of their mouths buttering bread for sandwiches. There they were, gossiping away about this, that and the other, and who was sitting in between them? Buttress the younger. Pop said it looked like I was watching a tennis match. When one said something I'd look at her, and then I'd move to the other. Mum and Pop just stood there watching me for about five minutes, completely agog.

I've met a lot of wonderful, wonderful people in my time, some with crowns and some with seven or eight names, but if I'm honest it's usually the ones towards the bottom of the pecking order who I get on best with, and it's through knowing people like this that I developed, from a very early age, a complete abhorrence for both ignorance and arrogance. You know the types: the Mr Bostons of this world. I can spot idiots like that an absolute mile off.

Now the last employer I'm going to tell you about from my young years was a Mr Ted Ockenden, who was a serious noise for the Bank of England. He and his wife Kitty were two of the nicest people you could ever meet, and their four sons all went to the John Fisher School the same as me. The only ones who are still alive are Neil and Keith and I'm still in touch with them to this day.

By the time I was fourteen years old I'd landscaped three different gardens for the Ockendens because, despite them having plenty of money, they only ever rented houses. This was on the basis that if Ted went first Kitty wouldn't have the problem of selling.

The first of the three houses was in the grounds of the school, and as well as me they employed a part-time gardener who was, shall we say, selective in what he did and spent all his time in the greenhouse. To be fair to him he could grow tomatoes, but when it came to everything else he hardly lifted a finger. Weeding? He wouldn't have known one if it had jumped up and given him a big kiss. Anyway, in the end I had to do the lot. Ted Ockenden was too nice to get rid of the old buzzard and so he paid me to do it instead. I didn't mind. It was money for old rope.

I remember one day telling Mr Ockenden that I was going to burn the rubbish heap. It must have been about six foot high, a lot taller than me, and I couldn't wait to get started. I mean, who doesn't like a big old bonfire? Do you know, he was so worried about me having to shift it all on my own that he made his son Neil take a day off work so that he could come and supervise. It wasn't that he didn't trust me; he just thought I might set fire to the house! He was a proper gentleman.

Old Pop used to sell half his blooming produce to Ted. Every few weeks he'd go round there with eggs, beetroot, tomatoes, cucumber. It all went to the Ockendens. There he was, a general manager at Norwich Union, flogging his eggs and veg to a bigwig at the Bank of England. You couldn't make it up.

Once he'd seen Ted, Pop would come back with the money and put it into an old Player's cigarette tin. Player's was Pop's brand and back then you used to be able to buy tins of fifty, and that was where Pop used to keep his seed money. As I said, he was old-school. He might have worked in the City but old habits die hard. He was careful, was Pop, unlike Mum. While he was selling veg and saving up to buy a few seeds she'd be putting her last shilling on a 100-1 outsider in the final race at Catterick. They used to go racing together sometimes and while she was off backing rank outsiders with big prices he'd always back the favourites. What happened? He'd have four or five winners and a tenner in his pocket and Mum would have naff all. She'd be there berating the bookmakers and the Tote. It was everyone else's fault of course. Then, every so often, some old nag would come in at 33-1 and she'd be happy. I suppose it was like playing golf in a way: hundreds of disappointments with the occasional miracle thrown in. That was Mum though, she was a born gambler. I inherited the best of both really because although I absolutely love my racing, just like Mum, I've never really been much of a gambler, just like Pop. Lucky, isn't it?

Although I've never been that interested in money, Pop's entrepreneurial spirit wasn't lost on me; in fact, watching him come back from the Ockendens time after time with a pocket full of cash eventually gave me an idea – cuttings. I mean, all gardeners like the odd cutting, right? Well, I started off with a few geraniums, whipped them round to Ted and – bingo! That became my seed money. He couldn't get enough of them, so it was the perfect arrangement.

Looking back, I should never have been doing half the jobs I got paid to do. I was fourteen going on forty! But the fact is that from the age of about ten I was a self-contained visiting gardener and, without wanting to sound like a big-head, I was bloody good at it. I used to have a bike and on the side of it hung this long bag, which is where I kept all my gear. I had hoes, rakes, spades and trowels. This was a serious business. I had a little book too, where I kept a record of what I'd earned. As I said though, it wasn't the money itself that turned my head, it was the responsibility and the work that floated my boat, not to mention the social side. Mixing with and working for the likes of Mrs Boston and Ted Ockenden was my education. School meant nothing to me except when I worked there during the holidays, but it's not as if I was roaming the streets making a nuisance of myself. No, I knew exactly what I wanted to do in life.

6. W. H. Fuller & Sons

Before I regale you with what I did after leaving school, let me just tell you a bit about Mum's family, because although I had a good relationship with my granddad, and with Pop of course, there was somebody on the other side of the family in addition to Mum who I became very close to.

As I've said, Mum was brought up in a place called Worthing in West Sussex and although her own mum was English, her father, Albert Raphael, was a German Jew who had arrived in the UK in the 1880s, eventually applying for citizenship in 1908. He'd been a brush salesman in France before landing here but ended up becoming the joint manager of the London Bank of Mexico and South America.

When Albert died in 1919 he left an estate worth over £14,000, which in today's money is about £750,000. They'd lived in Beckenham before he died but not long afterwards the family moved to Worthing, where they bought a big flat, so from the age of eight that's where Mum lived.

Mum had two sisters, Susie and Nora, and a brother called Robert, and with them in the flat lived Grandma and one of Grandma's sisters, Aunt Dot. Now all Aunt Dot did day in, day out was knit – and knit – and knit – and who do you think were the recipients of her creations? We were. She made us all kinds of colourful stuff. Some of it was all right but the vast majority either didn't fit properly or was some awful bright colour. Green cardigans with pink pockets, you know the sort of thing.

Susie and Nora had both been engaged during the war – one to a clergyman and the other to a soldier – and both of their intendeds had ended up getting killed. I mean, how sad is that? It completely devastated them of course, and neither aunt ever went out with another man again.

So living in the flat you had Grandma, you had Mum, you had Aunt Susie, you had Aunt Nora, you had their Aunt Dot and, last but not least, you had Robert. Poor old Uncle Robert. No offence intended, but you imagine living in a flat with five women from two generations. Talk about being henpecked. He never stood a chance! Robert was a gentleman, very kind and quiet, and he devoted his entire young life to just three things – his family, sport and hobbies. He had a job of course, he worked for the Canadian Imperial Bank of Commerce, where he looked after all their security systems, but family, sport and hobbies were why he got up in the morning. He could turn his hand to any kind of sport, could Uncle Robert. He could play cricket, rugby, table tennis, badminton – and he could ski. I know we've actually got a Swiss connection somewhere in the family because Robert used to go out there regularly, skiing, and while he was there he used to meet up with relations. Cousins, I think. Mum went over too at some point.

Anyway, when it came to hobbies Robert tried all sorts of things, but his two favourites were photography and hill climbing, which meant come Christmas and birthdays what did I get? Photographs of bloody hills and mountains! I have no idea why he used to give me them. It's the thought that counts, though.

Robert and I did have one connection, and that was cricket. I don't know if they still play there but back in the day one of Sussex's out-grounds was Worthing; once a year they'd play a match or two there and Robert would take me.

Now at the time the president of Sussex County Cricket Club was the Duke of Norfolk (I know, he must have got his counties mixed up), and he used to turn up to what was only really a council pitch. I can see the old boy now, doddering into the beer tent.

'Could somebody find His Grace a chair, please?'

'Thank you, my good man!'

He always looked like he was about to collapse.

Because Robert had no family of his own at the time, he would treat me like a son when we went to the cricket. I used to love it. He was generous to a fault and he introduced me to everyone – and, believe me, he knew everyone. Everything he did had a social aspect to it and so wherever he stepped foot he'd be with friends.

By the time Robert got to about fifty everyone naturally assumed that he'd remain a bachelor for the rest of his life, and I'm sure he thought that too. But then one day while he was on a walking holiday in the Lake District the strangest thing happened. He was about to step over a ravine or something when he heard this woman's voice.

'I'd be careful if I were you. You might fall.'

That voice belonged to a young lady named Sheila, and just a few months later they became husband and wife. It doesn't stop there, though, as about a year after they got married they had a daughter who they named Patricia. How about that? One minute Uncle Robert's a fifty-year-old confirmed bachelor and the next minute he's a family man.

Years earlier Uncle Robert had been head boy at Lancing College, which is one of the top independent schools in the country. That side of the family had money, you see, and so they could afford to give him the best. When Robert was there Lancing College was a boys' school but in 1970 it became mixed, and who do you think was the first girl to be accepted? Robert's daughter Patricia. How proud was he? Patricia even ended up getting married at Lancing and you should have seen the old boy's face. Grinning from ear to ear all day long he was.

The first time I ever wanted to leave school and go and do something else was about the age of four (or about five minutes after I started) and that feeling stayed with me for the next twelve long years. You can well imagine then, when I finally did get to walk through those gates for the last time, aged sixteen, the almighty sense of relief I felt. In my last year at school I'd done a bit of part-time work during the holidays for a local nursery named W. H. Fuller & Sons. They'd been operating since just before the end of the war apparently, after Mr Bill Fuller Snr had been given some land to rent cheaply by the council. They used to do that a lot back then, handing over land to small businesses like pig farmers, chicken farmers, salad growers and of course nursery owners, with a view to them providing for the local community. Supermarkets and the like saw an end to them all eventually but for a time it was a good arrangement.

So, anyway, when it came to thinking about which companies I might be able to touch up for something full time Fullers were top of the list.

'What do you want a job for?' asked Bill Fuller Jnr who then ran the place. He was a biggish bloke, who always reminded me of a head gardener: ready to get stuck in but whatever he did he was always smart.

'Well I've just left school. I've got to do something.'

Now he knew I wasn't frightened of hard work and so after a little bit of umming and ahhing he eventually made me an offer.

'I'll tell you what,' he said. 'I can't afford much in the way of cash but you'll be well looked after and you'll learn a lot. Good enough for you?'

'Yes, Mr Fuller!'

'I'll tell you what then. Let's give it six months and we'll see how it goes.'

I can think back now to that first conversation with Bill and I don't think I'd ever been as excited or as happy in my entire life. It was like every single birthday and Christmas present rolled into one but with a big win on the football pools thrown in for good measure. This place was like a professional version of Granddad's smallholding in a way. It was about four or five times the size and instead of only spending the odd weekend or the occasional holiday there I was allowed to stay full time. And I got paid!

Old Bill and his dad, Bill Snr, grew everything on that land, far too much to list here. In fact just to give you some idea of how big the operation was, the only things they didn't grow on site were a few trees and shrubs but that was it. We used to propagate all the alpines ourselves. This was done in an old propagation pit, which was basically a big hole in the ground with some glass over the top and a stairway leading down to the bottom. In addition to things like alpines we'd propagate all manner of seeds, cuttings and bulbs. It was always full, that propagation pit. It was primitive of course, but my word it was effective.

As you drove into Fullers, straight in front of you were five or six of those enormous wooden glasshouses that you used to see, and then running down the side were a couple of houses. In one of those houses lived Bill Jnr and his wife and on the other side of the road lived Bill Snr. What an old character Bill Snr was. Just after the start of the First World War he'd gone to join up and when the recruitment officer asked him what religion he was, he said, 'Whatever you're short of, sir!' That was one of his favourite stories, bless him. And who was one of the old boy's dearest friends? Canon Charles Byrne, my old eccentric headmaster. They used to live opposite each other and whenever Canon Byrne was out walking his dog he'd always stop by the nursery – prayer book in one hand, dog lead in the other and a great big smile on his face.

'You coming in for a cup of tea and a chat, Charles?'

'That's very kind of you, William.'

'Step this way.'

Once they were settled they'd talk for hours about politics and religion.

So what was my job exactly? Well, basically I was Bill Fuller's apprentice. Just like Uncle Robert before he found Sheila, Bill didn't have any kids of his own and so he too treated me like his own son. I absolutely adored the man and consider myself tremendously lucky to have known him. Think about it, though: here I am, the world's keenest teenage gardener, and I am absolutely desperate to learn and work. And who do I end up working for? Somebody who A) owns their own nursery and grows absolutely bloody everything and B) has no kids, loves football, cricket and rugby and likes the occasional drink. I'd fallen well and truly on my feet.

We were inseparable, Bill and me. Everything he knew, I learned. Everything he did, I did with him, and everyone he knew, I was introduced to. And he knew an awful lot of people, did Bill. It was one of those relationships where everything about it worked. Mutually beneficial, I think they call it. He needed an apprentice come surrogate son, and I needed a master. Do you know, I even used to go round to Bill's on a Sunday, which was the only full day we were supposed to be shut, and help him to maintain his garden. After that Betty, his wife, would sit us down for a big lunch and I'd be there for the day. Mum and Pop didn't mind. They were just relieved that I was working and keeping out of trouble.

I say supposed to be shut because, although he wasn't allowed to trade on a Sunday, Bill would still open the gates for an hour or two so people could wander round, and then if they wanted to put in an order they could. He'd leave little slips of paper lying around along with some pencils, and when the customers had made their selections they'd post their orders into a little box that Pop had made for him. People didn't always have time to browse during the week and so if they couldn't get along there on Saturday it was a welcome alternative.

Incidentally, years later when I went back to Fullers for a few months after studying at RHS Wisley, old Pop came and helped out there. Now Bill could be a bit funny with people sometimes and because I was his apprentice I thought he might have felt a bit threatened by Pop, or vice versa. But Bill and Pop were having none of it. In fact they used to get along marvellously together and I think Pop was grateful to Bill for allowing him to help. It was the closest he ever got to doing it for a living.

We grew our own roses: bush, standards, climbers, half standards and weepers. They all had to be budded – a propagating technique, where a bud from a desirable plant is attached to a briar, which forms the rootstock. In my first year with Bill we also grew about five thousand *rosa rugosa* for standard or half-standard bushes. Once they got to a certain height we'd lift them all and line them out, and this is where it started to get painful. You see, my job was to tie the stems back onto the bamboo canes, but I had to untie them and tie them back on again every week. They'd all grown a bit so it was a regular job. Well, you can imagine – all those bare stems and no gloves. Each week it was my hands versus about a hundred thousand razor-sharp rose thorns, and no prizes for guessing who won.

What we were basically doing was producing something that looked like a long prickly stick, because once a week I'd also have to take all the side shoots off. But that's exactly what we were after – just a long clean stem about five feet high.

Come November, when all the leaves had shed, we'd plant them out in lines and I'd have to untie the bloody things once again. Bill would bud them the following July. I remember the day he first showed me like it was yesterday.

'Watch carefully, Jim, you're going to be doing a lot of these.'

He wasn't lying. Do you know, I must have budded getting on for half a million roses over the years?

Bill, glasses balanced on the end of his nose, took the stalk of a cultivated rose, made a nick underneath the bud and then peeled the bud off like a sheath. After that he scraped the pith out from the back of the bud, made a T-cut in the briar and then inserted the bud. Then he'd turn it round and do the same thing on the other side. All the time his glasses would be sliding up and down his nose as his head moved. How they didn't fall off I'll never know. It was a perfect balancing act. After Bill had finished budding I'd nip in, using raffia to secure the buds. I used to stand there for days on end just watching Bill, playing with bloody raffia and listening to him harp on. And, my word, could he talk. I think he forgot I was there sometimes because hardly any of it made any sense. The highlight of this job was when Bill dropped the occasional bud. Honestly, you've never heard language like it.

'Sorry about that, Jim. I must have learned all that in the army.'

More like the Foreign Legion!

After a couple of years of doing this Bill came to a very sensible decision. Well, it was as far as he was concerned.

'I'll tell you what, Jim,' he said one day. 'I'm absolutely fed up to the high teeth of doing this and I'm sure there must be a quicker way. Do you know what I'm going to do? I'm going to hire a couple of Dutch blokes to come over and they can do it. I've had enough.'

Now, do you remember the French guys who used to come over and sell onions after the war? Well, back in the day, Dutch people would often come over to England and help out in nurseries and gardens. They're a nation of horticulturalists, you see, and always have been.

Despite Bill getting in some hired help I still had to do the tying-in, and I remember the first day those Dutch blokes arrived. I had to tie-on for both of them and was there from seven in the morning until seven at night. At the end of the shift my back was so stiff that they actually had to put me in a wheelbarrow to get me down to my bike.

Would you believe it, about a week after I eventually stopped breaking my back and having my hands ripped to shreds on rose thorns while buggering about with raffia they started introducing plastic ties. Basically these were just strips of plastic with a loop at one end, and all you did was slip one round the stem, loop the other end through, pull it tight and that was it – done. Neither an ounce of pain nor a drop of blood in sight. Typical!

One slightly more enjoyable job, not to mention easier on the back, was planting out wallflowers. We used to grow at least two acres of wallflowers. Bill's brother Cyril, who was a mechanic, used to drive the tractor and on the back he had a little planter. I'd sit on that holding a tray of plants, and as the machine moved the soil, I'd put them in and then it would cover them up. We did row after row for hours on end, then once they were all planted we'd have to make sure they were weeded regularly. You imagine taking a hoe and weeding two or three acres. I always made sure I kept on top of it because if you didn't you could be in for a rough couple of days.

If it ever got really wet, which it obviously did from time to time in early winter, we used to all go and work on the chrysanthemums in the glasshouses. Watering these could be quite an arduous task because you had to be very careful not to under-water the pots or splash water everywhere. Splashing can cause mildew, of course, and if Bill ever saw us splash while we were watering he'd give us a mouthful. To ensure that we hadn't under-watered a plant he'd follow us sometimes, carrying a little hammer. He'd tap that on the side of the pot and depending on the noise it made he could tell whether it was watered. You don't forget things like that.

Once all that was done, if the weather was still bad I'd get on with painting or mending the frames. Maintenance was a huge part of our job and so, in addition to honing my skills as a gardener at Fullers, I also became quite a useful little handyman. Every day a different challenge and every day I'd learn something new. You know that feeling of satisfaction you sometimes get when you've worked really, really hard on something? Well, I used to experience that every single day. We worked our absolute backsides off, me, Bill and the rest of his team but, I'll tell you what, we kept that place running. This kind of establishment is almost a thing of the past these days and that's such a shame. Everything now seems to belong to a chain, and the majority of what they sell is bought in from abroad.

Thursday was always one of the hardest days because, regardless of whether it was raining or not, we'd spend the entire day lifting out the next day's orders, whether it be roses, trees, shrubs or herbaceous plants. If it was piddling down with rain we'd wear flat caps and trench coats that Bill had purloined from the local council tip. We must have looked ridiculous.

We always used to get two or three hours' overtime on a Thursday, because once we'd finished lifting at about five or six o'clock we'd then have to make up the orders, which we'd deliver the next day. These were mainly for our regular customers.

There used to be this pig farmer just down the road and he would let Bill have all the sacks that his bran came in. We'd turn the sacks inside out, put the order in, stick a label on the front, then that was it, job done. The next day, if it was my turn, I'd go out with Cyril on the lorry and we'd deliver the lot, and there would be hundreds of them. It wasn't the hardest job, going out with Cyril, but it was a long, long day.

By the way, it wasn't just the trench coats, flat caps and sacks that were second-hand. If I had to hazard a guess, I'd say that well over half of the non-mechanical equipment we had at Fullers was second-hand; and in a lot of cases had originally been used for something else. I'll give you a couple of examples: dahlias for instance. When it came to lifting them and then moving them to the glasshouses we put them in wooden trays. We used to get hold of hundreds of those from the old council dump and they were perfect. I have no idea what they were originally used for but I'll tell you, that dump saved Bill a fortune.

Just down the road from where we lived in Purley there was a Drapers' School, and the caretaker of this school, Mick, was a pal of mine. My God, he was a character. Like Arthur Daly but with a proper job. His missus was drop-dead gorgeous and his daughter Cynthia even more so, which was one of the reasons I used to see this chap on quite a regular basis. I collected the football pools money for a while and so would pop in and collect his on my way home from work.

Anyway, one day while I was there he took me to one side.

'Look, Jim, I don't know if you're interested but I've got quite a bit of timber coming out of the school. They're relaying all the floorboards on the second floor and I tell you what, it's good stuff.'

So I said I'd have a word with Bill and the next day I did.

'I could be interested, Jim,' said Bill, 'if it's good stuff. You go and have a look at it for me and if you reckon it's worth a punt we'll put a deal together.'

Now I don't know if it's because drapers are generally quite light-footed or that they wear slippers or something, but those floorboards were as good as new, and they'd been treated and polished regularly.

'Take 'em, Bill,' I said to him. 'They're quality.'

Normally they would all have been skipped, but instead Cyril and I took the lorry up to the school, loaded it up, and that was that. Mick got a few quid, I got a drink from Mick and a sack of spuds from Bill, and he got all the new bench-ing he'd been after for the glasshouses. He couldn't afford to go out and waste thousands on this, that and the other, but even if he could, I don't think he'd have done anything differently.

We used to rotate the crops at Fullers, which meant that we'd grow roses in one of the fields one year, then the next we'd do potatoes which would clear the soil, and then the year after that we'd grow wallflowers; and then back to roses again. This meant that in each field there was always something different growing. Spuds were the hardest. We didn't dig them by hand of course; we used to follow Cyril in the tractor. He had this machine for taking up spuds and as he drove along we'd follow behind and pick up what it missed. After that we'd get them under cover and start sacking them.

At about seven o'clock, Betty, Bill's lovely wife, would come out and she'd do us cheese on toast, a mug of tea and a cake, and we'd sit there, have a fag and then go on again. Depending on how much we had to lift and how many orders there were to make up we could be there until ten or eleven o'clock sometimes.

The first job we had to do on a Saturday morning (having been on the ale all Friday night down at the Jolly Farmers in Purley!) was hose down and then sweep all the paths in the glasshouses, and once that was done we'd go round and clear up all the rubbish. This would be about seven o'clock in the morning, by the way, so you can imagine the state some of us were in. Bill was an absolute stickler for cleanliness but also for punctuality and so you didn't dare turn up late. That was Bill, though; he just wanted things done the right way.

Later on, we had a toilet put in for the customers and after we'd finished hosing, sweeping and cleaning we'd draw lots to see who was on toilet duty. Now, bearing in mind the number of people we used to get in – hundreds a day mainly – and the fact that it was only cleaned once a week . . . Well, you can imagine what kind of state it was usually in. More often than not, if I drew the short straw I'd end up vomiting. It's not what you need after ten pints of beer, some pork scratchings and six pennyworth of greasy chips!

Sometimes if we were especially hung-over Bill would suddenly decide that some manure needed spreading on one of the fields. He could be a mischievous old bugger when he wanted to be.

'Jim! Cyril's going to bring round half a ton of pig manure to the field where the briars are going. Go and spread it, would you? There's a good boy.'

When I stuck my fork into that pile I almost heaved. You see it wasn't just pig manure in there. Bill used to buy it from that local pig farmer I mentioned, and he'd chuck in all the entrails from the dead piglets and what have you. This would take me at least an hour or so to spread, so you can imagine what I was like at the end of it. White as a sheet!

The worst thing about this particular job was that he'd always make me do it just before I finished for the day, and hard as I tried I could not get rid of that bloody smell. I used to go straight to play football after work on a Saturday and my mates would say, 'Bloody hell, Jim! Have you fallen into a slurry pit or something?'

Well, they weren't that far from the truth, were they? Even while we were playing I could see the opposing players looking round as if to say, 'What's that bloody awful smell?'

One person who didn't seem to mind the smell of yours truly was a new recruit Bill took on about two years after I joined. Her name was Nickie and, to be quite honest with you, she was the first girlfriend I *should* have had, but I was always too busy playing football.

Her old man was a big noise at some pharmaceutical company, and her mum? Well, she was one of the chattiest people you could ever ask to meet. Always happy and always interested.

I'm still in touch with Nickie, and in fact I'll be going down to give a talk for her local horticultural society in Somerset just after this book comes out. I'd better be nice about her, then, otherwise they won't buy a copy!

Now, how much stick do you think a young girl doing a manual job alongside three working-class boys is going to get? Well, whatever you come up with, double it, because, seriously, we were beastly to that girl. Not that it made a blind bit of difference to her, by the way. No, she was more than a match for us blokes, as you'll find out in just a few pages' time.

When it came to customers, Bill used to serve the entire neighbourhood. It didn't matter whether you were after a box of tomatoes or enough plants to fill an entire garden, if you lived in the Purley area you went to Fullers. I was astonished by the amount of money some people used to spend. Mr and Mrs Edgerton were the biggest spenders. He was big in property, if memory serves, and they had some serious money, not to mention a five-acre garden. Mrs Edgerton called in one day and she ordered five hundred pounds' worth of bedding plants, and this was the early 1960s! I just stood there with my mouth open, trying to imagine what five hundred quid must have looked like.

The majority of these were a variegated geranium with a beautiful dark pink flower, called Caroline Schmidt; they're still going to this day. Mrs Edgerton would have somewhere in the region of three or four hundred lining the entrance to the house. Right on the very edge of the drive would be French marigolds but there'd also be lobelia (a variety called Crystal Palace, believe it or not), sweet peas and petunias. As I said, five hundred quids' worth!

Bill and I delivered them a few days later, and we ended up planting them all out for her. Mrs Edgerton was one of the loveliest women I think I've ever met. She was a proper lady and I remember her coming out every fifteen or twenty minutes just to check I was all right.

Do you know, their house was so big that they had a carpenter and a full-time painter and decorator working there, not to mention a staff of five full-time cleaners, maids and cooks. It wasn't quite *Downton Abbey* but it was north of *Upstairs, Downstairs*. That place would probably be worth tens of millions these days. The gardener they had there was a Spanish bloke, and he was worse than bloody useless. He'd never pulled a weed in his entire life; in fact, as a favour to Mr and Mrs Edgerton (but without them knowing), Bill sent me round there one afternoon to tidy up.

We supplied and planted out their front drive too, which went on forever, and after we'd finished it was just a sea of geraniums. We must have planted five or six hundred of them. It looked stunning.

We ended up spending a few weeks every year working for Mr and Mrs Edgerton. It was like painting the Forth Bridge: the moment we thought we'd finished, Mrs Edgerton would ask us to start on something else.

'I say, Bill. Would you mind having a look at this herbaceous border over here? I'd like it re-designing.'

'Of course, Mrs Edgerton.'

Now when you think about herbaceous borders at home

you might be looking at something between twenty or fifty feet, right? Well, this thing must have been all of a thousand because it ran either side of the main lawn. You should have seen Bill's face. I could almost see the pound signs jumping up and down in front of him.

Eventually old Mrs Edgerton passed away and when Mr Edgerton remarried he decided to downsize. Well, who do you think he asked to look after the garden while he was trying to sell the place? Me. I was working for the Greater London Council at the time, and the old boy called me up. My brother Pat and I ended up looking after it for him and for a time we had a nice little business together.

Incidentally, Pat ended up working in horticulture full time just like me, and he was good at it too. He studied at Oaklands College of Agriculture and Horticulture and was there the same time as my old mate Alan Titchmarsh. In the end he worked in local authority, the same as me, and he's retired now. Personality-wise Pat is just like our mum was: obstinate, but with a heart of absolute gold, and I love him to bits.

I have to say that as well as being a great all-round gardener Bill Fuller was also a fabulous salesman, but the difference with him was that he could walk-the-walk as well as talk-the-talk, if you see what I mean, and his reputation in local horticulture was second to none. This made him one of the go-to people in the area. These days I think he'd probably have to refer to himself as a 'gardening consultant' or something.

Anyway, getting back to the plot – so to speak – and to my mate Nickie. Our staff room at Fuller & Sons was an old shed, which must have been built about the same time they opened up, and before we went in there for our grub we'd dip our hands in the water tank in the glasshouse. Now there's health and safety for you. We always brought sandwiches in but Bill would let us pick a couple of tomatoes to go with them. After we'd finished our grub, me, Vic and Roy, who were the two blokes I worked with, would play three-card brag for pennies, and then after about twenty minutes and several cigarettes we'd get off back to work. That was until Nickie joined us. Now Nickie was an absolutely brilliant propagator, but unbeknownst to us she was also a pretty good card player, and she used to run rings round us. Not in an actual game of cards, by the way. No, this was something far more cunning.

To this day I don't know how she did it, but sometimes Nickie would deal the cards for us and when she did, Vic would get three queens, Roy would get three kings and I would get three aces. After that there'd be pennies flying absolutely everywhere and because I had three aces, I won. A few days later it would happen again and every time I'd come out the winner. Nickie gave nothing away so at the time we never really suspected foul play. It was only after the fourth or fifth time that she got found out. Clever? You bet your life she was.

Roy and Vic were both a lot older than me and so to a certain extent a lot more experienced, but they didn't begrudge the attention I got from Bill. To Vic and Roy it was just a job, you see, and so, in a way, they were probably just going through the motions and collecting a wage, but for me it was more a vocation really, or a way of life, and I think they found my passion for it all quite amusing. It could quite easily have gone the other way, though. I mean, think about it. A young upstart comes in and starts sucking up to the boss. They could have turned on me.

In the end, I think they could see how much it meant to me and they knew that I would never ever go out of my way to belittle them. I respected them, and what's more I always made sure I listened to them. They were fully grown men whereas I was just a boy, and if there's one thing Pop taught me, other than how to look after a garden or an allotment, it was to respect your elders. This didn't stretch to nuns of course, but then you can't have everything.

When I wasn't hard at it I was watching and listening, because, as I've said, everything Bill knew, he taught me, and he knew the lot. He was ex-Wisley you see, and, my God, was he proud of it. It was funny though. One minute I'd be painting the inside of a glasshouse or cleaning out that bloody awful toilet and the next I'd be standing there for two hours watching Bill graft some clematis. That was his legacy really. He didn't have much money and he didn't own either the house he lived in or the plot of land the business was on, and so what else did he have to leave behind but his knowledge? In me he'd probably found the world's most grateful recipient.

When it comes to my time with old Bill, there's one memory in particular that when I think back always has me in stitches. It centres around two words, and the words are – nicotine shreds. Nicotine shreds? I bet you're saying to yourself, here we go: he's on about cigarettes again. Well, no, I'm not. In fact if I'd ever tried to smoke one of these buggers – and I've smoked some pretty strong fags in my time – I'd most probably have coughed myself inside out.

These days if somebody suffers an infestation of, say, glasshouse whitefly, what would they normally do? Personally I'd probably try something like a sulphur candle first, but let's do things by the book, shall we? According to the Royal Horticultural Society, biological control is preferred to things like pesticides or sulphur candles on account of two things: the rapid reproductive rate of the pests and the widespread occurrence of pesticide-resistant strains. The RHS then goes on to explain which predatory mite is suitable for which pest – in the case of whitefly, something called *Phytoseiulus persimilis*.

It doesn't matter which pest lands in your greenhouse, the RHS can recommend a biological antidote, whether it be mites, parasitic wasps or pathogenic nematodes. It's marvellous stuff, it really is.

If only we'd had them at Fullers.

Once again I should point out that health and safety circa 1961 was somewhat different to how it is today and the same goes for pest control. In fact it didn't matter which bug or beastie came to visit – whitefly, red spider mites, mealy bugs or aphids – we dealt with them in exactly the same way: with me, a handful of nicotine shreds and a big box of matches. This was actually one of my favourite jobs at Fullers, because despite it not actually being terribly safe Bill used to take the whole process very seriously, and so I always felt quite important.

First I used to have to put some nicotine shreds in each corner of the glasshouse. Not too many, but then it was strong stuff and so you only needed a bit. Then, when Bill gave me the nod, I'd set them alight and then run like hell for the door. I remember that, once, the bloody thing jammed and I honestly thought I was going to be engulfed by smoke, never to be found again. Bill had to run over and get me out in the end.

By the way, do you know what I carried with me for protection, and Bill always made sure I had one? A handkerchief!

Well, what could possibly go wrong?

Anyway, within about ten to fifteen seconds the entire

glasshouse – and remember, these were big buggers – would be just acrid. Full of smoke!

'All right then, Jim,' Bill would say. 'You know what to do.'

Once I'd checked that the door was securely shut (you couldn't actually lock the thing) I'd put a small handwritten sign on the front that said: 'Do not enter! Fumigation in progress'.

That was about as much use as a rake made out of spaghetti. You didn't need to enter the glasshouse to be overcome by smoke, it was everywhere! It was coming out from under the door and from the eaves. It even came out from the gaps between the glass and the frames! From a distance it must have looked like a bloody house fire. What a palaver!

The other job that would have the Health and Safety Executive clambering for a notice to cease trading involved a delightful little invention called a sulphur lamp. Not a sulphur candle, by the way, which are perfectly harmless – a sulphur lamp. These were also used to get rid of pests on an industrial scale and were basically paraffin lamps with canisters of sulphur stuck on top. Once again I had to set them up around the glasshouse, light them all one by one, and then run for the door. The smell though! My God, it was strong. I used to light them just before we left for home, and when we went back in there the next morning it still reeked, and I remember there was always a film of burned sulphur on top of the water tank. Seriously, the lengths we went to to get rid of pests and diseases.

I haven't told you about the heaters yet, have I? Well, all of our glasshouses were heated by what were called Robin Hood boilers. We had three boilers, heating three glasshouses each. Each had its own boiler room of course, and it was my and Vic's job to stoke them up in the morning. These were serious bits of kit, by the way, and they used to eat tons of coke every week. We could have got jobs as stokers on the *Queen Mary* if we'd ever got fed up with gardening.

Before we could fire the boilers up each day we'd have to clinker them. This was done using a big six-foot metal grab (like a rake, just a lot bigger) and, I promise you, it was hard going. After that we'd have to remove the ash and, depending on which section of the boiler you were working on, this could take forever. These things heated three glasshouses each, remember, and so there were pipes running everywhere.

Once that was done I'd have to drop down into the pit below each of the boilers and then shovel out all the ash. I used to shovel it into these big buckets that had rope tied to the handles and then Vic would pull them out. There were no gloves or masks, by the way.

We used all the ash of course – that went on the flower beds – and we used to scatter the clinker on the paths in the winter. After a couple of years they went over to using oil burners. Relieved? You bet your life we were.

The most exciting bit about working at Fullers was getting your Christmas bonus. The whole thing was quite an event. At about four o'clock on Christmas Eve, once we'd finished the orders, we'd all pile into the van and go down to the local pub. Now, bearing in mind what Bill used to dress us in when the weather was bad, we'd often turn up looking like a load of tramps and we used to get some right funny stares. We didn't care though. Bill would always stand the first round and then after one or two more we'd all pile back into the van, drive back to the nursery and then Bill would shake your hand and give you an envelope.

'Happy Christmas, Jim,' he'd say, and away I'd pop.

We would all have been earning about five or six quid a week back then and there was always at least twenty or thirty quid in there. It was the jackpot!

After that I'd go straight back home, have a quick wash and change, and then I'd be straight down the local. The two most important nights of the year for me at that age were Christmas Eve and then New Year's Eve. They were the big ones and I don't mind admitting I'd get absolutely legless.

Talking of Christmastime, do you remember the winter of '63? Well, that's one of the abiding memories from my entire four years at Fullers. It's got to be one of the hardest we've ever had in this country. It started snowing on Boxing Day and, I promise you, it hardly stopped until early May. I remember this because the football team I was playing for at the time were top of the league on Boxing Day and, do you know what, we never kicked another ball all season – over four bloody months. How mad is that? We were under a blanket of snow and frost.

Now this only really occurred to me a couple of days ago but, during the whole of that period, Bill never laid a single person off; which, when you think about the business he was in, is unbelievable really. I thought about it because I heard somebody talking about these zero hours' contracts, and it's things like that make me realize just how lucky I was. All through that winter Bill had us cleaning out glasshouses, building frames and mending wheelbarrows – we did the lot – whereas these days the moment there's a drop of rain, that's it, you're off home. We just carried on. You didn't have to look hard to find things to do. We even finished up clearing snow from people's drives. A little bit of public service went a long way in those days.

7. Moving On

Not long after I started working at Fullers, Bill began dropping RHS Wisley into the conversation. At first I had
absolutely no idea what he was talking about, because as far
as I was concerned RHS Wisley was just a very famous
garden, but even when I eventually did twig that it also
had a college attached to it I didn't really want to know.
I'd just left my final seat of learning and to be honest I was
trying to forget about it.

Old Bill wouldn't let it go though, and as time went on
he'd relate everything we did to an experience he'd had at
Wisley.

'You see how I'm budding this rose, Jim?' he'd say. 'Well
I was taught that at RHS Wisley, and by one of the country's
most eminent horticulturalists.'

'Really, Bill?'

I did my best to pretend I was interested.

Looking back he must have had it all worked out from
the start, because after that he'd begin saying things like,
'You just wait until you go to Wisley, Jim.' At first I didn't
take any notice but then after a while I could tell he was
being serious.

'What do you mean, "When I go to Wisley", Bill?'

'Well, you want to go, don't you?'

'I haven't given it much thought.'

'Well it's about time you did, my boy. Best horticultural
college in the world, RHS Wisley.'

From then on I paid attention to Bill when he told me about his exploits at Wisley and even started making a few enquiries. Pop was first on the list.

'Wisley, boy? Best horticultural college in the world. Seriously, if you can get in there you'll have made it.'

At the time I didn't know that Pop would have ended up going to RHS Wisley had he been allowed to go and work for Gussie Bowles, so it's hardly surprising that he was so enthusiastic. Well, I thought to myself, if Bill and Pop thought it was a good idea, maybe I should go?

'The thing is, Bill,' I said, 'it's all about qualifications and as you know I'm not that studious.'

Now I know I always say that the only test I ever passed was my cycling proficiency but that's the truth. At the time I was a gardener, a beer drinker and a poor footballer – in that order!

'That's rubbish, Jim,' said Bill. 'I never amounted to anything at school but I got in. What's more, I passed with flying colours, and why do you think that is? Because I love gardening and because I was always willing to listen. As long as you keep your lugs open, boy, you'll be fine.'

My ears are like open taxi doors so there was no problem there.

At the end of the day I was just a younger version of Bill, and he could obviously see that. He'd really flowered at Wisley and was now running one of the most popular nurseries in the whole of Surrey. I was beginning to get excited. Once I started getting involved in Bill's chats about Wisley and showing more of an interest I could tell he was pleased. His plan was coming together, you see.

'I'll tell you what, Jim,' he said. 'If you're serious about going to RHS Wisley I think we'd better start sending you to some evening classes.'

Well, if that's what I had to do, that's what I had to do. Bill made all the arrangements and even ended up paying for the course.

'The Practice and Principles of Horticulture' was the first course he sent me on and it took place at Croydon Technical College. The teachers were all park superintendents and so they were able to teach me a few things on the practical side that perhaps regular teachers wouldn't have been able to: things I hadn't done before, like pruning. And on the other side of the coin they taught us some alternative methods of controlling things like bugs and diseases. I remember the class took place every Tuesday so I used to run home after work, wolf down some grub and then dart down to Croydon Tech. Two bloody hours it lasted! Mind you, to be fair to the teachers, they always managed to keep it interesting and, what's more, there was a lovely little pub over the road. Well, you've always got to have something to look forward to.

In the end I think I did three or four of these courses and then one day, when I was probably about twenty, Bill sat me down in his office and gave me the shock of my life.

'Look, I'm sorry, Jim,' he said, 'but I'm afraid it's time for you to move on.'

My face must have been a picture.

'What do you mean, Bill? I don't want to move on.'

I couldn't believe what I was hearing. Even with Wisley on the cards I just couldn't imagine a life outside Fullers.

'We need to build up your CV. Look, at the end of the day, the RHS are a bunch of bloody snobs [his words, not mine!], and if we were to put in an application that said you'd only ever worked in a nursery . . . Well, I doubt you'd even get an interview. You need to get some municipal experience.'

Now I'd been at Bill's about four years by this time and

you had to have six years' practical experience before you could even apply to go to Wisley. This tended to weed out all the time-wasters; after all, if you were prepared to work outside for six years and in all weathers, the chances are you were going to last the course, and hopefully pass it.

'What am I going to do then? I don't want to leave.'

'I'm afraid you're going to have to, Jim. Going to Wisley will be the making of you, you mark my words. Seriously, you've got what it takes to get right to the very top.'

To be honest, I had no idea what the top was. All I knew was that the two people I respected most in the world thought I was good enough, and at the end of the day I trusted them.

'All right, Bill. Where do I go?'

Once again he had it all worked out.

'Have you ever heard of a bloke called Upton? He's Parks Superintendent at Croydon.'

'Yes, I think so. Why?'

'Well he's ex-Wisley too, and what's more he's a pal of mine. I've had a word with him and he thinks he might be able to help. You're seeing him tomorrow at 3 p.m. OK?'

Well it would have to be. The blokes who'd taught me at the evening classes all worked for Mr Upton and they seemed like a good bunch.

'OK, Bill. I'll be there.'

'Good boy. I've talked it through with your dad and he thinks it's the right thing to do.'

So, the following day, off I went to Croydon Parks Office.

Looking back once again, Bill was absolutely right in sending me off to work for Croydon because the experience I'd gain there would be varied, to say the least. Instead of just growing and then selling bedding plants I'd be planting them out in parks and designing beds. Then there'd be maintenance, of course: looking after all the cricket pitches, bowling greens and graveyards. And I'd even get a crack at things like floral decoration. Just think about all the displays they have in the Mayor's Parlour, and what have you. They're all changed as regular as clockwork. No, the more I thought about it the more sense it made.

Bill had explained to Mr Upton what kind of experience I had, not to mention the courses I'd been on, and when it got to the end of my interview with him he seemed a bit embarrassed.

'Look, Jim,' he said. 'I like you, but to be honest you've probably got more knowledge than half the foremen I've got working for me, yet all I can really offer you is a labourer's job. If I brought you straight in as a foreman I'd have the unions on my back in half a minute. There'd be uproar.'

This came as a bit of a shock to me, although a nice shock all the same. You see, pardon the pun, I was probably still a bit green back then. I had never been assessed professionally (except by Bill, who was biased) so had no idea how good or bad I was. What's more, I didn't care. I just got on with it.

'A labourer's job would be fine, Mr Upton. I just want to work.'

'I'm really glad you said that, Jim. I was at Wisley with Bill and he's one of the best. I know how much you going there means to him and so if this job helps then I'll be very happy.'

I stood up, shook Mr Upton by the hand and walked out feeling pleased but also quite embarrassed. I'd never received as many compliments before.

When I started at Croydon they put me in the nursery first; a brand spanking new nursery. Hell's teeth, I thought, this is state of the art. This was as opposed to Bill's of course, which was state of the ark! It was made of aluminium instead of wood and there was a stove-house at the end of it. Everything was there; it was absolutely fantastic.

I suppose Mr Upton was right to be a little bit edgy about employing me as a labourer because, without wanting to sound like a big-head, I did end up gardening and not labouring. What a difference to Bill's, though. For a start there was the wages. At Bill's I got a little brown envelope every Friday with about five or six pounds in it, and now I was paying things like National Insurance and what have you. Welcome to officialdom! We had a canteen too. I mean, what about my garden shed? This was a different world. The first person I worked under was hilarious. He was ex-army and it didn't matter where he was or what he was doing his boots were always spotless. I could never work out how he did it. I'm not kidding; you could see your face in them. And he still carried his old kitbag with him. Mr Savage his name was, and, my God, could he dig. He must have dug the tunnels for the Great Escape or whatever during the war because I've never seen anything like it. He could get down six feet and about three yards square within ten minutes.

He was a fair old boy though, because when we were out working rather than send somebody else to go and make the tea, he'd always do it himself.

'I know exactly where we're up to so if you cool off while I'm away I'll know about it, OK?'

Well, the moment he was gone, out came the fags. We had him sussed, you see. He used to carry this little cane with him and when he went to make the tea he'd distract us and then put it in the ground where we were digging. We just moved it back a few feet. He had no idea.

'Well done, boys. Making good progress, I see.'

Not half. About two Capstan Full Strength each!

Do you know that near the nursery there used to be this

wonderful walled garden that we looked after? I used to adore working there. Any excuse. We would dig it all out, rake it, and then plant all these wonderful polyanthus we'd grown in the nursery. There were hundreds of parks and grounds we had to look after, anything from a graveyard to a hospital garden, so growing your own was the only way to do it. I remember a van would come down to the nursery every morning about nine o'clock and once we'd loaded up, the plants were delivered all over the borough.

My best pal at Croydon Parks was an old soak called Harry. He was a good few years older than me of course but then I always did get on with people older than me. Old Harry used to finish work at five o'clock every day like the rest of us but instead of going home and having some tea – again like the rest of us – he'd go straight into the local pub. What's more, he'd stay there until closing time. The following morning – or in Harry's case every bloody morning – he'd come in holding the cold fish and chips he hadn't finished the night before and he'd have them for his breakfast. Watching him used to make my stomach do flaming cartwheels. It was horrible!

I used to work with Harry quite a lot, in fact at one point we were known as the Compost Kings. We had to sterilize all the soil before it was used. It would come in bulk and then we'd put it through something called (and forgive me if I've got the name wrong) a Terrorforce Sterilizer, which was basically a very long cylinder that had a big flame burning at one end. Harry and I would load the soil in at the other end, light the flame and then switch on and spin the cylinder round for a bit until the soil had been sterilized. Don't ask me how we knew. We just did. The only thing you had to be careful with was the temperature, because if you overdid it the soil would be useless.

Now, do you remember the old time and motion studies? Well this was about the time they started introducing them, and because Harry and I had become so proficient at doing this we basically got paid extra. The bloke watching the process had decided – don't ask me how – that the job we were doing should have lasted an hour, say, and we were doing it in half an hour. That was then turned into money and we were earning another four or five quid a week. That was serious money to us. None of the other kids wanted to know because, quite frankly, the task was hot and sticky and made your arms ache, but me and old Harry couldn't care less. All he could see were beer tokens and a few extra betting slips. He was nobody's mug, old Harry, and if memory serves he thought up one or two other wheezes in order to take advantage of the time and motion. It all went straight to Mr Ladbroke and Mr Tetley of course.

This kills me when I think about it, but about fifteen years later I saw old Harry sitting on a bench on Croydon High Street begging. He looked absolutely dreadful, the poor old thing, and when I went up and handed him a tenner or whatever it was he had no idea who I was.

'Thank you, governor,' he said, which is what he used to say to the boss when he handed him his wage packet. It all came flooding back: the sterilizer and the cold fish and chips. What a character, but what a dreadful way to end up.

When it came to the extra money I earned – well, that all went on my car. You see by this time I was mobile. In fact I was the proud owner of a once new Ford Anglia 105e. Remember them? What a motor – 997 ccs of pure oomph! In actual fact it was probably about as powerful as a bloody hairdryer but at least it was mine.

Croydon got their money's worth from me though. Do you know, at 5 p.m. every couple of days a lorry used to turn up with a load of materials on the back of it, but because people tended to work to rule back then nobody would stay behind to unload it, except me. I just kept thinking about old Bill. That's what we'd always do with him, and if he'd thought I'd started working to a bleeding clock just because the others did, he'd have gone barmy.

I suppose I could have claimed for the time it took me to do it but what would have been the point? An extra couple of bob for twenty minutes or whatever it was? No, that wasn't the way I'd been either brought up or taught. You left when the job was done, and that was it.

Don't get me wrong, there were dozens of advantages to working at Croydon and I probably learned as much there as I did with Bill. I was certainly doing a lot more than labouring, which was what I was paid to do. It just presented me with a bit of a culture shock sometimes.

I think one of the turning points of my career in horticulture was when I was assigned to the decoration team to put up a display at the Fairfield Halls. To be honest I was dreading it because I never really saw myself as a flower arranger. I was happy enough landscaping gardens, of course. Working on gardens for people like Mrs Edgerton saw to that, not to mention the dozens of others Bill let me practise on. But when it came to the intricate, decorative stuff; well, I suppose I saw it as being a bit dull and perhaps too feminine.

It just goes to show how wrong you can be. I loved every single minute of my time on the decoration team and although I was never what you'd call an artist I always did my best, and I think I became OK at it in the end. Most importantly though, it provided me with another string to my bow and made me love my profession even more. It opened up a whole new world really.

Dad as a young boy
with his parents Owen
and Maud.

Mum and Dad
on their wedding day
in 1943.

My godfather,
sea captain
Stanislaw Lubez.

Uncle Robert and yours truly at Worthing.
West Mansions, where Robert lived with his sisters,
mother and aunt, is in the background.

Mum is holding me with, on the left, her sister Susie and
Auntie Dot, and on the right her mother and her sister Nora.

Mum and Dad with me, my sister Caroline and younger brother Patrick.

Myself aged about seven.

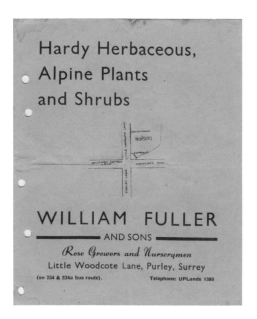

My first full-time job in horticulture
was at Fullers nursery.

Nicky in one of the greenhouses,
tending the chrysanthemums.

Fullers grew everything from scratch,
including these cyclamen.

With my old governor at
the GLC Bob Corbin, aged 100.
He was one in a million.

We may look like we're modelling gents' blazers, but this is
a group of students from Wisley on an outing to Stonehenge.
I'm third from the left, seated.

Our more natural habitat, on the Wisley trial grounds, aka Siberia.
David Fitton is on the left, I'm in the middle and
John Cromwell is on the right.

Chopping down hazel
at Wisley Common.

I'm MCing one of the many
social events I organized.

As Chairman of the London Garden Society I'm in the
background as part of the welcoming committee when the
Queen Mother (our patron) came on a visit.

I never stood on ceremony with my teams.
Bob Legge, who I exhibited with at Chelsea, is on the right.

Winning gold at Chelsea with the Royal Parks apprentices and
Bob Wadey (second from right on the front row). The false wall was
packed against two poles and swaying in the breeze.

Another gold medal, but this time I masterminded the exhibit.
Joe Woodcock, next to me, was my assistant superintendent.

Before that the closest I'd ever come to flower arranging was when one of Bill's customers, who had a flower stall somewhere, used to come and pick his order up. It was always on a Friday afternoon, I remember, and about an hour before he was due I'd have to walk up and down the glasshouses getting his bunches ready. I used to have to do single colours, then a few mixed colours. Once I'd done a bunch I'd wrap them up, put it under my arm and do another one, and when I had about six or seven done I'd take them outside and put them in a bucket. There you go. You could hardly describe that as floristry, could you?

I remember watching this bloke turn up. He was a proper old-school market trader and always had a fag hanging out of the corner of his mouth. Actually, do you remember Claude Greengrass, Bill Maynard's character in *Heartbeat*? Well if you do, that was him. He wore a great big trench coat, a flattened trilby and a roguish grin.

Once he'd chucked all the flowers on the back of his van he'd shut the door and say, 'Right then. How much, Bill?'

'That'll be thirty quid, Bob.'

'Have you got any trays of tomatoes?'

'Yep.'

'I'll take five. How are yer beans?'

'Yeah, we're picking.'

'Good enough. I'll take ten pounds.'

Then he used to bring out this wad of cash. Well, there must have been three or four hundred quid there. But regardless of how much it was he'd always give Bill an extra tenner.

'Give the boys a drink, will you, Bill? Right, see you next week.'

And with that he'd get back in his van and drive off again. The next day he'd be flogging the veg and the flowers in the market – for what, probably a couple of shillings a bunch?

I remember at the end of every rose season he would always come and pick up the runts. You'd always have a few in the crop, perhaps ten or fifteen a row, and so Bill would give the old boy a ring and then he'd come down and clear the lot. If he hadn't taken them we'd have just had to burn them all.

The first time he came to collect the runts I went up with him and Bill to the field.

'OK, Jim,' said Bill. 'Cut all the briar out, cut them back and then label them all.'

Then as I stepped up to carry out Bill's request Bob stopped me with an outstretched arm.

'Don't you dare, Jim! What the bloody hell are you thinking of, Bill?'

Poor Bill looked well and truly affronted.

'Well,' he said, 'that's what you do. You cut back the briar and . . .'

'Balls to cutting back the briar!' interjected old Bob. 'You do that and that's half the bleeding bush gone.'

'Yes, but the briar won't be any good,' pleaded Bill.

'I know that, and you know that, but my customers won't. And besides, what do you expect for three and six? Here, Jim, don't bother labelling the bloody things, just put 'em in a bag. They won't care what colour they are.'

Poor old Bill. I'm sure he preferred dealing with the Edgertons!

Anyway, in the Croydon Parks nursery during the winter we forced through flowers like hyacinths, daffodils and freesias. We grew the lot in there, and they were all used for decorating the Mayor's Parlour and the Town Hall. These days you've probably got something plastic sitting there, but back then that was a very, very important part of our job and I'm so glad I got involved.

One day the nursery manager pulled me to one side.

'Look, Jim,' he said. 'There's a big decoration job about to come up and there's some overtime in it if you're game?'

Is the Pope a Catholic?

'Count me in,' I said.

This is what I mean about doing something you enjoy. Getting paid for decorating the Mayor's Parlour was terrific, but then getting paid extra to do some more? I don't know. Somebody up there obviously likes me.

Each year one of the London boroughs would have to entertain the mayors from all the other boroughs, and this year it was obviously Croydon's turn. It all took place in the Arnhem Gallery, which is attached to the Fairfield Halls, and the plan was as follows: at each end of the hall was a bank of flowers and in the middle was a big circular dining area where everybody sat. Now in the middle of that – and this will give you an idea of just how big it was – we laid a full-size bowling green, and then in front of the seats and around the bowling green we built a flower bed that ran all the way round. The backdrop to all this, by the way, was about fifty conifers that were all about twenty or thirty feet high. We had lorry after lorry after lorry turning up from the nursery. Talk about ornate. I can't remember who designed it all but once we had it in it looked fabulous. In actual fact I think there was probably a little bit of one-upmanship at play because, let's face it, none of the boroughs wanted to be seen as the poor relation. There was pride at stake.

I remember standing there after we'd finished and in walked the nursery manager. We were all pleased as Punch by what we'd done and were expecting nothing less than a bombardment of thanks and congratulations. Well, we were going to be disappointed.

'I suppose you think you've finished, do you?' he said.

We all looked at each other and then one of us said, 'Yes, we think we have.'

'Then what the hell's that bamboo cane doing over there?'

I looked to where he was pointing, but couldn't see anything. Then two or three of us went over there. It took us ten minutes to find what he'd spotted and it was quite literally one bamboo cane that was about six inches out of place. That was the discipline they taught you there, and I wouldn't have had it any other way.

'I'll tell you what,' said the manager, 'you all have another look round and then come and tell me when you've really finished.'

What he meant was: 'I've spotted something straight away so I suggest you go through every inch again and make sure it's as it should be' – and we did. We spent another two hours checking it all.

Now some people might say that that's just nit-picking but I'd disagree. If you're going to spend so much time, money and effort on something as elaborate as that there's only one way to do it – the right way. Otherwise you might as well just not bother. Once you've done it the right way, that becomes the only way.

8. Wonderful Wisley

After being at Croydon for a couple of years I'd almost forgotten about Wisley. It still came up in conversation every so often, either when I saw Mr Upton or met up with old Bill, but that was rare. You see, not only did I put the hours in at the parks five days a week but I played football, cricket and was the social secretary for the John Fisher Old Boys. I was a busy boy!

Then one evening, completely out of the blue, I got a call from Bill.

'Right, Jim, it's time. I'll meet you in the pub tomorrow at seven o'clock. Don't be late.'

With that he just hung up. Now I can be a bit slow on the uptake sometimes and on this occasion I surpassed myself. I couldn't for the life of me figure out what he meant. Anyway, I turned up at seven o'clock as instructed and as soon as I'd shaken his hand Bill said, 'It's time, Jim. Get yourself a pint, sit down and we'll fill in your application for Wisley.'

Bleeding hell, I thought. Wisley! I'd forgotten all about that.

I went to the bar and bought myself a pint, but before I went to sit down I had a think for a bit. At the end of the day I was having a really good time at Croydon. Did I really want to give it all up to become a student, of all things?

Then I began to think straight again. Of course, I bloody well did. I was still a labourer at Croydon (in name and wage only!) and as much as I liked being there I wasn't being tested and, to be honest with you, I wasn't really learning much anymore. I think the attraction was the security, and perhaps the social life!

'What do I have to do then?' I said when I sat down.

'Not a great deal, thank heavens. Just answer a few questions. They'll fill in all the gaps at the interview. Here's a pen. Best handwriting, Jim!'

Bill was right, there wasn't a great deal to fill in – just your background and a bit about your experience – and so in about half an hour we were done.

Bill took the form back and put it in an envelope.

'I'll post this first thing tomorrow.'

'I can post an envelope, Bill,' I protested.

'You'll forget.'

He was right, I probably would.

After a couple of days I'd all but forgotten about Wisley again. I'd never even been to the place and so even though I'd filled out the application form it just didn't seem real to me.

That lasted about another five days or so, because after a week I received a letter from the college asking me to go down for an interview. The letter had arrived during the day of course and so by the time I got home Mum was almost having kittens. In fact she was waiting for me at the front door.

'What's wrong, Mum?' I asked. I thought somebody had died.

'There's a letter for you, Jim, and it's got RHS Wisley printed on it. Open it, Jim, open it!'

'All right, Mum, calm down.'

Pop was there too and I could see that he was as excited as she was.

Now this was a horrible moment for the simple reason that I was sure it was going to say something like:

Dear Mr Buttress,

Thank you for your recent application but I'm afraid that on this occasion it has been unsuccessful.

May we wish you every success blah blah blah.

You know the kind of thing.

Anyway, when I opened it I got the shock of my bloody life.

'They want me to go for an interview!' I said.

'When boy, when?' asked Pop.

'Says here next Tuesday.'

That's the moment it all became real, I suppose. You should have seen the looks on Mum and Pop's faces. They were a picture.

'Make sure you ring Bill,' Mum said. 'He'll be so pleased.'

Bill was pleased all right, but he was also realistic.

'It's just an interview, Jim. The hard bit's still to come. You need to concentrate on next Tuesday. Make sure you speak to Mr Upton first thing tomorrow to get the day off.'

There was no way I was going to forget that. Mr Upton was delighted for me and I got the day off no problem.

'Make sure you prepare, Jim,' he advised. 'You know what they say. If you fail to prepare you prepare to fail.'

Well actually I wasn't aware of that particular saying, but it made perfect sense. The thing is, how? I knew what I knew. There weren't any books I could read. In the end I just tried to forget about it and get on with my life.

Come the morning of the interview I was actually surprisingly calm, which is more than can be said for Mum, Pop and Bill. They'd been behaving like expectant parents ever since I'd got the letter and they'd been making my life a misery; but in the nicest possible way of course. They were just excited for me.

The main four questions they asked me were:

'What are you going to wear, how are you going to get down there, what time are you going to set off', and 'What are you going to say?'

But they didn't just ask me the questions once. They asked me again and again and again!

The answer to the first question was easy. I had one pair of smart-ish trousers, one smart shirt, one sports jacket and one pair of shoes. It wasn't Savile Row but I reckon I scrubbed up OK.

The second question was also a doddle. I was going to take my Ford Anglia 105e. Mum wasn't convinced.

'But what if you break down, Jim?'

'It'll be fine, Mum. Stop fussing!'

The next question was a bit trickier. I mean it was only about twenty miles, but that was about the top speed of my old Ford – twenty miles an hour! To be fair it was a bit faster than that, but just to be on the safe side I gave myself a good hour.

And the last question could be answered with the initials A.N.I. – absolutely no idea. At the end of the day I had no idea who was going to be interviewing me and no idea what they were going to ask me, so what was the point in trying to second guess the questions? I was just going to be myself and if that was good enough, great, and if it wasn't, no hard feelings. I'd just carry on.

Anyway, there were the four questions answered. With a bit of luck I'd get there looking presentable, and with another bit of luck I'd get in.

I was supposed to be going on my own to Wisley, after all it was a work day and so Bill and Pop wouldn't be available. Then, about two hours before I set off – this would have

been about seven o'clock in the morning – Pop came in looking all flustered.

'I've decided, boy. I'm coming with you. I'll call work and
tell them something's come up.'

He was a bag of nerves, bless him, and I'll tell you what,
for my Pop to take a day off work . . . well, it had to be a very
special occasion. Either that or a death!

'You don't mind do you, boy? I'm sure you could do with
the company and I'd be worse than bloody useless if I went
in to the office.'

'Of course not, Dad,' I said. 'I'd love you to come along.'

And so an hour or two later me and Pop hopped into my
Ford Anglia and off we went.

What a journey that was. Although it was only twenty
miles it seemed like a hundred and the closer we got to the
venue the more nervous I became. In the end I had to stop
for five minutes and have a fag.

'Come on, boy,' said Pop. 'You don't want to be late.'

By the time we arrived at Wisley I'd got over the nerves,
thank goodness.

'Just remember to keep smiling,' said Pop. 'And if you get
stuck on a question, ask them one.'

I had no idea whether that was good advice or not but it
was all I had.

As we got out of the car, instead of going straight to the
main buildings we had a walk down to Bowles' Corner. This
is an area dedicated to Pop's mentor, E. A. Bowles, that has
within it all the plants he either discovered or was famous for
growing. When we got there Pop turned to me and took me
by the shoulders.

'For heaven's sake, son,' he said. 'Go and do something I
was never allowed to do. Do it for me, eh, boy?'

The look on his old face said it all. Forty years in insurance when all the time he wanted to be working in a park or a garden. And he could have been too.

'I'll do my best, Dad. I'll do my level best.' And away I went to the main building.

I was almost in tears seeing my old dad like that. He wasn't a very emotional man by any stretch of the imagination and, as you know, he could be a proper disciplinarian. He was just old-school though.

By the time I got to the main building I'd pulled myself together and was beginning to feel a little bit more like my old self again. And it's a good job I did, because when I arrived the people I encountered were pretty businesslike.

'Excuse me,' I said to one of them. 'I'm here for an interview. Could you tell me where—' but before I could finish asking my question she pointed at a chair. 'Sit down there, would you. Somebody will take your name and you'll be called in due course.'

Sure enough, after about ten minutes another woman came up to me.

'Mr Buttress?'

'That's right.'

'The panel are ready for you now. Follow me.'

I don't mind admitting that by this time I was absolutely terrified.

As I walked through the door I saw three people sitting at a table. There was Frank Knight, who was a director at Wisley and the main man. He was the chairman of the panel. Then there was a chap called Chris Brickell, who was one of the teachers there, and finally a man called Mr Everson, who was the Parks Superintendent down at Brighton. Apparently you always had to have somebody independent on the panel and so poor old Mr Everson got to interview me.

'Good morning, Mr Buttress,' said Mr Knight. 'Thank you so much for coming. Sit down there, would you.'

They started off by asking me some random gardening questions. Things like 'When should you prune holly?' and that sort of thing. Well, that was like falling off a log to me, I got all of them on the button. No problem.

Now after about fifteen or twenty minutes I thought I'd done quite well. I'd answered all the questions correctly, had spoken only when asked to and hadn't used a single swear word. For somebody who likes a chat and who uses the occasional expletive, that must have been some kind of record. The funny thing is I still got the feeling that I'd blown it because whenever I answered a question Mr Knight and Mr Everson just looked at me like I was some kind of numbskull. Must have been the accent, I suppose?

Just then, after yet another question about pruning or whatever, Chris Brickell suddenly piped up.

'Right, that's enough of all that,' he said. 'Now what do you do when you're not gardening, Mr Buttress?'

'You mean socially?'

'That's right, in your spare time. What are your hobbies, Mr Buttress?'

Well, I thought. Eyes down for a full house! If you want to know about my social life I'll give it to you. And so with that I sat up, leaned forward in my chair and I gave them the lot.

'Well, sir,' I began, 'I play football on a Saturday for my local club and I play cricket on a Sunday, and I'm on the social committees for both. I help organize the social events, the Christmas parties, the end of season presentations and the booze-ups. I also help host all the events and am in charge of the fundraising. On top of this I like to go and watch the Palace play and afterwards . . .'

I gave them chapter and verse – my entire social calendar.

After about ten or fifteen minutes I was done, and so I sat back in my chair and waited for the next question.

The reaction to my short lecture on the comings and goings of a sports-mad gardener who likes the odd pint was the same as a football match really – a game of two halves. Mr Brickell had taken in every word and had been genuinely enthralled by what I got up to.

'How fascinating,' he kept saying. 'You really do all that, Mr Buttress?'

Unfortunately, Chris's enthusiasm was not shared by his two esteemed colleagues and the more I spoke the more uncomfortable they both became. It was like Lord and Lady Tiddlypush being locked below stairs with the servants. As I said, though, I was only going to be myself and if they didn't like it, there was nothing I could do. I wasn't going to pretend to be something I wasn't.

Eventually they sent me on my way and when I got back to the car and told Pop what had happened he suddenly got all moody on me.

'They were obviously embarrassed by what you told them about gardening so they had to make something else up, boy. Looks like you've blown it.'

Now as you know I thought I'd done well with the questions but, to be honest, I still didn't fancy my chances much; certainly not after Pop had finished with me. What a pessimist. No, as far as I was concerned I'd tried my best but I probably wasn't their kind of person. It wasn't the end of the world.

By the time we got home the mood hadn't changed – if anything it had got worse.

'You may as well give Bill a ring and tell him you've blown it,' said Pop. 'He won't be happy.'

In actual fact Bill was quite a bit more optimistic than Pop and I.

'They're like that with everyone, Jim. A right bunch of snotty buggers. They have to be though. They can't give anything away. Look, if you answered all the questions correctly, like you say you did, then you stand as good a chance as anyone else. Keep your chin up, Jim. You might just be surprised.'

Good old Bill. If it wasn't for him I wouldn't have been able to spell Wisley, let alone have been for an interview there; and here he was cheering me up. He was one in a million.

Well, I think you know what happened. About ten days later – by which time Pop had convinced me that I'd be staying at Croydon for life – I received another letter with the words RHS Wisley on the front. Here we go, I thought. At least I can put us all out of our misery.

Dear Mr Buttress,

We are pleased to inform you that you have been accepted . . . Blah blah blah.

'Here, Dad,' I said. 'Read that.' And then I handed him the letter. Suddenly tears welled up in his eyes.

'I knew you'd get in, boy.'

I thought, you cheeky old devil! He had thought the closest I'd ever get to Wisley would be playing football away at Byfleet.

What a fantastic moment that was. Was I proud? Well of course I was, but my pride was reserved for Bill Fuller. He'd given me a future in gardening – something I loved more than anything else in the world, including football – and that was the greatest gift anyone could have ever given me.

Instead of phoning him I jumped in the car and went straight round to see him. I wanted to tell him in person.

'Didn't I say that you might just be surprised?'

'You did, Bill.'

'Seriously, Jim, there might be a few nobs and snobs up there but there are also a lot of good people at Wisley and there are as many people like you and me to come out of there as there are academics. You're in there on merit, Jim, and don't you forget it.'

This was the late summer of 1966 and not long after the World Cup Final, so for an Englishman who was fanatical about both gardening and football . . . well, let's just say there was quite a bit of celebrating to be done.

As you know, Purley was about twenty miles away from Wisley and because I owned a car that, although roadworthy (just), wasn't what you'd call speedy, there was no way I could commute. I'd have to live in. I don't really remember how Mum was when I left home but I remember Pop was thrilled to bloody bits! He thought I treated the place like a hotel and, to be honest he probably had a very valid point. I was a busy boy though, as well you know. Some nights I didn't get in until gone 2 a.m., and if I ever woke the old boy up, God help me. Pop used to give me a right ear bashing. He was a big lad, my old man – a lot bigger than me – and although he was an early riser he liked his kip. Waking him up was as good as starting an argument with a grizzly bear. The truth is, I was as keen to move out as Pop was to see me go, as with such a busy life the last thing I needed to do was worry about what time I got in.

I left Croydon Parks on a Friday of course, a couple of days before I was due to arrive at Wisley, and so spent the weekend saying all my goodbyes; not only to my mates at Croydon but to all my chums at the football club I played for as well as the cricket club. I'd spent many happy years with all of the above, and I don't mind admitting that having to say goodbye to them had me welling up like a good 'un.

In between all the pats on the back I suddenly remembered that I had to pack, and so at about eight o'clock on the Sunday evening, after one or two final goodbye drinks, I set about chucking all my worldly goods into a bag. I didn't have much – just a few clothes, an alarm clock and my shaving gear – and so before long I was in bed dreaming about what was to come. The following morning I had a bit of breakfast, threw my bag into the car and off I went. It was a funny feeling. You see, even though I was only moving about twenty miles away I'd spent almost all my life within the confines of either Haywards Heath or Purley. Wisley could have been Australia as far as I was concerned.

The journey from Purley down to Wisley was a lot smoother this time. I didn't have to stop once and even when I drove through the entrance I don't remember feeling nervous. I was just excited and full of expectation.

We all received a wage of £10 a week for the work we did at Wisley (it was like any modern apprenticeship in that way) and £6.50 of that went on your digs. The accommodation there was run by the YMCA and the warden was a man called Mr Lane. He was a cheerful old thing, Mr Lane, and once the new batch had all arrived he got us in a line and then told us first what we'd be doing day-to-day, followed by where we could find our rooms. There were eighteen of us altogether, which would normally have meant nine rooms of two, but for some reason I got a room on my own.

'I thought it was best to give you a single room, Buttress,' said Mr Lane. 'Is that all right?'

'That's fine, sir. I don't mind where I sleep so long as I've got a bed.'

'Well it said on your application you're a Catholic so I thought that was probably safest.'

Probably safest! For who?! What the hell he was getting at I have absolutely no idea. It gave me a bit of a Catholic complex though.

We were all split up into groups after that and then told which section we'd be working on first. You spent about three months on each – glasshouses, rock and alpine, trial-grounds, etc. – and so over the course of the year you covered everything.

Incidentally, in order to supplement my income at Wisley I used to operate one or two schemes, once I'd got to know the right people. One of the first people I befriended was the landlord of the Hut Hotel, which became my local, and just before my first Christmas there he took me to one side and asked if I could get hold of any greenery for him.

'No problem,' I said. 'Just you leave it to me.'

That evening I waited till everyone had gone to bed and then went round with a torch and secateurs and set to work. I think I collected about four sackfuls in all.

'Bloody hell,' said the landlord. 'Thanks a lot, Jim!'

What I didn't know then was that every year Frank Knight arranged a Christmas lunch in the Hut Hotel. What's more, some of the bits I'd snipped were only to be found – in Surrey at least – at RHS Wisley!

Fortunately, when Frank Knight questioned him about it the landlord told him he'd bought it all from a traveller.

That was a close one!

The course itself was for a two-year Diploma in Practical

Horticulture. I later found out that one of the reasons I might have been accepted – apart from being a perfect candidate of course – was because of a rather problematic 'them and us' situation. I'll explain. Over the previous few years Wisley had accepted an awful lot of students who were, shall we say, academically inclined, and had no ambitions to work in the practical side of gardening. To them the course was really just another notch on their academic bedpost, and in a way that belittled both the course and the subject. On top of this, the academics generally kept themselves very much to themselves and refused to mix with either the students who *did* want to forge a career in practical gardening or the staff. They were up themselves a bit by all accounts, and so, in an attempt to level things up a bit and keep the brainboxes to a minimum, they decided to bring in a few more members of the great unwashed. People like me! I didn't mind one bit when I was told about this. In fact it made me feel quite pleased with myself. I've nothing against academics but I'm every inch a hands-on gardening man, and being considered as such was a compliment.

This situation had also affected the social scene at Wisley, which until a few years before had been buzzing. In fact ever since the place had become overrun with scholarly types it had turned into a ghost town. There was very little football and very little cricket; the entire social scene was limited.

Now it was all starting to fit into place. The interviewer who'd taken such a keen interest in my social life? Well, he knew exactly what he was doing, didn't he? Let's get young Buttress in. He'll sort them out.

Anyway, that's exactly what I did. As most of the course was practical at the beginning – which was easy-peasy – that gave me plenty of time to resurrect Wisley's football and cricket teams, as well as all the social events. I was like Wisley's very own Redcoat, I suppose, and for the first few months I was there my feet never touched the ground. I was ringing up the secretaries at all the local football and cricket clubs trying to arrange friendly matches. It was a big old job.

This wasn't just for the benefit of the students, by the way. Oh no. Wisley's a community in itself, and so in addition to the students getting involved we had not only the teachers but the regular staff-members too. The Redcoat comparison wasn't a joke – I got the social scene at Wisley well and truly buzzing.

Some of the best events we ever had at Wisley were the dances. They used to attract students, teachers and staff members, and as well as helping to organize them all I used to compere them too. Basically, if there was a social gathering of any kind at Wisley, the social committee and I would be responsible. About a week before the Christmas parties took place I'd ask some of the more creative students to make wreaths and then auction them off in the staff canteen.

Once I was off there was no stopping me. In fact, thinking about it, that and compering the events was probably the training ground for my career as a public speaker. It's in the genes you see. I didn't mention this before but if Pop's side of the family were responsible for any talent or enthusiasm I might have as a gardener, it's Mum's lot who are to blame for the gob.

Do you remember the old film and stage actor Fred Emney? He was about twenty stone and always wore a monocle. Well, he was a relative of mine – a first cousin of my mother's mother, I think – and was the latest in what had been a long line of family thespians. Mum always said she could see a lot of Cousin Fred in me, especially when I used to take part in the school plays.

'You're just like him, you are,' she used to say. 'A great big show-off!'

It wasn't showing off. I just like talking to people and entertaining them.

That's another thing I didn't mention – my early career as an actor. Basically, as with gardening, if anyone needed a volunteer for a part in a play I'd be the first to put my hand up and during my time at the John Fisher School I ended up playing all sorts of different roles, even female ones! Believe it or not, I actually scrubbed up rather well as a member of the opposite sex and if I hadn't gone into gardening, who knows? I might well have given it a go as a pantomime dame.

Anyway, back to Wisley. The facilities we had there were absolutely first class. The changing rooms for instance were spot on – a lot better than I'd been used to – and the cricket and football pitches were fabulous. Well, bearing in mind where they were and who'd be looking after them, they'd have to be, wouldn't they? If those pitches had been any-thing other than perfect we'd have been a laughing stock. As it was, we were by far the most popular place to come and play. I mean, come on, what better place to have a game of cricket or football than Wisley? The opposition used to love playing us because they could bring their wives and kids with them. Normally the majority of the wives would keep out of the way, thereby avoiding the inevitable six hours of bore-dom, but when they played Wisley it became like a family day out. You see, while the blokes were all playing cricket the women and children would go off and have a good look round the gardens and what have you. They weren't sup-posed to, mind you. Sunday was a members-only day and so we used to sneak them in through the staff entrance. If there's anybody from Wisley reading this then I can only apologize, and pretend to mean it! There was no harm done. Anyway, after that we'd all have a great big tea in the pavilion and everyone went home happy. I mean, who could ask for more? It couldn't have been better.

The football was just the same, except there'd usually be a few more libations involved after the sport was done. The cricket teas were lovely of course – terribly English – and we'd still have a few jars afterwards. The football, though. It didn't matter who we played or whether we won, drew or lost, there was always a celebration afterwards. Well, that's what life's all about, isn't it? Once you're gone that lid's down a long time.

Once again, we used to get the world and his wife turning up to the football, especially when we played the clubs that weren't that far away. I remember once playing a team from a company called Byfleet Engineering. Now the bloke who owned Byfleet Engineering was a big noise at Chelsea Football Club at the time and so he must have had some serious dosh. Well, I assume he wasn't short of a bob or two, because when the Byfleet lot turned up not only did they have about a hundred fans in tow, not to mention rattles, scarves and all that other malarkey, but they had a couple of future Chelsea players too! I'm not kidding.

There was one bloke playing called Ian Hutchinson. He passed away about thirteen years ago, sadly, but, my God, could he play. He was just a trainee for Byfleet at the time, but he ended up making over a hundred first-team appearances for Chelsea and despite his young age he could do things with a ball that I never knew were possible. He could take a throw-in from the halfway line and it would reach the goal. I just stood there thinking, what the hell happened there? Of course he went on to score about ten goals and after trying to hack him down, which didn't work, we just let him get on with it. It was men against boys, really, except half the men were boys!

Now the only person who seemed to have a problem with what I was doing on the sports and social side was the director of RHS Wisley, Mr Frank Knight. He loved me like a son, did old Frank, a son who had just dropped out of Oxford so he could sell programmes at football matches. He couldn't stand me!

He was a double for Captain Mainwaring really, and in every way imaginable. He was short, about five foot nothing, and had a tummy, a comb-over and wore those little pebble specs. I told you, Captain Mainwaring! I was his nemesis, and he mine. He used to say to the teachers, 'Why have we got a joker like him here?'

Old Knight was an academic, you see, and was all for piling more and more of them into Wisley. I'll never forget the first time he spoke to me. It wasn't long after we'd started and I could tell that he'd been dying to let me have it.

'You do realize that there were literally hundreds of applicants this year, Buttress?' said Mainwaring, tight-lipped. 'And for reasons which I confess are beyond me the panel decided to choose *you*.'

Nice to meet you too! I mean, fancy saying that to a student?

He was a clever man, don't get me wrong, and I swear to you I had an awful lot of respect for him, but at the end of the day he had a very clear vision of the kind of student he wanted at Wisley and unfortunately that vision didn't include people like me.

Anyway, I just ignored the daft old beggar and carried on regardless.

As old Pop used to say: 'Son, you can't please everyone all the time. If somebody doesn't like you, that's their problem.

Don't make it yours.' What do you reckon, wise words? That was good enough for me.

Of the eighteen people who were in my group at Wisley there's one person in particular who I'd like to tell you about, and that's a chap called Bobby Golden. Now I flatter myself but I reckon I can sniff out a character at about a thousand paces, and when I first met Bobby Golden I was absolutely fascinated. He won't mind me saying this, but do you know who he used to remind me of back then? Little Lord Fauntleroy! He's a tiny bit older than me, about five foot three, and used to wear a waistcoat, a little trilby hat and he always had a scarf tossed over his shoulder.

'Good morning, James,' he'd say, when I was hung-over at breakfast. 'I suppose you've been playing in one of those beastly football matches again?'

'As a matter of fact I have, Bobby. How about yourself?'

'Oh, I had tea with the Queen Mother yesterday.'

Now at first I always thought he was pulling my leg until one day he pulled out a little card with 'Clarence House' printed at the top.

'Dearest Bobby,' it read. 'I so enjoyed tea yesterday. Look forward to seeing you again soon. I am, yours sincerely, Elizabeth R.'

Well, you could have knocked me down with a feather. It turned out little Bobby knew the lot.

From then on every time I picked up the *Telegraph* or *The Times* and they were reporting on some royal event, there he was! 'In attendance this afternoon: Lord Tiddlypush, Viscount Pardew of Selhurst and Mr Robert Golden, a good friend of Princess Alice, Countess of Athlone.'

But it wasn't just Clarence House and Kensington Palace where Bobby had connections; he had them all over the shop and used to organize visits to places of horticultural interest that wouldn't usually be on the cards.

Old Knight used to absolutely hate this because he didn't have the connections Bobby had, and that used to drive him mad. I, on the other hand, used to love it!

Never could the term 'opposites attract' have been more appropriately used than with Bobby and me, because despite the fact that on the face of it we had naff all in common we became great pals at Wisley and have remained so ever since. He's one of the most generous, entertaining people I've ever met.

The assistant curator at RHS Wisley at the time was Christopher Brickell, now Christopher Brickell CBE, who had been part of my interview panel. You might well have heard of him – he's a very learned gentleman. Chris is about fifteen years older than me and as well as being the assistant curator he also taught botany at the college. He was, and still is, a boffin of some repute. Seriously, old Chris has written dozens of encyclopaedias for the RHS over the years and God knows how many instructional books. He's the real deal.

Now in addition to having a brain the size of a football, Chris was a pretty nifty fast bowler, but during the week he had the unfortunate job of having to teach things like botany to the likes of me. Well, by the time it got to Sunday I think all the venom and frustration he'd built up trying to impart his vast knowledge to us just exploded inside him and he ended up bowling like Fred Trueman. They were like bloody missiles and his strike rate was absolutely fantastic.

During his classes Chris used to ask us to identify certain

plants – about twenty if memory serves me correctly – and as we came in he'd have them all lined up in the room.

Believe it or not, me and some of the other 'hands-on' types used to do rather well at this, and do you know why? Well, the evening before the lesson Chris and one of his colleagues would sneak out into the gardens and start choosing the plants they'd want us to identify, and we'd follow them. It was as simple as that. They'd pick their samples and sneak back in and then we'd pick the same samples and try to find out what the hell they were. We'd learn their Latin names, the lot. It didn't always work as sometimes we couldn't get close enough to see what they were picking. Unfortunately they eventually got wise to our skulduggery and so sometimes used to swap the samples at the last minute. We did get a few right though, and my Latin improved immeasurably.

The closest I ever got to excelling at anything resembling horticultural theory was during those plant identification classes. To start with, as I've just said, we used to follow Chris Brickell into the gardens and try to get a head start, but after a while I realized that, actually, I didn't need to do this. Believe me, nobody was more surprised than I was.

They were all very hotly contested these identity parades, and once we thought we'd identified all the flowers, trees and shrubs and had included all their scientific classifications we'd stand back and try to make sure nobody could see what we'd written. As if anyone would want to copy from me?

I admit I never beat the top boys but once I'd found my feet I was always up there. This was a real victory for me because I had to actually think about things for a change and I do believe – shock horror – that I might even have read a page or two from a couple of text books.

As I said before, when we first arrived at Wisley we were split into groups and followed three-month rotations in all the different sections. It was almost like doing another apprenticeship really, but at the end of the day that was what we were there to do – learn about the practical side of horticulture. In many ways it was just like being at Croydon. They had lots of foremen there like old Savage, not to mention labourers, and because of all the social events I was organizing I got to know everyone really well. These were all seasoned Wisley staff, by the way, who'd been working there for an age and they all lived in the village. I suppose it was like a monastery, only without the silence, abstention or prayer. All right then, it was nothing like a monastery, but you see what I'm getting at. It was a wonderful little community, where people not only lived together, but worked together.

From a practical horticulture point of view my first three months there were pretty flat; in fact I spent the vast majority of the time sweeping leaves in Seven Acres, which is one of the gardens there. From September right through to November that was virtually it. I did think to myself on more than one occasion, what the hell am I doing this for? But at the end of the day it was part of what practical horticulture was and it had to be done.

The bloke I worked with most closely during my sweeping-up sessions was an old boy called Ernie Martin. Now Ernie had been working at Wisley since about 1785 and he knew the place like the back of his hand. Quite often in life it's not what you know, but who you know, and with Ernie being Mr Wisley, so to speak, this was definitely a case in point. Never mind sucking up to the headmaster and all the teachers; you can do that in the classrooms. If you want to get on somewhere the first thing you have to do is get to know the people who are at the very heart of the place.

Do you know, despite Ernie being a labourer, just like I was at Croydon, he still had his own office. The thing is there was only me and him who knew about it. This still makes me laugh even today.

Once Ernie and I had got to know each other a bit and had begun having the odd fag break together he gestured to me one day from in front of a large conifer.

'Here, Jim, over here. Do you fancy a cup of tea and a slice of homemade cake?'

After I nodded in the affirmative he pulled aside a branch or two on the front of this conifer and walked in. I thought, here we go, it's the Secret Garden! But do you know what he'd done? He'd cut out the whole of the inside of the tree and there in the middle was a seat made from a plank of wood. There you go then, one ready-made canteen. It worked an absolute treat.

Ernie's boss, Mr Clayton, who was also a really nice bloke, used to wander past wondering where we were.

'Shh,' Ernie would suddenly say. 'It's 'im. It's Clayton!' And we'd sit there silently like naughty little schoolboys.

After my three-month stint with old Ernie my group was moved down to the vegetable trial grounds, and do you know we might as well have been in Siberia. These grounds were situated down in the village and basically it was just a large flat dust bowl. But in the winter, my God, it got cold! We had to put straw bales all around the circumference to act as a wind barrier; and then once that was done we used to dig, and dig, and dig! It was never ending. They used to trial absolutely everything down there, from beetroot to broccoli. All the seeds would be provided by the big seed companies and once a crop was ready a team of judges would come down from all over the country. If they liked what they saw over a period they'd award the veg a merit, which would of course be mentioned within the seed company's next catalogue.

There used to be some absolutely beautiful old glasshouses at Wisley, and when we started I couldn't wait to get into them but by the time our turn came around it was summer, the hottest time of the year. I mean how typical is that? Spent all winter out in the cold and as soon as the good weather comes along it's 'Here you, get indoors.'

They're not there anymore those glasshouses, but they were situated right in the middle of the gardens and they used to grow some unbelievable stuff in there.

All the colleges used to exhibit at Chelsea at this time, so when one of the members of staff at Wisley, a chap called Ken Aslett, asked me if I'd like to take part I snapped his hand off. I remember old Pop was absolutely over the moon when I told him, and he even came along to see how we got on. He'd taken me to Chelsea lots of times as a spectator, but to exhibit there? I really thought I'd made it.

I'd been singled out by Ken because as you know I didn't mind getting my hands dirty. If we ever had to work late I was always the last to leave and so he must have thought, let's have him. Believe you me, when it comes to devising, building and then installing an exhibit at the Chelsea Flower Show – the biggest and most prestigious gardening show in the world – it takes a lot of hours and a lot of hard work. I was more than up for it though.

We ended up building this wonderful Japanese Garden, Ken and the team, and although we weren't allowed to win any medals at the show I think we did ourselves and the college proud.

Old Frank Knight wasn't too happy about me being there but that was one thing he didn't have any control over. I remember him sniffing around while Ken and I were building the exhibit and all he did was criticize.

'I'm not sure you're doing that correctly, Buttress. Oh no, no, no . . .'

My God, that was hard work though. Once Ken and I finished on an evening we'd then have to catch a Green Line bus which would drop us just outside RHS Wisley, but the moment we got on the bus we'd fall straight to sleep; not before we'd asked the driver to give us a nudge, of course.

'Your stop, boys,' he'd shout. 'Come on, off you get!'

We were there for about a week prior to the show and by the time it opened to the public we were done in. We looked awful too, like a couple of tramps. I remember standing there on the first day. We'd only had about three or four hours' sleep and I was starting to wobble a bit. Then all of a sudden Ken piped up.

'Here, Jim, look lively. We've got a royal visitor.'

I looked up and there, coming straight towards us, was Princess Alexandra, surrounded by all the RHS hierarchy.

'What the hell do we do?' I said to him.

'Don't worry, Jim; she'll probably just walk on by. Just smile and nod.'

But she didn't. She came over and started chatting with us. You should have seen the RHS bigwigs. They were horrified. To be fair we did look pretty rough.

'What are you boys doing here?' she asked.

'We're from RHS Wisley, Your Highness. And this is our exhibit.'

'Oh, how absolutely splendid!' said the princess. 'You have done a good job. I simply love Japanese gardens.'

'Thank you very much indeed, Your Highness.'

'Who designed the garden?' she asked.

'We did,' I beamed.

I looked over and grinned at Ken and there, standing next to him, was Frank Knight. He looked like he was about to explode! This was his worst nightmare, as not only was he being ignored in favour of a student, but that student was me, his grubby little nemesis!

Incidentally, years later, while I was exhibiting for the Royal Parks, one of our bigwigs, who shall remain nameless, did a very good impression of Knight, except this one took it to extremes. Basically he would find out the route of whichever Royal was visiting, and then stand there like a horse tied to a stake at every bleeding corner. 'Look at me, Your Royal Highness, look at me!' Bob Wadey and I used to absolutely howl with laughter. The world's full of Mainwarings.

Princess Alexandra ended up chatting to us for about fifteen minutes and once she found out I was a student, that was it; she wanted to know the lot. Where I was from and what my parents did, etc. Since then I've met her at dozens of events and each time she's always the same: chatty, cheerful, interested and knowledgeable. She certainly knows her stuff! Best of all though, Princess Alexandra is the patron of Perennial, a charity that supports people who work in horticulture, and she's done some wonderful work for them over the years.

Slowly but surely I began to get to grips with becoming a student – or at least one half of it. Practically, I was as sound as a pound. After all, that had been my life ever since I could remember. It was the theory I had problems with. No surprise there of course. At that point I think the only thing I'd ever read cover to cover was a Crystal Palace programme and a selection of sports pages, so that didn't make things easy when it came to studying. I just didn't have the patience. I'd start reading a book but within about a page and a half my mind would be elsewhere.

On the theory side of things (and you can thank Bobby Golden for the details) we had lessons on things like biology, botany and general sciences, and then we'd have the dreaded lectures of course. Miss Brooks, who was the Wisley pathologist, used to lecture on the identification and eradication of pests and diseases, and then Mr Walker, who was also Wisley-based, would talk about the cultivation of fruit and vegetables. Every so often we'd have guest lecturers who covered all kinds of strange subjects; things like behavioural sciences and the like. Needless to say I don't remember a single word. Thank goodness for Bobby! One of the visiting lecturers was from Reading University and was called Mrs Quinn. We used to call her the Mighty Quinn on account of her being a big strapping lass. She lectured on landscape design, which is probably why I remember her. That was about the only bit of theory I was interested in.

Let me tell you about a typical day at Wisley, because we had an awful lot to pack in. After breakfast we'd start off with some practical gardening at about 8 a.m., whether that was in the glasshouses, the rock gardens or wherever. All throughout this period we'd receive instruction from a member of staff as well as the odd lesson, but it was almost all practical; at least ninety-five per cent. Then at about five o'clock we'd have tea, which for me was usually sausage, egg and chips and a mug of tea, followed by a bun and then a fag, and then after that you'd go for lectures. Such was my enthusiasm in the gardens that by the time I sat down for the lectures I was fit for one thing – kip! I was just exhausted. You see quite often, once the lectures had finished, I'd have to go off and meet somebody about a dance or a football match and so my days usually lasted about fifteen or sixteen hours. On top of that I didn't go anywhere either at the weekends or during the holidays and so I never, ever had a day off. Now don't get me wrong, this was completely out of choice and I never got roped into doing anything I didn't want to. Apart from, that is, the lectures, and as what they were supposed to be teaching me would be making up a size-able percentage of my overall mark . . . well, it doesn't take a genius to work out that I might just have been heading for a fall. Do you know, I've got all my lecture notes somewhere and I promise you there can't be more than about fifteen words per sheet.

I promise you that I tried though. After tea I'd have a fag, walk around a bit and try and wake myself up, but by the time I sat down again in the classroom I was doing ten rounds with the bloody sandman again.

I remember old Chris Brickell delivering a lecture on botany one evening, and a very fine lecture it no doubt was – if only I'd been awake to hear it. One minute I was sitting there trying to take it all in and the next minute – *bang* – I was woken up to the sound, not of leather against willow – which is what I was used to with Mr Brickell – but of blackboard rubber against blackboard.

'Buttress! Do try and stay awake.'

'Yes, sir, sorry, sir.'

It was no use. I was back in the land of Nod again within seconds. I think Chris and the others just gave up in the end.

The other students managed to find a balance between practical and theory, taking it nice and easy during the day so that by the time it came to theory they had more than enough energy left to get them through. Me, on the other hand – the old whirling dervish – went at those flower beds or whatever like a bull in a china shop and didn't come up for air until I absolutely had to. That was where I was in my element, I'm afraid. I knew I wasn't really fulfilling the remit but I just blocked it out and carried on doing my own thing. 'It'll be all right,' I used to say to myself. 'You'll get through.' Who was I kidding?

Funnily enough, one of the things you had to do at Wisley before you received your final mark was to deliver a lecture in front of the teachers and all the other students on a subject of your choice; and it didn't matter whether the lecture was on the dos and don'ts of garden bonfires or on Cumberland turf – a lecture was what you had to give, so that was that.

Now here's an irony for you. Despite not listening to many lectures in my time I'm actually more than happy giving them. Funny that. But one lecture I did listen to at Wisley, and what's more I'm very glad I did, was delivered at the start of the course by a visiting teacher. It must have been at the start because I remained awake for the whole thing!

It was actually a talk on how to deliver a presentation or a lecture, and the chap who spoke said that in order to do it well you need to remember four things:

1) Know your subject.
2) Don't use notes unless you have to.
3) Always face your audience.
4) Keep it interesting, don't say more than you have to, and add humour where appropriate.

Now if I'd known then just how important those words would become to me, I'd have slipped the bloke teaching us a pocket full of fivers. As it was I didn't, and so he'll have to make do with a few words of gratitude! You see, over the past thirty years or so I have delivered about a hundred and fifty horticultural talks every year and those four points have served me very well indeed. They're the rules of the game.

By the way, you're going to read more about my talks later, whether you like it or not!

Anyway, when it came to delivering this final lecture we were told you could choose your own subject, give or take, and the audience you had to deliver it to would be made up of two elements: guests of the RHS and your fellow Wisley students.

I'm rarely short of a few words and so instead of spending hours and hours preparing for my lecture I decided to just wing it. I know what you're thinking: if he's just going to wing everything, how can he ever expect to get on? For the simple reason that in addition to being a confident speaker I also knew my subject inside out. And what subject do you think I chose for my lecture?

Budding roses of course!

Twenty minutes? I could have done twenty hours.

I kept it informative, or so I hoped, and at the same time added a nice sprinkle of humour to it. Most importantly though, I stuck to those four golden rules, and it worked like a treat.

Despite all the confidence, I was actually terrified before I gave that talk, especially when I saw old Knight sitting there, and so when I eventually got to the end it was like being told I'd been asked to run a pub and manage a football team. Pure joy!

It seemed to go down well though. There were laughs in all the right places and, do you know, I genuinely think that one or two of them learned a thing or two. Job done!

After I'd finished waffling I sat back and watched some of the other boys. Some of them weren't public speakers, bless 'em, and they weren't big when it came to humour.

One chap, a lad from Cumberland, got up four times to give a talk on Cumberland turf, but each time he stood up the only words that would come out were – Cumberland turf! He'd stand up, say 'Cumberland turf' and then sit back down again. It was a two-worded lecture.

Wisley paved the way for what I've become today: a reasonably knowledgeable, good old-fashioned practical gardener. And do you know, by the time the course had ended I was doing all the budding demonstrations. The chap teaching them had only done a few whereas I'd done hundreds of thousands. It had been my job for nigh on six years. He didn't mind and I was in my element.

Unfortunately, this little victory wasn't quite enough to get me through, and as a consequence of not making myself familiar with the theoretical side of practical horticulture I ended up becoming one of only three people who failed to get the required mark. I think you needed sixty per cent to get a pass and be awarded your diploma and I got something like fifty-eight per cent. I was three sheets to the wind when I found out – we all were – but I wasn't upset. I think I knew I was never going to pass and so I'd prepared myself for the inevitable.

But despite not getting that bit of paper I had two brilliant years at Wisley, and in addition to doing my first ever Chelsea Flower Show I met more characters than you could wave a trowel at and worked alongside a fantastic bunch of people, some of whom – i.e. the ones who haven't pegged it – have remained pals of mine to this day. What's more, I got to spend every working day, and it has to be said almost every non-working day, in what I believe is one of the most beautiful gardens in Britain, if not the world.

The passing-out parade, which took place after the presentations was a right giggle. You didn't have to attend if you hadn't passed – in fact it wasn't really expected – but I thought, bugger that! This had been my life for the last two years and I'd had a ball. I wasn't going to miss it for the world!

When I and my two fellow flunkies found out we hadn't passed, one of them, who I can't really name because it would be unfair, left the room, packed his bags, and went home there and then. We never saw him again. He was devastated, the poor chap. Not long after he left the other lad got up to do the same. This time though I was having none of it.

'You're not leaving me on my own,' I said to him. 'We've done the two years. Diploma or no diploma, we're going to that passing-out parade!'

And so we did. We put a big smile on our faces and in we went. And who was the last person I saw before I left that day? Who else but old Frank Knight.

'Aah, Buttress,' he said. 'I think we both know why you didn't pass, don't we?'

'Yes, I suppose we do, Mr Knight.'

'You've done wonders for the football team here of course, Buttress, but then Wisley isn't Wembley Stadium?'

'No, Mr Knight,' I replied. 'Wisley isn't Wembley Stadium. Wisley is a stunning garden that I have had the pleasure of working in these past two years. And do you know what, nobody can ever take that away from me.'

What he said then I'll remember for the rest of my life.

'Do you know, Buttress? Despite not passing your diploma I've a funny feeling you're going to get on in gardening. What's more, I rather hope you do.'

With that he shook my hand, turned on his heels and left.

I, on the other hand, went straight to the pub. I needed a drink!

9. Man Management

There's a very wise old saying you often hear being bandied about and that's 'Never go back', but unfortunately, when I left Wisley, that's exactly what I did. Most of the other boys from my intake at the college went straight into what was then called the Institution of Recreation and Parks Administration, which had been started by an old parks administrator from the Stockport area. He figured that unless you intended to either stay in education or go and work at your family's nursery or stately home, you were probably going to go into – as it says in the name – recreation or parks administration. Courses mainly lasted a year or so and prepared people for jobs with local authorities. It was like a horticultural finishing school, I suppose. Parks and recreation was a much bigger concern in those days and privatization was still a long way off.

Now although I considered going straight to the Institution with the others – because you were all but guaranteed a job when you came out – I eventually decided that it just wasn't for me. I can be a pig-headed so-and-so sometimes, and because it didn't feel right, I didn't go. I'm a great believer in following your gut instinct, you see, and at the time mine was saying *Don't do it*. As you can imagine this went down like a lead balloon with the family. I remember having a meal with Mum and Pop one evening not long after I left Wisley and all the way through he kept on at me.

'What are you going to do now, boy? Your mum and I can't support you.'

'I don't know, Dad. I haven't decided yet.'

'You're no use to anyone just moping around here.'

He always chose his words very carefully did Pop.

'I'll tell you what,' he said. 'What about going back to work for Bill?'

'Come on, Dad,' I protested. 'Wouldn't that be a bit of a step backwards?'

Pop didn't like that one little bit.

'A step backwards is when you go to somewhere like RHS Wisley and then turn down the chance to train for a perfectly good job. Beggars can't be choosers, boy. You've got to pay your way.'

He was right of course.

Anyway, funnily enough, just a day or two later, Bill phoned me up and asked me to meet him. I had no idea what he wanted to see me about and when he told me I got the shock of my life.

'Jim, I want to offer you a partnership at Fullers.'

I couldn't believe it.

'A what?'

'Look, I can't go on forever, Jim. I need somebody to leave the business to. Think about it. It's the perfect solution.'

At first glance I suppose it was the perfect solution. After all, Bill had no kids, the business was surviving (although in need of a bit of a push) and I needed a job. It ticked all the boxes. Unfortunately it was slightly more complicated than that because although Bill's offer of a partnership seemed to be the answer to all of our prayers, once you scratched beneath the surface a bit there was actually no partnership to be had. It was just idealism really. A bit of a fantasy.

For a start, the land Fullers occupied was owned by Surrey County Council and they'd leased it to Bill's father with a view to it being passed down to the Fullers of the future, so to speak. Passing the business on to an outsider wasn't an option and so any arrangement that was put in place would only last as long as Bill remained alive. Fair enough, I thought. All I want to do is get my hands dirty again!

Then a bit later when Pop had a look at the books, it became clear that there wasn't really enough money in the business to sustain two equal partners; not unless we both worked for a pittance. I'm not money orientated, as you know, but if I was going to be left with nothing when Bill retired I wanted to at least be on a decent whack. But I decided to give it a go, and over the next year or so I put everything into trying to build up the business so it could sustain us both. I gave up playing football and cricket and I even stopped going to watch Palace! I mean, how's that for dedication? Seven days a week I worked and, what's more, I absolutely loved it. The business wasn't exactly on its knees when I came back, but as I said, it was in need of a good push, and we gave it our all. Vic was still there, bless him, and between him, Bill and me we got that place buzzing again. I also got my first taste of man management, which was interesting.

In addition to Vic there were two or three newer members of staff there and their attitude towards me was, shall we say, a little bit lukewarm. Actually it was more like the Arctic! They couldn't stand me initially, and if looks could have killed I'd have been head first into Bill's propagation pit five or six times a day.

They thought that because I'd been to Wisley I'd have my head up my whatsit, but nothing could have been further from the truth. As you well know, I was not your typical Wisley student. Anyway, once they found out that I didn't mind getting my hands dirty they eventually came round, and when they found out that I didn't get my diploma they thought I was the bee's knees!

Old Bill was absolutely thrilled to bits having me back there again budding the roses and what have you, and of course I was dead pleased to see him so happy. This would have been about 1968, by the way, because the diploma course at Wisley lasted two years.

So where did it all go wrong? Well, despite the business doing quite well again, at the end of the day there just wasn't enough money coming in to support two partners and so to all intents and purposes I was in exactly the same position as I had been five or six years ago; just with more hours and more responsibility. Poor old Bill was desperate for me to stay but the truth was you can't get blood out of a stone, and so I had to move on. Do you know, he was so worried about me going that he even gave me an envelope one day with about £400 in it. God knows where he got it from but, seriously, what a gesture. I couldn't accept it of course, and eventually Bill came to terms with me having to leave. What a shame though. So there I was, back at the old drawing board again.

The first job I applied for after leaving Bill again was with a local authority somewhere and as disasters go, this was quite a size. As I arrived for the formal interview this bloody great big tractor pulled out in front of me and almost squashed me and my Ford Anglia. You should have seen the idiot who was driving the thing. He was shaking his fist and effing and blinding. I don't mind saying it shook me up a bit.

Once we'd finished exchanging pleasantries I parked up and made my way to the offices, but as I opened the doors to go inside there he was again, shouting the odds. I couldn't possibly repeat what he said to me, of course, but let's just say that he seemed to doubt the marital status of my parents. Not being one to shy away from confrontation I decided enough was enough, and so once he'd finished saying his piece I laid into this moron big time and finished by telling him exactly where he could stick his tractor. Well, not only did he turn out to be one of the men who I'd have had working for me but he was the shop steward! Needless to say I didn't get the job, and, to be honest, I'm quite glad.

After another couple of interviews which, although less confrontational than the first, turned out to be no more successful, I eventually came across an advert for a Garden Supervisor with the Greater London Council (exactly the kind of job you'd be offered through going to the Institution of Recreation and Parks Administration). It sounded OK and so I got on the phone to County Hall and arranged to go in for an interview. Now, believe it or not, the man who interviewed me for that job – and who subsequently became my next boss – turned one hundred years old in 2015. Bob Corbin's his name, and in a way he became my new Bill. He was also ex-Wisley and so he knew his stuff, but more importantly than that he was just a really great bloke. He still is! He was into everything though, was old Bob. He was chairman of the Institute of Groundsmen and God knows what. He barely stood still. Some people used to accuse Bob of being a bit of a know-it-all but his argument was always, 'If you don't tell them, how will they ever know?' and I was right behind him on that. It was just professional jealousy.

Bob was heavily into photography back then and almost every day he'd go down to the nursery with his camera. Once there he'd ask a member of staff called Tony Fleming to demonstrate certain tasks. 'I think we'll do some seed sowing today, Tony,' he'd say. And so, while Tony just got on with it, Bob would take photographs of the process. He ended up with the biggest horticultural slide library in the world. He used to get calls from everyone, be it *Amateur Gardening* magazine or one of the newspapers.

'You wouldn't have anything to go with an article on propagating geraniums would you, Bob?' and he'd sort it out for them.

Funnily enough, Bob's daughter, Anita, is also a photographer, except that she does it for a living. When I was guest of honour at the Taunton Flower Show in 2015 I popped in to see Bob and she took a photo of the two of us. It was just before his hundredth birthday and there's a copy of it in this very book. Anyway, I'm digressing slightly.

The job for which Bob interviewed me and then offered me was basically overseeing the maintenance of various council estate gardens. The first one I went to see after I'd got the job was the St Helier Council Estate, which is in Carshalton, and basically there were just rows and rows of council houses all with a privet hedge and all with a tarmac path leading to the door. You know the kind I mean. My team used to have to cut every inch of every hedge during the summer and, believe me, that was one heck of a job. The other big job they had was cutting the grassland, because as many of you will know these council estates often came with acres of it, and it all had to be pristine. All in all I was responsible for six or seven of these estates and had to manage all the individual teams who looked after them. These teams would be made up of about nine or ten blokes and each team would have a transit van (or the equivalent) and a trailer on the back. In there would be the mowers and what have you and in the back of the van all the tools. In the morning they'd report to me, I'd give them their tasks for the day, and then away they'd go.

As it turned out, my job had about as much to do with
horticulture as it did with hairdressing. It was just man
management and pen pushing really. I remember my first
day as if it were yesterday. As I pulled into the yard, which
was on Thornton Road in Carshalton, all the curtains in the
men's mess room started twitching and as I parked up I
could almost hear them gossiping.

''Ere's the new governor. Bet he won't last.'

Then, the moment I got out of my car, out came the
men, hands in pockets and faces like thunder. Here we go, I
thought. I tried saying good morning to them all but I didn't
even get as much as a nod. They just got into the vans and
scarpered. Things weren't much better in the office. I had
two old charge hands working with me in there and once
I'd tried my best to introduce myself to them I asked where
I was supposed to sit.

'Over there,' one of them eventually said, and then
pointed to the end of a long desk in the corner of the room.
'That's your bit.'

Well he wasn't lying. 'Bit' was the operative word. I literally had the end of a desk. Not the whole desk, but the end
of it. I think I even had to pinch a chair from somewhere.

That was a day of firsts for me really. It was the first day
of my job of course, the first day I'd ever worn a tie, and it
was the first time I'd ever turned up to work and wanted to
go straight home again. I love old Bob to bits, you know, but
at that moment in time all I wanted to do was go along to
County Hall, walk into his office and hand him my letter of
resignation.

It was about to get worse.

About an hour into the day I was just deciding which
bridge to jump off – Tower Bridge or London Bridge – when
this bloke walked into the office. At first I thought he was a

tramp who'd wandered in off the road to borrow the price of a cup of tea. He had a shirt on which, when it was new, could have been one of about fifteen different colours and he sported a jacket that would have shamed a scarecrow. His trousers weren't much better either and as for his boots . . . Well, let's just say that they were probably about the same age as me.

'You the new governor?' he said.

'That's right.'

'Well I 'ope you're better than the last one. He was bloody useless.'

'I'm sure I'll do my best. What can I do for you?'

'Here,' he said. 'Look at this.' And then out of one of his jacket pockets he took a pair of secateurs. 'Look at that,' he said indignantly. 'There's no bloody spring. How am I supposed to work with them?'

He had a point.

'Well,' I said. 'I'm going to start as I mean to go on. You can only do a good job if you've got the right tools.'

And so I asked one of the charge hands to show me where the stock room was and I got him a new pair.

'There you go,' I said to him proudly. 'One brand-new pair of secateurs.'

'Thanks very much,' he said. 'Now what about these?' And he pulled out a trowel with no handle, a small fork with a couple of teeth missing and two pairs of gardening gloves with holes in them.

'Just a minute,' I said. And off I popped to the stock room again and sorted him out.

Now you know what was happening, don't you? I was being done.

As soon as I'd finished making a note of exactly what

I'd given my new dishevelled friend, one of the other lads walked in. Eddie was his name.

'You're the new governor, ain't you?'

'That's right,' I replied, expecting the worst.

'Well here's a tip for you. You know old Wally? Looks like a tramp and smells like a horse.'

'Bit of an interesting shirt?'

'That's the one! Well for heaven's sake don't give him anything new.'

'Why not?' I asked.

'Why do you bloody think? He'll be selling it down the pub later. He's an old soak.'

Come in, Buttress, your time's up! He'd caught me hook, line and sinker. It could have been worse I suppose. He could have asked for a new lawnmower. It turns out old Wally was a bit of a legend round the yard and was about as shifty as they come.

'I'm afraid it's too late,' I said to Eddie. 'He's had me.'

'Oh hell! What did you give him?'

'Some gloves, a fork and a trowel.' I felt like a right berk.

'You got off lightly!' he said. 'He did the last governor for two rakes, a spade and a hoe. And he touched him up for ten bob.'

'He did what?'

'He's famous for it!'

'OK. Well thanks for the tip, Eddie.'

Now I thought this was just a bit of fun at first and had he stopped it there and then I'd have let it go, but I'm afraid old Wally obviously thought he was on to a good thing with his new boss and just a few hours later he came in to see me again.

'Sorry, governor,' he said, 'but all my tools have gone.'

'What do you mean, gone?'

'Just what I say, gone. There's a public toilet just up the road and I went in there for a pee. I had to leave my wheel-barrow and all my tools outside of course and when I came out they'd all been nicked.'

'Well, it's probably just kids,' I said. 'They'd have chucked the tools in a bush somewhere and they'll be pushing each other round in the barrow.'

'No, you don't know the area like I do. Everyone's a thief round here. Mark my words, they'll be long gone.'

I could tell by the look on his face that he thought he'd got away with it but I was as tenacious as he was dodgy and what he didn't yet know was that I knew the area quite well, and although it wasn't exactly Mayfair it was not what you'd call a den of thieves.

'I'll tell you what,' I said. 'Why don't you show me exactly where this barrow went missing?'

'Why do you want to know that? I've already told you. My word not good enough for you, eh?'

'For heaven's sake, Wally,' I said, pretending to get a bit irritated. 'I've got to make a note of all this and then log it. Then there are the police of course.'

'What do you mean, the police?' *Now* he was ruffled.

'Well if you're right and the tools and the barrow have been nicked, we've got to report it.'

'That's never happened before.'

'How do you mean, before?'

'Well, on the odd occasion when things have been nicked, they've just been replaced. As I said, this area's well dodgy. No point reporting anything to the police. They'll just ignore it.'

'Oh, I don't think so, Wally,' I said, looking him straight in the eye. 'Things are about to change around here.'

As we were walking up towards the scene of the crime he stopped me.

'Now look 'ere,' he said. 'I hope you don't think I nicked 'em.'

'I didn't say that, did I, Wally?'

'That's what you think though. Right, when the shop steward comes round I'm going to tell him about this and, what's more, he'll support me. We'll all be out by 3 p.m.'

What?! I'd only been in the job a few hours and they were already going on strike!

Any rate, while he stood there grumbling I walked on by myself and a minute or two later I came to the local pub. Now I'd been told by Bob that some of the men liked a lunchtime drink – which was fair enough – but that this could often last all afternoon if you weren't careful and so it was always a good idea to stick your head round the door about two, just in case. Well, it was about two, and so as I was there, I thought I'd pop my head round the door. And what do you think I saw? That's right: a wheelbarrow, a bag of tools, two pairs of gardening gloves, a trowel and a fork. He'd flogged the lot for beer money.

As I closed the door he was just catching up with me.

'Right,' I said. 'That's the last time, Wally.'

'What do you mean? 'Ere! Just you wait till the shop steward hears about this. We'll be out for a week!'

'Look, mate,' I said to him. 'I've got you bang to rights so don't you dare try and threaten me with all that union rubbish.'

It was just bluster of course. He knew it was over.

'This time I'm not going to report it but just you remember, I know – all right?'

He must have thought all his Christmases had come at

once, but at the end of the day I just couldn't be bothered with all that. It was probably just the thin end of a very long wedge as far as he was concerned but the most important thing was he wouldn't be doing it again.

'Yeah, all right,' he said, and then he scarpered.

On top of being a bit of a tealeaf Wally was also a compulsive liar and in the first month I was there his mother died six times. He couldn't help himself. He was an alcoholic, you see, just like old Harry in Croydon, and so as soon as he finished work on an evening he'd go straight down the pub, and that's where he stayed. Then in the morning it'd be stale pie and peas from the night before and then back to work.

The second or third time he came in late I said, 'If this carries on, Wally, I'm going to have to dock your pay.'

'Don't be too hard on me, governor,' he said, trying to squeeze a tear out. 'I'm afraid my old mother went last night.'

'You told me she died last week.'

'No, no, you don't listen. I told you she was ill.'

Believe it or not, I actually got to like old Wally. He lived in a world of his own, bless him. He was a proper Walter Mitty character.

So that was the world I'd gone into. I talk about it as though it was a bit of a laugh but, to be honest with you, it was anything but. From a physical point of view I hardly lifted a finger, and for somebody who'd always thrived on being outdoors and grafting that was a definite negative, but it was the stress that almost did me in. I'd done all that training at Wisley and all those years with Bill and at Croydon Parks, and what was I doing? Filling in forms and pulling men out of pubs or cafes. It was the job from hell really, and the unions were just the icing on the cake. They couldn't give a toss if people didn't pull their weight, yet the moment one of them had a so-called 'grievance', all hell was let loose. They just went looking for it.

Protecting working men or women from being exploited by companies and local authorities is all good and well, but when they're sat on their backsides doing nothing it's just taking the Mick. We did have one or two good ones there but even they were bullied by the unions. It was endemic. Do you know, they used to put soil in the fuel tanks of the mowers so they wouldn't work, just so they could have a skive. Honestly, everything was too much trouble to those men. I became a mechanic almost overnight when I started there. I used to turn up at a job somewhere and instead of them getting on with it they'd all be standing round smoking.

'Why aren't you using those mowers?' I'd ask.

'They're knackered.'

'What, all of them?'

'Yep.'

'Well, here you are,' I'd say, and then I'd hand them a load of hoes and what have you. 'Now get out there and do some bloody work!'

'You can't speak to us like that. The shop steward's going to hear about this.'

I remember going to Mum and Pop's for a meal not long after I started there and before we even sat down I just broke down in tears.

'I think I've made a big mistake,' I told them. 'I hate it!'

Do you know, I came within a hair's breadth of jacking that job in yet when it came to me writing out my letter of resignation I just couldn't do it. I was going through purgatory with those men yet there was something inside almost urging me to stay. It was quite a pivotal moment in my life, to be honest, because at the end of the day I had two choices: either I caved in to the idiots and went to work somewhere else or I took that role by the scruff of the neck and made it into a success. Fortunately for me (but possibly not some of the men I had working under me) I chose the latter and what's more I'm damn glad I did. It was the making of me. I went back in to that job and I started treating those men like gardeners, because, like it or not, that's what they were. I started gardening clubs in the evenings for those who wanted to learn a bit more and I also went out on jobs with them. Not so I could stand over them and tell them what to do, I just wanted to get involved; and because I showed an interest in what the lads were doing day-to-day they started to take a pride in their work. Some of them even used to ask me to come and inspect what they'd done for that very reason.

I remember one of the lads calling me over one day and pointing towards a long privet hedge.

'What do you think of that then, governor?' he said. 'You could put a spirit level on top of that hedge and the bubble would be dead centre.'

Do you know, that was probably one of the proudest moments of my entire life. There I was public enemy number one – the scourge of the unions and all ready to resign – and now look at me. I'd got a group of lads desperate to show me how well they could cut a privet hedge. I can't begin to tell you how gratifying that was.

There were one or two people who didn't want to know, of course, but I made it clear to them: either pull your finger out and get involved with the others, or bugger off. Simple! A fait accompli, I think they call it.

Most of the blokes thought I was mad when I took on the bad eggs, but because the majority were now pulling their weight and actually enjoying what they were doing there was no hiding place. Game, set and match to common sense.

Some of these lads really were desperate creatures, though. I remember one poor soul who used to come in every morning with either a black eye or a bloody nose. At first I thought he was just another drunk who liked a bit of argy-bargy when he'd had a few, but Eddie, who'd tipped me the wink about Wally, told me otherwise.

'It's his missus, guv. She's on the game.'

'I beg your pardon?'

'Exactly what I said, guv. His missus is on the game.'

Well, I'd heard about some pretty desperate situations in my time but this poor devil's predicament really took the biscuit. How she got into it I have no idea, but she and he lived in a little council house somewhere and while he was at work she'd have a steady succession of lorry drivers popping by. By the time he arrived home she'd be half cut and would end up laying into him. You couldn't make something like that up, could you?

I actually met his missus once and the moment I laid eyes on her I could tell that she was a wrong'un. He'd been off sick that week, which was a rarity, and so on the Friday she came into the office to try and collect his wages. There were no introductions.

'I've come for my husband's money,' she barked. 'I'm his wife.'

'Well I'm afraid you can't have it,' I told her.

I'd rather not repeat what she said next. Suffice to say she wasn't best pleased.

'Wages have to be signed for by the employee,' I said.

'Well that's no bloody good to me. What's he supposed to do?'

Luckily she'd caught me in a good mood.

'I'll tell you what,' I said. 'You give me your address, I'll take it round to where you live and he can sign for it, OK?'

I had the address somewhere of course, but my filing system left a lot to be desired! And so after a bit more whinging she reluctantly gave me their address and I told her I'd be round later.

I thought I'd better leave it a while just in case she had any other 'appointments' and so about half past five I went round there. Their son answered the door, and from first impressions he'd been to exactly the same charm school as his dear mother.

'Yeah. What do you want?' he said when he opened the door.

'I'm your dad's boss. I've brought his wages. Can I see him, please?'

After a couple of grunts and a sniff I was instructed to go down the side of the house to the garden.

He must be up and about again, I thought, but he wasn't.

When I met the young master in the garden he just pointed towards a shed at the back and said, 'He's in there.'

Fair enough, I thought. He must be either having a nip or planting a few seeds.

When I got to the shed I looked through the window and there he was, sitting in a chair surrounded by what I assumed were all his worldly possessions. He lived there!

'Hello, Mr B,' he said. 'What are you doing here?'

'I've brought your wages.'

You could hardly move in that shed. He had a camp bed in there, a chair and a table, a little Baby Belling cooker and about five or six bloody canaries. I'll tell you what, by the time I left that shed I was covered in feathers and millet.

That poor old devil. He was obviously terrified of his wife and son and they treated him like a dog.

*

We had another lad there, called Tony, and he used to suffer badly from fits. Now I'm not sure what kind of fits he had but every so often and without warning he'd go off on one; and let me tell you, when he flipped he was all over the shop. Things could get very violent at times and if you were on your own with him when he flipped you really had to watch yourself. As far as I know his parents had had him very, very late in life – into their fifties I think – and he'd never really been right from birth. He was a good-looking boy and when he was well he was as good as gold, but because of the unpredictability of these episodes, not to mention the severity of them, we couldn't let him go out with a team. This meant that I always had him based with me in the yard. It was a big old place and there was always plenty to do so it was a good arrangement really. I certainly kept him busy.

A few months after Tony joined us his fits started becoming more regular and because his parents had both passed away I decided to take it upon myself to go and see his doctor. These days you could never do something like that, of course, but back then I didn't know who else to turn to. There were no HR departments. The buck stopped with the line-manager.

Now Tony's doctor was like something out of a Dickens novel. Honestly, he was hilarious. You remember I told you about Canon Byrne's office, that was stuffed with mad animals and bits of tat? Well this doctor's surgery was exactly like that, just a lot worse. He must have been ninety if he was a day and the poor old boy couldn't see a bloody thing. I kept on having to wave at him so he knew where I was. In the end he told me that he'd recently increased Tony's medication but had a suspicion he wasn't taking it.

'Fair enough,' I said. 'I'll leave you to have a word with him.'

Something had to change though, because as things stood I was going to have to let Tony go and that was the last thing I wanted to do. But think about it, we had chainsaws, pitchforks and all sorts of dangerous pieces of equipment in that yard and everyone was terrified of him. These days he'd no doubt receive a lot more help but this was the very early 1970s.

Anyway, about the time that I took young Tony on, the powers that be had decided I needed some transport and so had issued me with one of those little Mini vans. You remember the ones? It was a terrific little thing and although it was quite small it couldn't half shift.

A few days after going to see this dotty Dickensian doctor I had to take some tree stakes down to the estate in Carshalton and when I got back young Tony was waiting for me outside the office, and he didn't half look angry.

'Hello, Tony,' I said. 'What can I do for you?'

He was so worked up that he could hardly get the words out.

'Have y-y-y-y-you been to see my d-d-d-d-d-doctor,' he said. He was literally shaking with anger at this point.

Bloody hell, I thought. He's going to lose it.

'No, you've got it wrong, Tony,' I began. 'I only ever speak to my own doctor and that's once in a blue moon. He or she must have got the wrong man.'

'The doctor rang me and said my governor had been to see him and had been asking about my medication.'

He was at breaking point now, and as the charge hands had both gone home I had to think on my feet.

'Now why would I do that?' I said. 'You know me. I don't go poking my nose into other people's business. Look, Tony, I've got a meeting with these two blokes now.'

And with that I opened the door to the office slightly and

proceeded to have a two-way conversation with some imaginary colleagues.

'Are you still there, George?'

'Yes, Jim.'

'Good. Did you make yourselves some tea? I shan't keep you a minute.'

I had no idea I could throw my voice like that but I was bloody glad I could.

'Is there anything else, Tony?'

'Well, if you're sure you didn't call him.'

'Course I didn't! It's none of my business. Anyway, must crack on. See you tomorrow.'

Talk about breathing a massive sigh of relief. I was terrified. There was only me and Tony in the yard at the time and so if he'd lost it and gone at me, my money would have been on him.

Talking of money, the GLC were still rolling out this time and motion malarkey while I was there, and what a load of rubbish all that was. The Americans had ditched it as a bad idea and so what did we go and do? Anyway, it resulted in me having to be a little bit creative when it came to doing the time sheets.

'What's this?' I hear you cry. Buttress was on the fiddle?

Well on paper, yes, I suppose I was. Allow me to explain.

You see I had six foremen working for me in that role and three of them were, shall we say, a little bit past it. Don't get me wrong, they were all good blokes. They were just a bit old really, and so when it came to having to trim a hedge or replace a flower bed they'd take a bloody age. I mean, what was I supposed to do, lay them off? I couldn't do that.

This meant that when it came to working out the time and motion bonuses, which were calculated collectively, they were in danger of losing not just themselves money, but the entire department, and so in order to maintain the status quo and keep everybody happy I simply added on the odd yard or two. It's hardly the Brink's-Mat robbery, is it?

It used to take me an absolute age to fill out those time sheets, and to be honest that was the only thing I could never stand about my line of work – pen pushing. Saying that, had I not had to fill in a few forms here and there I might never have met my Linda. She won't like me talking about her too much, but as she's involved with pretty much everything you're going to read from now on I'll just give you a few words about how we met.

As I said, I met Linda through, shall we say, the administrative side of my job? She was a clerk to the GLC's building surveyors and was based in an office close to our yard. If we had to take down a tree anywhere I had to fill in a form first, and it was Linda who had the dubious pleasure of taking the form from me and then processing it.

Well, as matches go, I suppose you could say that we were nigh on perfect really. She liked a good laugh, a smoke, the odd glass of lager, and, best of all, she was a supporter of the finest football team ever to boast the initials CP. Bingo!

You see, until I met Linda I don't suppose I'd had time to form any serious relationships. I'd been far too busy working, playing or watching football or going to the pub. And to tell you the truth I'd always been a bit put off getting into anything serious in case I got henpecked. I'd seen it too many times before. We'd get to the end of a game of football and I'd say, 'Right then, who's coming for a pint,' and the look of horror on some of these poor devils' faces. It was as if I'd asked them to jump into the Thames. 'Naaaa, sorry, Jim, got to get back to the missus. She'll kill me if I'm not back.'

Now don't get me wrong, I'm sure these wives and girl-friends of theirs had good reason to want them back as soon as the final whistle had blown, but watching them scurry away like that used to just make me want to confirm my allegiance to bachelorhood. Linda was different though, because not only would she come and watch a game of football – whether that be Crystal Palace or my own Old Boys team – but she'd stay and have a few drinks afterwards. Her youngest brothers, Colin and Tony, even used to play for our team when they were at school and I'd let them have a beer or two afterwards. Do you know, Linda likes watching cricket as well, and if any further proof were needed that we were more than a little bit compatible she also has more than a passing interest in gardening. Mad, isn't it? Linda's definitely the brains of the outfit, though, and I have no problem admitting that without her I'd be well and truly lost. She means the world to me. There, what a soppy old sod, eh?

I'll tell you what though, it very nearly didn't happen.

When I first asked Linda out on a date we arranged to meet in a pub in Cheam and I was almost two hours late! I'd got caught up with some work, I think, and of course there were no mobile phones in those days.

When I eventually got to the pub I remember looking through a window very nervously, and there, sitting at a table reading a book, was Linda. I thought she would have been long gone by then, but no. It must have been a very good book! And so, after thanking my lucky stars, in I went to try and apologize. Now although Linda doesn't suffer fools I think she could tell I wasn't telling porkies, and so instead of giving me what for, she very graciously allowed me to buy her a drink, and I'm damn glad she did. Now normally, at the end of a story like that you'd say something like, 'And the rest, as they say, is history,' but in our case it's not quite as simple as that.

Without going into too much detail, Linda and I split up

for a time in the 1980s and I ended up getting married to a policewoman called Geraldine. Although Geraldine and I are still good friends I don't mind admitting that it didn't really go according to plan, and I know for a fact she'd tell you the same thing. First off, because of the hours we worked, she'd often be going to bed just as I was getting up for work, and so once you took into consideration all of our social comings and goings we never saw hide nor hair of each other. It was just one of those things, I suppose, but I should have known it would never work, especially given the fact that Geraldine was and still is a diehard Pompey supporter! I'm only joking of course. She's a really good egg is Geraldine and I'm so pleased that we were able to stay friends.

Just after I first met Linda in 1974 I went for an interview to become a Garden Inspector for the GLC. This was basically the role directly above me, where, rather than looking after the manpower at a yard with four or five teams attached to it, I'd be looking after the blokes looking after the teams, if you get my drift. The job was based out of County Hall, which is where Linda now was after being promoted to the position of rent assessor, but instead of sitting behind a desk five days a week I'd probably spend three of them out on the road. This made the job just about bearable, because if I'd been office-bound I think I'd have gone barmy.

Once again I had my little van, and because I covered so many different areas I was doing hundreds of miles every week. It was like being a troubleshooter in a way. One of the Garden Supervisors would ring me up and say, 'Jim, we've got a problem,' and regardless of what that was I'd have to go out and help. Now I enjoyed that to a point, as just occasionally I'd be required to get my hands dirty, but at the end of the day I was just a problem-solving pen pusher. Horticulture? I think by that time I'd forgotten how to spell it.

Now when I said Bob was like a new Bill I wasn't kidding, because in 1976, after I'd been with the GLC for about seven years, Bob called me into his office one day and told me it was time for me to leave.

'You've done a great job, Jim,' he said. 'And there's one thing about you: if you're asked to do a job, you do it, but I think it's time for you to move on.'

Talk about déjà vu! It was 1964 all over again.

'Really, Bob? What have I done wrong?'

'Nothing, Jim,' he said. 'I just think it's time you went back into horticulture.'

It's true I was just going through the motions as a Garden Inspector and had got myself into a bit of a rut. The thing is I didn't actually realize it and so it took somebody sitting on the outside of the tent to do something about it. What a lucky boy I am. Not one, but two careers advice specialists! Seriously though, if Bob hadn't said anything to me I could have been doing that job for the rest of my working life.

'I've heard a whisper,' he said, 'that there are some jobs coming up in the Royal Parks, and if you went for one, I reckon you'd have a very good chance.'

What Bob was basically saying was that he'd had a word with the bloke at the Royal Parks and as long as I didn't make a fool of myself in the interview I should be OK. This wasn't just because we were friends, by the way. Oh no. Bob had his reputation to think of. He could only recommend me if he thought I was the right man for the job; but even so, that's a lot of faith to put in somebody.

I'd had a good run with the GLC and what's more I'd enjoyed most of it. I may not have been knee deep in daisies day in, day out but I'd met some great people, including Linda of course.

Sure enough, along I went for the interview and got the job.

Now here's a story that will make you laugh. When I left the GLC I was due a lump sum for the seven years or so that I'd worked there and I was looking forward to getting my hands on it. It was something to do with my pension, I think, and I could either cash it in or transfer it to my next job. Well, everything I had was second-hand at the time. My car was falling to bits, I'd never had a holiday and I had holes in just about everything I wore. I thought to myself, This is it. At last! I'll have a new-ish car, a few days away and I'll even buy myself a new pair of wellies.

No chance!

A few days before I left the GLC Bob said to me, 'Jim. I've never met your parents and you're always talking about them. Any chance I could meet them before you leave?'

I said, 'You'd be very welcome, Bob,' and so I arranged for him to come round for dinner one evening at Mum and Dad's place in Purley.

Pop was in his element. He showed Bob round his garden and his greenhouse and Mum made us a lovely meal. Then, towards the end of the evening, Bob came out with the real reason that he'd asked to meet them.

'I don't want you to think that I've just come here for a free meal, Mr and Mrs Buttress, but without wanting to make your Jim any more big-headed than he already is, I'd like you to know that I'm very proud of him. He's done a fantastic job for me these past seven years and I think the least I can do is to make sure he goes to his new position in good shape. Now I don't know if he's told you but Jim's about to receive a lump sum from his pension and my advice to him will be to transfer that money to his new position.'

My little heart sank without any trace whatsoever.

As soon as Bob left, Pop said, 'What sound advice, boy. That's what you'll be doing then?'

I was almost thirty-one years of age yet I couldn't bring myself to go against Bob and Pop. Not because I was scared of what they'd say but because at the end of the day I knew they were bloody right! A new car? Who was I kidding?

Sure enough, because of Bob's advice I was actually able to retire from full-time employment at just fifty-one years of age, which meant I could dedicate all my time to judging and doing talks. Not bad, eh? I mean, how many governors would go to that much trouble? At the time though, I felt like I'd lost a fifty-pound note and found a fifty-pence piece. I just sat there wanting to cry my eyes out. I reminded Bob of that story when I went down to see him and he remembered. What a diamond.

A few years ago I had to give a speech at the one hundredth anniversary of the Garden Club at Wisley, which is basically a club for ex-students, and Bob was in the audience. I said, 'There's one of my old governors in the crowd today. There he is, Mr Bob Corbin. He's one in a million is Bob. He taught me the difference between right and wrong. He was always right and I was always wrong.' I looked over at Bob and he was crying with laughter.

Before we move on to the Royal Parks I just want to tell you one little story about Pop. After Bob's advice regarding my pension he obviously thought he'd get in on the action, and one morning, just as he set off to work, he said, 'I'll have the forms for you to sign tonight, boy. You're still coming round for your tea, aren't you?'

I said, 'Yes, of course I am. Hang on, what forms?'

'Life insurance, boy! You've got to have life insurance now you're at the Royal Parks.'

Then about a week later he did the same again.

'What are they for this time?' I asked.

'They're doing a special offer on investments. It's about time you were putting something away.'

Before I'd even collected my first pay packet there was hardly anything left!

Anyway, a few years ago in about 2009 this investment policy Pop had sold me matured and it turned out that, as with the pension, I'd been right to keep my mouth shut and go along with it. The investment had done quite nicely and so at last, there was my lump sum. It was thirty years late of course but I'm not one to complain.

Linda and I decided to spend some of the proceeds of Pop's policy on a holiday to South Africa, and it was only when I was standing on my own on Durban Harbour one afternoon when Linda had gone shopping that it came to me: this was where Pop used to arrive when he came in on the *Nieuw Amsterdam* during the war. It is a very different place now, of course, but I could just picture him on that ship, sailing in from the Indian Ocean.

'Flaming hell,' I said to myself. 'And I'm only here because you made me take out that policy! Thanks, Dad.'

10. The Royal Parks

The chap who interviewed me for the job in the Royal Parks was a man from the Department of the Environment called Bob Hare. You see it didn't matter where in the country they were situated, back then, each and every royal park or garden was the responsibility of Whitehall and so had nothing whatsoever to do with local government.

Now Bob Hare was a real gentleman and, what's more, he'd do anything for anybody. I'd always tried to be the same but watching Bob was a reminder of exactly why you'd do it. It makes people feel good. Members of the public used to get in touch with him and ask for advice about their own gardens and he always made time for them. In fact, if memory serves, he'd even visit them in his own time if he could.

While he was in charge of the Royal Parks Bob was asked to write a weekly column for a little local newspaper and he never accepted a single penny for it. He was offered payment but always flatly refused. In that respect he was a real one-off.

The interview itself was more like a chat really, although he certainly put me through my paces. Bob Corbin had recommended me and that was a good start but Bob Hare still had to make doubly sure I was the right man for the job, and somebody he could work with.

The list of parks and gardens that fall within the Department of the Environment's responsibility isn't quite as long these days as many of these places are now looked after by English Heritage or the National Trust, but back then the Royal Parks department had within its number the likes of Bushey Park, Regent's Park, Green Park, St James's Park, Hyde Park, Richmond Park, Greenwich Park, Hampton Court, Primrose Hill, Kensington Park, Buckingham Palace and Clarence House.

The post I was interviewed for was Superintendent of the Central Royal Parks, and because of the size of the job they ended up splitting the role between me and another bloke. He looked after Kensington Gardens and the nursery therein, and I looked after Green Park, Hyde Park, St James's Park, Buckingham Palace, Clarence House and the nursery down at Richmond Park. With Buckingham Palace and Clarence House, which I'll come on to a bit later, I was just a figurehead really as they each had their own head gardener. I think it was the BBC who first started referring to me as the 'Queen's Gardener' but it's something I've never actually claimed to be.

Now with this kind of job you're usually given a house to live in with a peppercorn rent and I have to admit that was one of the things I was really looking forward to. At the time Linda and I were living in a self-contained flat above my mate Paul's dental practice down in Purley, and as grateful as we were to Paul for letting us rent it from him we were really looking forward to living in the centre of London.

The first person I was introduced to when I started was my new boss, who worked directly under Bob Hare and was the Superintendent of the Royal Parks, and one of the first things he did was arrange a time to show me and Linda our new accommodation. Brilliant! I thought: we're almost there.

Unfortunately the accommodation in question, a gatehouse close to the Knightsbridge Barracks, wasn't fit for a dog, let alone a member of staff and his better half, and when we first saw the place we were devastated. Basically it was one room with two cupboards, a kitchenette and a curtain down the middle. Linda took one look and said, 'If you think I'm living in that you've got another thing coming.'

I turned to my boss. 'You've got to be joking,' I said. 'We can't live here.'

'Well, that's all there is. The house we had earmarked for you is still being occupied by your predecessor and until he finds alternative accommodation you'll have to make do.'

Well, there was no way in the world that was going to happen and so until the old boy we'd taken over from had sorted himself out it was back to Paul's place. Incidentally, the chap who'd been employed alongside me had a young family and so he'd been given the other Superintendent's property, which was already empty. That was fair enough though.

In addition to us being offered something not much bigger than a dog kennel I was now working more hours than I ever had in my life. God, I was miserable. I had to be in the yard at Hyde Park by 7.30 a.m. and so while I was living in Purley I had to set off at about 5 a.m. Any later and I'd have hit the rush hour traffic head-on. Coming back was no better. If I set off at 5 p.m. like everyone else it would have taken me over two hours to get home and so there was no point leaving before about 6.30 p.m. Not unless I wanted to sit in traffic. In addition to this I had to come in to work on a Saturday morning, so you can imagine how I was on a Sunday. Useless! I couldn't get the train, unfortunately, as more often than not I needed the car. It was just about bearable for the first month or so but after that it started getting me down. Fortunately for me I had an ally.

As well as Bob Corbin putting in a word for me with the

Royal Parks, another friend, ex-Wisley student Bob Legge, had done the same. He's no longer with us, I'm afraid, but Leggy had been at Wisley a year or two before me and after we'd been introduced somewhere we ended up keeping in touch. He was the governor up at Regent's Park now, and so because he was also employed by the Royal Parks I thought he'd know what to do.

'You've got to apply a bit of pressure, Jim,' he said. 'At the end of the day you're entitled to a house. Just tell 'em!'

I was still a new boy and so didn't want to go shouting the odds but Bob was right, I was entitled to somewhere decent to live, and preferably less than twenty miles away and with more than one room.

After a bit of toing and froing we were eventually offered a vacant lodge in Orme Square, right next to the Russian Embassy just off the Bayswater Road. It still wasn't ideal and so, until we got the place they'd originally promised us, we decided that Linda would stay on in the flat above Paul's and I'd join her at weekends.

Because of this there was no point furnishing the place on Orme Square and so it didn't have any carpets, curtains or furniture inside; not that I cared much. It wasn't in Purley and so I wouldn't have to commute.

It won't surprise you to know that the first Christmas I was in that job I decided to organize a big party – the first Christmas party the staff there had ever had, by all accounts – and at the end of the evening I invited them all back to my place. I say all of them. There were quite a few who were either working or couldn't make it but we still had a good number. You should have seen the looks on their faces when they saw the state of it. As I said, I had no carpets, no curtains, and worst of all, no glasses. I only had two cups and so everybody had to drink out of a bottle. It was like a winos' convention! On top of this I only had two chairs in the house and so most of my guests had to sit on the floor. What I didn't tell them was that I'd nicked those two chairs out of the office.

In the end I managed to salvage an old wardrobe that was going to be thrown out and I even got hold of some carpet. A mate of mine called Colin, who I still see today, had his own carpet business and one day he rang me up. 'I've just done a job at a convent, Jim,' he said. 'Some of the kids spilt glue in one of the classrooms and I've had to replace the carpet. You're welcome to it if you want. It's a bit of a mess but it'll be better than nothing.'

He was right, it was a bit of a mess, but I took it off him. After all, waste not, want not!

It has to be said that while I was there that lodge in Orme Square probably looked like Compo's place out of *Last of the Summer Wine*.

When my predecessor eventually did find somewhere else to live our new address was Cumberland Gate Lodge, Marble Arch, London. The original Cumberland Lodge, which was designed by the architect Decimus Burton, had to make way for Marble Arch back in 1851 and when they built the current one nearby – the one we ended up living in – it started life as a public convenience. We were living in a lav, then! But this hadn't been just any old public convenience. At the time it was the most ornate in London and ended up providing the well-heeled of the city with somewhere to spend a penny for over a hundred years. Then, in 1961, it was taken down again and moved brick by brick just a few hundred yards away, which is where it stands today. From now on though it was to be used as the home for whoever's in charge of Hyde Park. After a bit of a clean and a refurb, of course!

What capped the building's interesting past was that we were right on the edge of Hyde Park and so my commute was no more than about thirty seconds. Linda and I loved living in Cumberland Lodge and we ended up having ten very happy and eventful years there.

There's one other thing Linda and I have in common that I haven't told you about yet and that's a love of dogs. We're both barmy about them, and so shortly after we first moved in together we decided that we should go out and get one – and what an absolute nightmare he turned out to be. We ended up calling him Selhurst (what else could it have been?) and he was a rescue dog. Well, not to put too fine a point on it, Selhurst was as mad as a bleeding hatter. He was a Staffordshire bull terrier cross and had he been alive today I'm afraid that he wouldn't have lasted two minutes. He terrorized not only every dog he ever laid eyes on but also every human, cat, horse, rabbit, and anything else you care to mention.

Every walk I took him on would turn into a bloody incident and I must have had to apologize about a million times on his behalf.

'I'm so sorry, madam. Was that your leg?'

'Sorry, governor! He's usually quite good around horses.'

You get my drift?

Now my favourite story involving Selhurst took place in Hyde Park one evening shortly after supper. There was this woman who always used to walk her dog about the same time as me and, honestly, she was elegance personified. She always wore a fur coat, high heels and had her nose pointing straight towards the sun. I later found out that she was some kind of supermarket heiress – well out of my league! Anyway, there I was, shuffling along minding my own business when all of a sudden I heard yelping.

Oh Christ, I thought. SELHURST! Now what's he done?

I looked up and there in the distance was – surprise, surprise – Selhurst trying to mount this woman's Labrador.

'*SELHURST!*' I shouted. '*Put that dog down and come here!*'

Naturally he took absolutely no notice of me whatsoever, and desperate to stop him doing any proper damage I broke into a trot, still yelling. As I passed this vision of grace and sophistication she said, 'Sandhurst, eh? You must have army connections.' And then she just turned away and carried on walking.

In the end Selhurst became such a pain that Linda and I had to go back to the dog shelter to try to get some advice.

'What he needs is a bitch,' they said.

'What, another dog? You're joking.'

'Well, it's the only thing that'll quieten him down.'

Well, what else could we do? We couldn't have him put down.

So about a week later we welcomed Crystal into the fold. She was a beautiful Labrador cross, was Crystal, and sure enough, the moment Selhurst stepped out of line, she was on to him like a flash. Basically Selhurst was just a big old coward, and she ruled the roost right from day one.

The last dog we got while we were living at Cumberland Lodge was Terry, as in Terry Venables. He was the manager of Crystal Palace at the time and so once again it seemed like a natural choice. Terry (the dog, not the manager) was delivered to us one day by a man called Ron Keating, who was one of my team in Hyde Park. I'm going to tell you a bit more about Ron in a page or two, but he'd seen a bag moving one day in one of the litter bins and was just about to put a fork through it, thinking it was a rat, when all of a sudden he heard a barking noise. He looked inside and there was Terry, a mongrel terrier just a few weeks old. Somebody had abandoned the poor little mite and so she ended up coming to us.

I used to take the three of them out into Hyde Park of an evening once I'd finished work and as soon as I thought it was safe to do so I'd let them all go. Nine times out of ten this went without a hitch but there were a couple of occasions when I almost turned and fled. This was the time when the Arabs were taking over most of Park Lane and Mayfair, and Selhurst – who, to be fair, seemed to have given up mounting and biting by then – always made a bee-line for them. He was only trying to be friendly but to the Arabian ladies and gentlemen of central London he probably looked like the Hound of the Baskervilles. You should have heard the screams when they saw him coming. It was pure fear! Cue yet more apologies and frantic shrieks of '*SELHUUUUURST!*'

Anyway, let me tell you a little bit about this job of mine. As I said, I was a Superintendent of the Central Royal Parks and so if any of the park managers within our remit had a problem, whether that be a disciplinary issue or a need for some new equipment, they'd come to me. In that respect it was quite similar to my last job with the GLC. The difference being that I now had some horticultural responsibilities, which is why I was recommended in the first place. None of these were practical, more's the pity, but as opposed to just checking up on people and supplying plants and shrubs I was designing beds and the like.

It was like being back at Croydon really, just on a much, much bigger scale, and just like Croydon, we grew everything ourselves. At the nurseries in Hyde Park we grew spring and summer bedding to a level I never thought possible. It was industrial, but at the same time it was completely professional and the whole thing just oozed quality. Everywhere else I'd ever worked before the bedding had been grown in boxes, whereas here it was all grown in individual pots. Then there were things like standard geraniums, standard fuchsias, heliotrope and abutilon. The geraniums in particular were stunning. Until then I'd only ever grown from cuttings but these were all grown from seed and were far more consistent. Being involved in something so broad and professional was just marvellous.

Because these plants were all individually grown in pots we could afford to plant some of them out in flower and the reason we did that was because you had tourists coming from all over the world and the last thing they wanted to hear was us saying, 'Come back in a week and that bed will look stunning.' We simply treated the geraniums with a growth retardant and so they just kept on coming.

It didn't stop with flowers and plants though. We had a blacksmith and some carpenters who basically made and repaired everything.

You remember the decorating team I told you about at Croydon? What did we have there, three or four people? Well, imagine what it was like at the Royal Parks. We must have had twenty or thirty of them working in the decoration team and, my God, were they busy. They had Downing Street, not to mention the whole of Whitehall, to deal with. And then there was Buckingham Palace, of course, and Clarence House and Kensington Palace. They were responsible for decorating dozens and dozens of these places, sometimes on a daily basis. Then there were all the functions. Places like Buck House, Downing Street and all the departments on Whitehall used to hold receptions for foreign dignitaries and what have you, so it was never ending. Nine or ten phone calls a day I'd get, and all of them had to be serviced; first, via the nursery, which grew almost everything we needed, and then, via the decorations team, and believe you me, with the amount of practice these boys and girls got they were some of the best florists in the business.

I'm not sure about these days but back then, if any foreign heads of state came to visit they'd arrive at Gatwick Airport, get the royal train up to platform one at Victoria and then be driven up to Buckingham Palace, and it was my job to ensure that we always prepared a big floral display in the flag colours of whatever country they came from. That was yet another task for our intrepid decoration team and it wasn't just a case of choosing the right colours. These things had to be designed. They all did. And, once again, all the flowers and plants would come from our own nurseries.

We used to grow three out of the four seasons of flowers in the Royal Park nurseries. With spring, at the beginning of the year, we'd plant daffodils, tulips, crocuses and pansies, etc. Then, for all the summer displays we'd grow bedding plants, things like Busy Lizzie, antirrhinum and rudbeckia. It was never ending. After that, in between the summer display and getting ready for the next spring, we'd do a late autumn display. Here we'd have Korean chrysanthemums, which we'd lift out of the fields and then plant straight into the beds. You've never seen anything like it. I'm telling you, those nurseries were just a constant gift.

Believe it or not though, if there was ever anything on that we didn't think we could do justice to, we wouldn't do it. Back then we always had to set a precedent, and pride and reputation came before everything. Today it's different, and regardless of how big or difficult the job is they have to try and make it work. It's all about budgets these days. I suppose the trick to my job was coordination, as I had to keep the whole operation moving. When it came to purchasing things like bulbs it was done on an almost biblical scale. We used to buy millions of them. I'd put out a tender to four or five companies and then they'd all put in a bid for the order. Seriously, it was like selling off British Gas! It was the same when it came to buying anything we didn't grow in-house. I'd have to visit the nurseries and meet all the owners, etc. Supplying the Royal Parks was a much sought-after contract and so they all went out of their way to impress. Once again, though, I met some real characters doing that job, and because the horticultural element was so much more prevalent I was as happy as Larry.

Two of the biggest characters I had working under me at the Royal Parks were the storeman, Barney Miller, and the aforementioned Ron Keating. Now Barney Miller was also the union rep for the Royal Parks and he'd have been the first to admit that he made Red Ken look like Norman Tebbit. There was a difference with Barney, though. He wasn't blinkered like a lot of them and he always made sure everyone pulled their weight. He was awesome was old Barney, and although we didn't necessarily see eye to eye politically, we came to an understanding very early on.

Because he was in charge of the stores, petrol, machinery, bulbs, tools and clothing, etc., Barney had literally dozens of ledgers that had to be filled in, and I remember him bringing these in to me one day not long after I started. He was a big East Anglian boy with dark hair.

'You the new gaffer?'

'That's right.'

'There you go then,' he said. And with that he just chucked them all on my desk.

I was getting used to these warm welcomes by now.

'What do I want all these for?' I asked him.

'You've got to check 'em all and then sign 'em.'

I said, 'How long have you been doing the job, Barney?'

'I've been here thirty-two years.'

'And has anybody ever queried the ledgers?'

'No, they bloody well haven't!'

'Well in that case you can pick them all up and take them back again. I'm not wasting my time looking through that lot.'

He looked puzzled

'Really?' he said. 'Why not?'

'Well, for a start, Barney, I don't know what I'm looking for, do I? And if you have been fiddling for the last thirty-two years, you've done well, mate!'

From then on Barney and I got on like a house on fire, and all because I'd put some trust in him. Surely he'd earned that after thirty-two years? He knew I'd have to check the ledgers when it came to balancing the books and if something was amiss I'd know about it. I didn't need to see them every week though. That was just ridiculous.

From then on I had people who worked with Barney coming up to me and saying, 'I don't know what you've done to old Barney, governor, but I've never heard him say anything nice about a boss before!'

My other mucker at the Royal Parks, Ron Keating, was basically a hard-drinking horticultural version of Leslie Phillips. He was always immaculately turned out was Ron, and in addition to a neat little moustache and Brylcreemed hair he had as much charm as about ten David Nivens. No woman was safe when Ron was around! Best of all though, he knew and got on with everybody in central London, or that's how it seemed. He was just one of those people who appeared to click with everyone.

Walking down Oxford Street with Ron was an experience in itself. For a start it was impossible to hold a conversation with him because every ten paces or so he'd either be stopped by somebody, shouted at from a taxi, or waved to. Every doorman, shop assistant, cab driver and road sweeper seemed to know Ron. What's more they all seemed to know what he was up to.

'Morning, Ron!' one of them would shout. 'What time did you get off last night?'

'Oh, about elevenish. Good night, wasn't it?'

Then a few paces later there'd be another.

'Watcha, Ron. How's your old mum?'

'Surviving, just!'

And so it went on.

When I'd been there about a week or so he popped his head round my door one day just before lunchtime.

'Don't suppose you fancy a snifter at lunch do you, governor?'

'OK, Ron, why not.'

'I usually pop next door to the police station. They have quite a nice bar there and are always very accommodating.'

This just got better and better. Now I'm not belittling the position of a park foreman in any way whatsoever, but the way Ron waltzed into that police station bar you'd have thought he was the Chief Constable!

'Afternoon, inspector,' he said to one bloke. 'Will you join us for one?'

'Sorry, Ron, no can do. See you in the pub later though?'

'OK then.'

He even had his own bloody stool! Seriously, this bloke had more front than Southend Pier.

Do you know who else Ron reminded me of? Private Walker out of *Dad's Army*. Whatever you wanted, he could get, and whatever you needed doing, he'd sort it. The only difference being that he didn't seem to make anything out of it. He just did it as a favour.

That first time he took me to the police station bar he was approached three times by coppers asking for stuff.

'Did you manage to get hold of those plants, Ron?' one of them asked.

''Ere, Ron,' I said. 'What are you up to? Tell me you're not lifting plants.'

'Of course not, governor! It's all proper and above board. This lot are always asking me for stuff and as the nursery was over on a few I thought I'd offer them round. You can check if you want.'

I remember him once having a pop at me about a jacket I was wearing. He was Mr Sartorial Awareness of course, and he used to pull me up all the time.

'Bit big for you that, isn't it, governor? Hope you don't mind me saying.'

'Not at all, Ron. I suppose you're right. Do you know anyone who could alter it?'

'Yes, of course, guv. You know Mr Khan who looks after the Gents in the middle of the park?'

'Yes, of course I do. He works for me.'

'Well he used to be a master tailor back in India. Give it to me now and I'll drop it in to him this afternoon.'

Ron Keating was the Oracle.

Now some of you will remember this and some of you won't, but up until about thirty years ago you used to get washroom attendants who all but lived in these conveniences. They had a little room with a chair and a kettle in it, and they'd be there from the crack of dawn until last thing at night. These days you get blokes in posh restaurant toilets smothering you in aftershave every time you so much as look at the soap, but back in the day it was a full-time position and a job for life, if you wanted it.

Anyway, because Mr Khan spent so much time 'below sea level' he'd sometimes do a bit of alteration work when he wasn't busy, just to keep his hand in. I didn't mind, as long as it didn't interfere with his work, and he did a lovely job on my jacket.

Every Friday Ron used to do the fish and chip run, which, for him at least, would last about two or three hours. About ten o'clock he'd collect the money and the orders and then off he'd go. Nobody knew where he went but he used to come back with the most amazing fish and chips you've ever tasted. I didn't mind him going AWOL for a bit because Ron was a grafter and if I ever needed anyone to stay behind he was always the first to volunteer.

After a few months he said to me, 'Look, guv. One day I might be off sick or something. I think it's about time I took you on the fish and chip run.'

This was like being accepted into a private club.

'OK, Ron. Let's go,' I said.

Where did he take me? Straight to the Swan on the Bayswater Road.

'Morning, Ron. The usual?'

'Yes please, Gerald, and one for my governor please.'

'Your governor, eh? We are honoured!'

Once again he seemed to be at the centre of everything that went on. He was my foreman but I felt like his apprentice! I didn't mind. In fact it was fascinating.

I know I'm probably going on about these old colleagues of mine, but they're what made me tick. I just love people.

I was in two minds whether to tell you about what became of Ron, and in a moment you'll see why. I'm afraid that all that fast living began to catch up with him and ended up having a detrimental effect on his capabilities.

Once this started to happen I was put under pressure to get rid of him but I wasn't having any of it. He'd been there thirty years or more yet the powers that be wanted to dump him just like that. Well, that wasn't going to happen, I'm afraid. Ron had been a terrific employee for as long as I'd been there and what's more he was a friend of mine. If I sacked him he'd have been dead within six months. His entire life was in that square mile around Hyde Park.

I lay awake at night for ages trying to figure out what to do with him and in the end it came to me. We had a nursery just a few miles from where Ron lived that used to supply us with trees, shrubs and all sorts of stuff. It was just on the edge of Richmond Park. Now Ron knew that he was on the cusp of being sacked and when I called him in to the office to tell him about my idea he feared the worst.

'You getting rid of me then, governor?'

'Am I buggery, Ron. You're going down to the nursery in Richmond, mate.'

'Really, governor?'

'Yep. Consider it being put out to graze, Ron.'

'Thanks, guv. I won't let you down.'

And he didn't. Ron went in and he virtually ran that place. A drinker he might well have been but he was also a damn good gardener and in the end he had a few good years there. They grew all our wallflowers down there, not to mention some of our spring bedding. Then there were the trees and shrubs of course. He did a terrific job. Do you know, there was even a little pub about a hundred yards or so away. I used to go down and see him every so often, just to make sure he was OK, and when I arrived he'd stop whatever it was he was doing and beam at me.

'Afternoon, governor! Would you care to accompany me on the fish and chip run?'

'Why not, Ron. You're buying though.'

One other part of the job I adored, having been one myself, was involvement in the new apprenticeship scheme. This was one of the finest schemes of its kind anywhere in the country at the time and helped nurture some big, big talents. They were all boys and girls in their late teens and early twenties and they had their headquarters down at Eltham Palace, which was also part of the Royal Parks. Do you know they even had their own apprentice master? They're now a thing of the past of course, as for the most part are apprenticeships, more's the pity, but it was that person's job to train the apprentices and ensure that they passed the course. A kind of teacher and headmaster all rolled into one.

Each apprentice would be based at a certain park, where they'd help out with all the day-to-day stuff and then once or twice a week they'd go down to Eltham Palace where they'd get taught things like fruit tree pruning or propagation. They'd finish up with something like the RHS General Certificate in Horticulture, which would set them up for a local authority job.

My job here was to coordinate the interviews with Bob Wadey, who was the apprentice master, and then he and I would conduct the interviews and choose the students. Bob was and still is a great, great friend of mine and was perfect for the job as he'd started off as an apprentice himself down at the Brighton Parks Department. During the interviews we each had a different role: he'd find out about their horticultural knowledge and ability, and I'd find out what made them tick. It worked too.

Bob always used to go first and once he'd finished with them he'd hand over to me, and my first question was always the same.

'Right then, on to the important stuff. Who do you support?'

'Charlton Athletic.'

'What!? You're joking? Get out!'

Do you know, it didn't matter if they were male or female, that question always used to break the ice. These kids were terrified when they came in and Bob and I wanted to see them relaxed.

I remember once we interviewed this young lad who hailed from the East End, and believe me he was super confident. In he walked, all swagger and chewing gum. I said, 'We've got a right one here, Bob. Hold on to your hat.' He was only about sixteen.

Once Bob had finished the official chat I got to work.

'Right then,' I said. 'Who's your team?'

He looked surprised. They all did when I asked that.

'Well, if you must know it's Millwall.'

'Millwall?' I said. 'What a load of rubbish. I don't know how you dare show your face.'

After that he gave us a little smile. Now he was getting it.

'Who are you then?'

'I'm Palace through and through.'

'Palace?! Well, you're not much better, are you?'

He was a real card this boy.

'So come on then,' I asked. 'Where does your interest in horticulture come from?'

'It comes from my uncle.'

'Really? And what does he do?'

'He's got a stall down the market.'

'Really? What does he sell?'

'Well, he does trees, shrubs and a few bedding plants. I used to help him out sometimes and I thought, I like that. I think I'll have a crack at it.'

So I said, 'Does he do it all year round?'

'No, no, no, no,' said the boy. 'In the winter he does fur coats, leather jackets and handbags and that. It's good money.'

'OK,' I said. 'Let's go back to the gardening. Where does he get all his plants from?'

He looked at me straight in the eye and said, 'Ooh, you don't ask questions like that.'

This boy was sixteen years old!

I said to Bob afterwards, 'We've got to have him, Bob. He's dynamite.'

These days we'd probably be hauled up before God knows what and God knows who for conducting interviews in that way but to us it just worked. Bob's apprentices were always a happy bunch and that was down, in no small part, to how they were spoken to.

Our boss, who let's just say was not really a fan of mine, always tried to get Bob to conduct the interviews with somebody else, but Bob always insisted.

'Sorry, but Jim brings out the best in them.'

Actually, *we* brought out the best in them. It was a partnership.

You'll read quite a bit more about Bob and his apprentices in the next chapter but in the meantime I want to give a quick mention to the police, because they're as important to the day-to-day running of the Royal Parks as anyone else.

As you know, their station in Hyde Park – and the all-important bar – was situated right in the middle of the park, just like our yard was, and once Ron had introduced me to a few of the coppers I used to go round there for my lunch. Good grub it was too.

'Any chance of a few plants, Jim?' one of them would ask.

'Yeah, once we've finished the season. Let me see what we have left.'

So like Ron, I started building a few new relationships. After all, we were all batting for the same team. What's more, they were really nice people.

Now you know what's coming, don't you?

Jim Buttress plus a load of young, fit people equals social and sporting opportunities. That's right – the Redcoat was about to come out again. Before too long I started to arrange one or two cricket matches, and then after that one or two football matches. It was Wisley all over again. After a few months we had all manner of teams and fixtures set up: Police versus Apprentices, Foremen versus Managers, Apprentices versus Labourers – you name them, we had them playing each other – followed, surprise, surprise, by a drink or two.

Now just you bear in mind how big this organization was. We didn't have tens of people working there like we did at Wisley; we had hundreds, and so from a social and sporting point of view the possibilities were endless.

Eventually I got to know the bloke in charge of catering at Hyde Park police station and so when it came to organizing the food for our social gatherings he was the first person I spoke to. In fact, we came to a nice little arrangement. He'd look after me and then I'd look after him with a few plants or what have you. Nobody went without and nobody got hurt. It just worked!

Some of the get-togethers we had were legendary.

Remember the first Christmas party I told you about, where a few of them came back to our place? Well, a year or two on from that we'd have had to hire Buckingham Palace if we'd wanted to arrange a bit of 'after hours'. They became epic!

As you can imagine, the security back then was quite tight, what with the IRA still being active, but fortunately I was never on the receiving end of any of the attacks, nor did I have to witness any of the aftermaths. One thing I was involved in, though, was the Iranian Embassy siege, which took place in 1980. Remember that? Something had been going on over the far side of Hyde Park, which is where all the bowling greens and football pitches were, for a few days but we'd been told in no uncertain terms to stay well away. In fact the entire area was being patrolled twenty-four hours a day and so we knew that whatever it was it must be something serious. To be honest there was always something like that going on in London – this was when the IRA was in full swing – and although we sussed out that it was the Iranian Embassy the police and army had been watching, we had no idea what was going on. Then we started hearing about it on the news of course, which is when it all became very real.

About five days after they first cordoned-off the area I remember getting a telephone call about three o'clock in the morning. Mum was ill at the time and when I first heard the phone I feared the worst. She's gone, I thought. But when I picked it up it was actually my boss.

'Don't ask any questions,' he said. 'I want you to meet me outside the yard underneath that big horse chestnut. Make sure you bring a torch, a pen and a piece of paper.'

'What, are we going on a treasure hunt?' I said to myself.

I had absolutely no idea what was going on but I did as I was told.

When I got to the horse chestnut my boss was already waiting for me.

'Right, you stand here with me. A gentleman from the armed forces is going to brief us. Just you make sure you take it all in.'

Now I was really foxed, and if the truth be known just a little bit scared. Being out in the middle of the night with my boss was bad enough, but the armed forces? Anyway, after a minute or two along came this commander.

'You've heard about the siege at the Iranian Embassy?' he said. 'Twenty-six people being held hostage?'

We nodded. 'Well I don't know if you're aware but one of the hostages has now been killed and the Prime Minister has instructed the SAS to rescue the remaining hostages and bring the siege to an end. In order to do this we're going to need help accessing various areas and so we're going to need your assistance.'

Over the next twenty minutes or so I made notes of exactly what the commander needed doing – clearing areas of equipment and making space for vehicles generally – and then went back to the office and started calling up all the staff that lived nearby. Within about half an hour or so they were all present and correct, and so under cover of darkness we set to work carrying out these orders. Now obviously I wasn't allowed to say a word to any of them about what was going on, which meant these poor kids of mine were absolutely terrified. I think they thought World War Three had started!

Anyway, not long after we'd finished, it all began: soldiers abseiling down from the roof, etc., and just seventeen minutes later the SAS had rescued all but one of the remaining hostages and had killed five out of the six terrorists. They'd lost another hostage but it could have been a heck of a lot worse. It was 5 May 1980 and although I didn't actually see or hear the rescue take place I remember watching it on the news. Doesn't everybody?

Fortunately for everyone concerned these kinds of episodes gradually became less and less but that didn't make the job any less eventful. Good God, no. If you wanted excitement mixed in with a lot of hard work you may as well go straight down to the Royal Parks. It was nonstop!

One of the most exhilarating parts of that job, not to mention tiring, was being involved in all the official events: Trooping of the Colour, the Queen's Silver Jubilee, Beating the Retreat – not to mention Charles and Diana's wedding. You see the day-to-day stuff like coordinating what went on between the nurseries and the park managers, not to mention all that bulk buying of bulbs, etc., was just the tip of the iceberg. It was like working in a city within a city.

Charles and Diana's wedding was just madness, as I'm sure you can imagine. The majority of the hard work took place in the run up to the big day and in particular the events which took place the night before. You reckon the wedding was big? Just wait till you read this.

Tuesday, 28 July 1981, was the date in question and I remember it as if it were yesterday. Not only had they planned the biggest firework display ever in British history, in Hyde Park, but there was also going to be live music, street parties and all sorts of other shenanigans. We virtually brought London to a standstill that night and it took me and my staff about a week to recuperate.

The police reckoned there must have been well over a million people in central London that night and the vast majority of them were split between The Mall and Hyde

Park. The royal family were in attendance of course, first at Buck House and then Hyde Park, as were the majority of the wedding guests, and so in addition to this firework display being the biggest we'd seen it was also the largest gathering ever of official heads of state. Security? I think half the British army must have been on duty that night. Nowadays I don't think they'd allow something like that to go ahead.

My job, by the way, was once again to coordinate everything: from the people planning the fireworks through to the TV companies and the chaps running security. You name it, I had to be all over it like a rash. Talk about logistical nightmares. I must have made and received about ten thousand phone calls in the lead up to that event. We had a cast of thousands, an audience of hundreds of thousands and a budget of literally millions.

In Hyde Park they'd built this facade which resembled Buckingham Palace, and behind that sat all the fireworks and the detonators. This facade was absolutely gigantic – like something you'd find in a film studio – and you could have destroyed half the world with what they had hidden behind it.

Now before they started blowing everything up – this would have been about 8 p.m. – the Queen had to be brought from Buckingham Palace, but because there were so many people on the streets they just couldn't get her through. I think it took about half an hour in the end.

The idea was that once she arrived she'd take her place in a stand they'd had built with all the other royals and heads of state, and then once everyone was ready – *BANG!*

I remember standing at the side of this stand, where they'd put the control point for all the TV companies. Honestly, I've never seen as many TV screens in my entire life – one for every camera, I presume. It was like Dixons shop window!

Anyway, once the Queen eventually arrived and took her seat there was a drum roll, after which a marching band started to appear from either side of the facade. So far, so good! Then, once they'd finished playing, the master of the band retreated to a rostrum where he was supposed to press a button that would give the signal to start the display. Well, he certainly pressed the button all right; in fact he must have pressed it around a hundred times. But instead of a load of bangs going off and shouts of 'Ooh' and 'Aah', all I heard were a couple of raspberries.

You see what the firework people hadn't taken into consideration was the fact that the band were going to be marching not only over the wires linking the start button to the detonator, but the wires linking the detonator to the fireworks. And so what happened? Well, because they couldn't see where they were going this band marched straight over the wires and pulled the lot out.

It gets worse.

In a desperate attempt to try and rectify the situation people began shoving all the wires back in and then they started pressing buttons, but instead of the display going off as it should have done – one firework after another – it all started to go off at the same time. This would have been all good and well if the marching band hadn't still been out there, but unfortunately for them they were.

Because of what was going on in the skies at the time I think the only person who had their eyes at ground level was me and you should have seen those poor buggers scarper. And the language! That was even more colourful than the fireworks.

As atmospheres go, that night was absolutely electric and I can say in all honesty that I have never seen as many happy, smiling faces in one place at the same time. It was just wonderful.

Now the chap who used to mastermind all these extravaganzas was Major Michael Parker (now Major Sir Michael Parker KCVO CBE) and in a way he was the Bernard Delfont of the services. He was a fixer was Major Parker, and on first-name terms with just about every Royal, politician and VIP you can imagine. He produced the Royal Tournament for twenty-seven years in total and had been doing this since the early 1970s.

Now as I've said, it was the lead up to Charles and Diana's wedding that caused the most stress, not least for Major Parker. He'd been having a running battle with Westminster City Council, who granted all the permits and licences, ever since he put in the application to host the fireworks display and just a few days before it was due to take place they called him down for a meeting. Now I was there when he got back from that meeting, and if I hadn't known who he was I'd have been desperately scrawling out a few goodbye letters to friends and family. He went ballistic!

'Those b******s have now said that the security isn't tight enough and unless we adhere to their recommendations and put up yet more fencing they won't grant us permission.'

'That is bad news,' I said. 'Can't you get your boys to carry out the work?'

'Of course I bloody can't! I thought we were done and so I sent them all home.'

'What's going to happen then?'

'What's going to happen? Well if this display doesn't come off, Jim, I'll probably be sent straight to the Tower. And you, by the way, won't be far behind me.'

Now I couldn't possibly say if this was true or not, but there was always a rumour going round that Westminster City Council hated the Royal Parks because it was them who picked up all the litter, and us who got all the praise, and some people presumed that was the reason for the last-minute demands.

True or not, Major Parker and I were in trouble and unless we came up with a plan pretty quickly we'd be for the high jump.

'How about some of your staff, Jim?' asked the major.

'They're all stacked out,' I said to him. 'And besides, what about the materials? They want another mile or two of fencing put in, don't they?'

'Don't you worry about the materials,' he said. 'All I need are bodies. How about offering some of your staff overtime?'

'We couldn't do that,' I said. 'Though you're freelance, so maybe there is a way to swing it. But how would they get paid?'

'No problem,' said the major. 'What are your initials, Jim?'

'JCB. Why?'

'We're going to set up a new company for this very task and that's what we'll call it. You send me an invoice for whatever the staff cost and I'll pay it straight away.'

'Well it'll have to be cash,' I said. 'A lot of these blokes don't even have bank accounts.'

'No problem. I'll need ten of your best men, Jim, OK?'

'OK.'

Later that day I got my ten best men together and I told them what was occurring.

'So tonight, lads, as soon as you've clocked off you go straight to Major Parker and he'll tell you what to do.

There'll be no breaks and there'll be no messing around. Got that?'

'Yes, governor.'

The following morning Major Parker turned up at my office carrying a briefcase. It was like something out of James Bond. I gave him the invoice and he opened the briefcase and handed me the money. If we did something like that these days we'd have been locked up, Major Parker and me, or there would at least have been a steward's enquiry. We got the job done though. The fencing went up and he got permission.

One or two of the lads who'd done the overtime were big drinkers – and I mean big – and so instead of giving them the money all at once I'd spread it out over a week or so. If I hadn't they'd never have made it in the next day!

One of the first really big events Major Parker organized that I had the pleasure of working on was the celebrations for the Queen's Silver Jubilee, and I don't mind telling you it almost finished me off. What a nightmare! We had kids by the thousand; we had street parties, garden parties, jelly, ice cream, elephants. That's right, elephants! Major Parker had organized a circus and so we had about ten of them tethered up at the top end of Hyde Park. Did you know that elephants only drink warm water? It's true. What's more they drink quite a lot of it. What a palaver that was, because by the time we got the buckets over to them the water had gone cold. It took me an age to figure out how we could heat the water where the elephants were tethered. And the dung! You could have filled a football stadium with what they deposited. Actually, that was a bit of a bonus really, because as soon as it came out I got one of the lads to shovel it up and it went straight onto the flower beds.

The biggest problem we had to contend with, though,

was the rain, which must have started about a day or so before the event took place, and it just didn't stop. Out of sheer desperation we literally smothered Hyde Park in ton after ton of tree bark. Little did I know, however, that when you put tree bark on top of grass it kills it. Somebody made me aware of what was happening a day or two later, and I almost died. So almost as soon as we'd put the stuff down we had to scrape it all up again! The show had to go on though, and somehow we muddled through. Years later there were still some areas where the grass hadn't grown back and I used to wince every time I saw them.

Do you know, we were like an industrial double-act, Major Parker and I. Bodge-it and Scarper! What an amazing man, though.

Years later when I was working down at Greenwich I was asked to help organize a one hundredth birthday celebration for P&O and when I arrived at the first meeting for the event there he was.

'Jim!' he cried.

'Oh my God,' I said to him.

'The old team back together again, eh? I'll tell you what though, definitely no elephants, OK?'

11. Chelsea

In 1976 when Bob Corbin said to me 'I think it's about time you got back into horticulture', what he meant was: it's time you started using some of your knowledge on a day-to-day basis. Never in a million years did I imagine I'd get the opportunity to work on some of the exhibits at Chelsea, let alone win a gold medal or two. What a lucky boy, eh?

But in addition to getting involved in the practical side at the show it also put me on the radar of the Royal Horticultural Society, and if it hadn't been for that I might never have become a judge. Now there are probably one or two people in the Harrogate area, not to mention one or two others, who will be cursing Bob Corbin for getting me into the Royal Parks, but there we go, that's just the way it is.

I'll come on to all the Judge Buttress stuff in a bit, but first let's concentrate on Chelsea, shall we? My spiritual home!

I first started visiting the Chelsea Flower Show back in the 1950s and have exhibited there more times than I care to remember. Do you know, it's difficult to think of anything that even compares to the Chelsea Flower Show. I'll have a go though. You see to me it's more than just a flower show. It's an organic art gallery. Imagine persuading some of the best artists in the world to gather together and paint something special, and then have a buffoon in a bowler hat judge it all! That's what it's akin to in my opinion – the ultimate competition. But you need a lot more than just gardening skills to do well at Chelsea. You need to have an imagination

– a big imagination. It's the gardening skills that help you interpret that and bring it all to life.

Some of the ideas they come up with these days are literally out of this world. In 2011 Diarmuid Gavin (the Damien Hirst of horticulture), who's probably one of the best garden designers in the business, came up with the idea of having a garden suspended in the sky, and do you know what, it worked! It was the shape of an eye, this thing, and must have been about ten yards wide by five yards high. According to Diarmuid the garden was supposed to represent the rolling green hills of Ireland and had as its main feature the plant *Carpinus betulus*, otherwise known as the common hornbeam, clipped into cone shapes and occasionally with stripped stems. In addition to this he included groups of *Taxus baccata* (English yew), *Buxus sempervirens* (common box) and various ornamental grasses. He'd also put two benches inside, which meant you could even take a ride on the bloody thing if you wanted! I decided to view the garden with my feet firmly on terra firma, thank you very much, but he got a gold medal for his efforts, and well deserved too.

The first one or two Chelseas I did when I joined the Royal Parks were with Bob Legge. The first one was for the Silver Jubilee in 1977 and that was pretty memorable. The biggest site at the Chelsea Flower Show is the monument, which is situated right in the middle of the grounds next to the hospital. It's the one that a company called Hillier's normally have. Anyway, that year, because of its significance, Hillier's very graciously handed the site over to the Royal Parks and Bob Legge came up with the idea of building a crown around the monument using purple violets and silver foliage. He never drew up any plans, by the way. With Bob it was all done on the back of a fag packet. Seriously, I remember when it came to the build, Bob pulled out four or five cigarette packets and on the back of each were a few sketches and notes.

'Right then,' he said. 'Gather round and have a look at these, Jim. I think it should all make sense.'

God only knows how, but it did. I only wish I'd nabbed them off him and kept them.

So in came all these African violets from the Royal Parks nursery and away we went. My God, that was hard work. We had to make it look like this crown was sitting on a cushion of ermine and that too had to be made out of flowers. We must have used enough wire mesh to house about a million chickens.

I remember Her Majesty coming round that year and she looked as pleased as Punch when she saw the crown. It was the centrepiece of the entire show.

Then after Bob packed in, in came Bob Wadey and his apprentices. Well, because Bob and I had struck up such a good friendship, when it came to him being asked to manage the Royal Parks exhibit at Chelsea he asked me to come on board. I honestly thought I'd struck gold when he suggested it.

He and I were like the Brian Clough and Peter Taylor of horticulture – him being Cloughie and me Peter Taylor – and our team were the apprentices. What a great bunch of lads and lasses they were. Keen as mustard and always smiling – exactly how I was at their age.

Bob was the one who called the shots and sat on his backside all day, and I was the one who tidied up, fetched and carried and kept the apprentices' spirits up. I'm only joking, Bob! We were a crack team he and I, and I learned a hell of a lot from him. We did quite a few Chelseas together, at least four or five, and we all had a whale of a time, especially the apprentices. They couldn't wait for Chelsea to come round.

As opposed to them just labouring, Bob and I used to get them involved with every aspect. They helped to design the exhibits, plant them, and then build them. We even had them managing the garden while the show was on: shaking hands with the bigwigs and giving them the story behind the design and all that. We were one big happy family.

Once Bob Wadey took over it was a very different dynamic. With Bob Legge we'd cross over with regards to roles, but with Bob Wadey everything was more defined. He liked being left to get on with what he had to do and so it was my job to make sure that happened. Then there were the kids of course, and that's what really made it for me.

Do you know, they were probably some of the happiest times I've ever had. Let me just explain how it all happened. First of all Bob would call a meeting about six months before and there'd be me and all the apprentices who were helping out in attendance. Then they'd explain the idea for the garden and then ask for input. Everyone would go away and think about it and we'd reconvene a week or so later. Once we'd agreed on the design it was then a question of growing the materials and a lot of this would be done by the kids: sowing, potting-on and dead-heading, etc. Timing is a massive issue here, because everything has to happen at the right time and that takes a heck of a lot of skill. I believe they call it squeaky bum time!

Instead of building the garden elsewhere and then transferring it to Chelsea, what we'd do is build a dummy garden instead. First of all we'd rope off an area the same size as the plot and then we'd put sticks in for the trees and pots in for the shrubs, and so on. This was to give us an idea of how it might look in real life and would stay in place right up until the day we started setting up. By the time we got to the plot at Chelsea we were so used to how it was supposed to look that we could have planted it all with our eyes closed.

Setting up was always great fun although it was hard work. We'd start about seven in the morning and work until about ten or eleven o'clock at night. Eventually I'd say to Bob, 'That's it, mate, we can't do anymore. The kids are just about fit to drop.' And then I'd bundle the apprentices back into the back of the minibus and take them all back to their homes. You should have seen them. It was like me on the Green Line all over again. The moment they sat down, they were gone. We'd be up again at five though.

'Come on, you lot, get in,' I'd shout when I arrived to pick them up.

There'd be a bit of whining at first, but once we'd got a cup of tea and a bacon sandwich inside them the banter would slowly start again and away we'd go. I think it was a mixture of camaraderie, excitement and adrenalin that kept us all going.

Once the show had finished the apprentices and I would start ripping it all down and so they were literally there from start to finish: inception to construction to deconstruction.

Now have you any idea what a mumper is? Well, basically, a mumper is somebody who can blag literally anything from anyone and I'm proud to say that I'm probably one of the best.

'You couldn't spare a few of those, could you, governor?'

'Yeah, all right. For you, Jim.'

'Thanks. I'll see you right.'

That's horticulture though. Everyone helps everyone else.

Anyway, one year at Chelsea, Bob, the apprentices and I built a garden that was modelled on Kensington Gardens. We even managed to get permission to use a model of the statue of Peter Pan and around that we built a pond. One day, as we were building this garden, Bob called me over.

''Ere, Jim,' he said. 'You couldn't go and mump some cement for me, could you? We haven't got enough for the pond.'

Well of course there were dozens of other exhibitors using cement for the show and so I knew I'd be OK.

'Yeah, of course, Bob,' I said. 'How much do we need?'

'About two barrows?'

'No problem.'

And so off I popped to see a few mates.

Unfortunately, the cement I'd borrowed wasn't strong enough to hold water for more than a few hours and so when we came back the next day we'd virtually flooded the place.

The woman in charge was absolutely furious.

'What have you done?' she cried.

I thought it was best to make myself scarce.

A year or two after that we did a garden based on the work of the famous garden designer Gertrude Jekyll, and for this we needed a brick wall. But instead of building the real thing we had a false one made out of ply. Now because of the site we'd been given, the only place we could put this wall was in the middle, next to this old marquee, and I had to pack it in against the two poles that were holding the thing up.

Just after I'd finished this old boy came up to me. ''Ere,' he said. 'You don't mind me giving you a bit of advice, do you?'

'Of course not. What's up?'

'You see those poles that you just packed that false wall into? They move in the wind.'

I looked back to my lovely wall and, sure enough, there it was, swaying gently left to right.

'Oh dear,' he said. 'It looks like something out of a Fun House.'

I didn't have much fun unpacking it all, I'll tell you that!

The prize that all the local authorities were vying for back then was the coveted Wigan Cup, which is awarded to the best exhibit shown to the Society by a local authority. Old Bob and I won it once, with a lot of help from the kids of course. I think it was 1982 when we won it and that was the last one we did together. After that Bob handed the reins over to me, and so from then on I was the one who came up with the initial ideas. I always enjoyed the design side but not on my own. I work much better as part of a team and once everyone else was involved I was a lot happier.

Believe it or not, the third and final win Bob and I had together with the kids was achieved with just a simple Cottage Garden. I'll quickly explain how we built it.

First me and the kids got a huge piece of plywood and screwed a load of dead branches onto it. Then we grew five or six *Tropaeolum*, which have flowers that look a bit like canaries, and put them onto the ply. It looked a lot better than it sounds, I promise you. Anyway, once they were all fully grown we lifted the whole thing up like a stretcher, took it to Chelsea, and then built the garden round that. It was quite an informal design, if I remember rightly, and featured a well, some dense plantings and a mixture of ornamental and edible plants.

Bob doesn't give away compliments lightly, but when he first saw what me and those kids had created he just beamed. 'That's marvellous,' he said. 'Do you know, I reckon we'll get a gold with that?' And we did of course. I'll tell you what, the kids couldn't believe it. Most of them were only in their very early twenties at the time, and they'd won a gold medal! Instead of bundling them all into the back of that minibus again and taking them home I took the lot of them to the pub, and my word did we celebrate! What a night that was. I was so proud of them.

When we first started exhibiting at Chelsea, themed gardens were the in-thing and, believe it or not, it was the local authorities who were the pioneers. There aren't as many now but back then there were probably seven or eight who exhibited regularly – from big councils like Birmingham through to much smaller ones like Newham. It was all down to the Superintendent of the Parks Department. If he or she had it built into their budget, you were in.

I remember exhibiting opposite Ayr borough council. They always put on a good show and this year had built a garden depicting the end of a race at Ayr racecourse. What a masterstroke that was, especially the colours they chose for the winning jockey. You see the patron of the RHS back then was HRH the Queen Mother (or to my mate Bobby Golden, Elizabeth R!) and when she realized that the winning jockey in the garden was actually wearing her colours, she was absolutely cock-a-hoop. The rest of us were green with envy!

Now while we're here let me tell you a little bit about how I came to be a judge, because as I said before, this all happened about the same time, *and* because of what Bob and I had been doing at Chelsea.

After we'd been exhibiting with the kids for a couple of years we began to attract the attention of one or two members of the RHS old guard. They weren't all a bunch of uppity snobs, you know. In fact one of them, a lovely lady named Carolyn Hardy, became a big, big fan of what we were doing; and we became a big, big fan of hers. Carolyn was the RHS's Vice President back then and a big hitter. I remember she always made a point of coming over to us and making a big fuss of the apprentices. It didn't matter if she was judging us or not; she'd be there. It wasn't hard-core horticulture, it was theatre, and it was fun. What's wrong with that? There were no airs and graces with Carolyn. She was just a good old-fashioned gardener.

'Hello, you lot!' she'd say. 'What have you come up with this year? You're going to have a job topping last year.'

You should have seen the kids' faces. 'Look sharp, you lot,' I'd shout. 'Vice President of the Society in attendance. Stand to attention!'

As I said, it was theatre.

So before I have a little gripe about how things used to be at the RHS let me just put on record that there were some absolute diamonds within that organization, none more so than Carolyn.

Anyway, after a while some of the other RHS bigwigs began wandering over to Bob and me, and pretty soon we were recognized by the Society, or at least some of them.

'We do admire you getting so many young people involved, Mr Buttress. You and Mr Wadey are setting such a wonderful precedent. What an absolutely splendid show!'

This worked both ways because, in my opinion, having the kids on board gave us the edge. All they were interested in were flowers, and so instead of getting carried away with props and what have you like some of the exhibitors did we tried to let the flowers do the talking. We used the odd statue of course, as with Peter Pan, but first and foremost this was and is a flower show and the boys and girls especially never let us forget it.

Now as Bob and I were making a name for ourselves with the kids I suddenly received a letter, as did Bob, from the RHS Council, inviting us to join the Floral Judging Committee. They have judging committees for every aspect of gardening at the RHS, and each one has to have several experts on it. The moment I opened the letter I called Bob.

'Have you got one?' I asked him.

'Yes I have. I can't believe it, Jim. You do know this is going to cause a real stir.'

He wasn't wrong.

The RHS circa the late 1970s was akin to the MCC circa the late 1870s, in that if you hadn't been to the right school and didn't possess at least two surnames and your own gardener you were highly unlikely to be welcomed into the fold. Honestly, there were more lords, ladies, counts and countesses in that society than there were in the Palace of Westminster. It was a closed shop – or so we thought. Carolyn Hardy, impressed by the progress we'd made with the kids, had obviously applied a bit of pressure.

We later found out that our shock inclusion was also partly down to our fellow exhibitors. None of us like being judged by people who haven't earned their stripes and it has to be said that at the time hardly anybody at the RHS had. They were just enthusiastic amateurs really, and the exhibitors who belonged to commercial organizations had apparently started complaining; and who could blame them? After all this was their livelihood. It was like a hairdresser refereeing a football match. Bob and I had been on the coalface, they argued, and would be able to relate to exhibitors without giving anything away.

To be fair, and without wanting to blow my and Bob's trumpet, that's exactly what happened. We didn't always agree with the exhibitors, of course, and that's pretty much the same today, but generally speaking we get along fine.

'There's one thing about you, Jim,' they'd say. 'You don't beat around the bush. You've told us the truth and we'd as soon hear it from you as from anybody else.' And that's the way it should be. I'm one of them, you see.

At the end of the day though, my purpose as a judge is to reward excellence and help people improve, and in order for me to do that properly I need to be willing to lend an ear occasionally. As I'm walking through a show, whether it's Chelsea or any of the others, they'll often pull me to one side.

'You haven't got five minutes, have you, Jim?'

'Yeah, of course.'

'What do you reckon to this?'

And so I'll have a look for them.

'Ooh, I'm not sure that's going to work, mate.'

Now if I was the only person judging these exhibits and deciding who should win what then this could be seen as being suspect, but at the end of the day I'm just a small cog in a very big wheel. You can't be all aloof when you're judging, you have to be consultative.

Anyway, I'm digressing . . . When I told both Pop and Bill Fuller that Bob and I had been asked to go on the Floral Judging Committee they were absolutely over the moon. They couldn't believe it.

'I'll tell you what, boy,' said Pop. 'For a working-class boy like you to be invited to become a member of the RHS Floral Committee – well, that's really something.'

I do believe the old boy was proud of me!

Bob and I couldn't wait for our first assignment, if only to see what kind of reception we'd get. It was a September show at the RHS headquarters, Vincent Square in London, if my memory serves me correctly, and there must have been at least twenty people on the committee.

When we all got together in the hall prior to doing the rounds it was like the living room of an old people's home. Half of the committee weren't paying attention and the other half were talking. It was just a joke.

'OK then,' said the chairman. 'We'll do the introductions when we meet to ratify our decisions. Is everybody ready to go?'

After one or two sniffs and shouts of 'Oh, raaaather,' off we all trotted.

The next twenty minutes was a real eye-opener for us because these people weren't enthusiastic amateurs after all. In fact they weren't even novices. They were just titled people with big gardens.

Until then, their idea of balancing things up had been getting an academic in there, somebody authoritative but much closer to them socially. I remember seeing one of these people waxing poetic about an Icelandic poppy once. 'Oh, this is simply marvellous,' he cried. 'I haven't seen one of these for years. Well done! I shall be recommending gold of course.'

That would have been all good and well if it had been a stand-alone entry, but it wasn't, it was just part of an overall stand, and because they all got so excited about the Icelandic poppy they took no notice of anything else.

Not surprisingly, there was a hierarchy in this group. A little fat bloke stood at the front next to the chairman, and it seemed that whatever he nominated was more often than not accepted.

'Gold medal, Mr Chairman?' he'd bark, and then that would eventually get fed down through the ranks.

'Gold medal here?'

'Oh yes, I think so, definitely a gold medal.'

These people hadn't even reached the stand yet! They just went along with it.

Eventually we got to some Korean chrysanthemums, and let me tell you they were covered with pests. In fact if there'd been an award for Most Diseased, they'd have won gold.

'I think a silver here, don't you, Mr Chairman?' said the little round bloke.

Well, by this time I'd had enough.

'Excuse me,' I said to them both. 'What are we doing this for?'

'I beg your pardon, Mr Buttress?'

They just looked at me as if to say, 'Good heavens, we're being addressed by one of the servants!'

'This is meant to be an example to the public,' I continued, 'and the exhibitors should have to earn the right to be here. But this is awful!'

I then shook these Korean chrysanthemums and as I did a cloud of white smoke puffed out followed by whitefly. It was like I'd just lit a cigarette. They were suffering from something called leaf miner, which is the larva of an insect that lives in and eats the leaf tissue of plants.

'They're ruined,' I said. 'Not even worth a commendation.'

Pinky and Perky obviously didn't like being told they were wrong, and so instead of saying 'fair enough' and walking past the chrysanthemums, they gave them a bloody bronze medal!

Next up were some Icelandic poppies, but unfortunately they were all tight-bud, and didn't have a single flower in sight.

'If we come back in a week or two they might be worth

a medal,' I said. 'But at the moment, I'm afraid they're just not ready.'

'Gold medal, Mr Chairman?' came the cry.

'Oh undoubtedly, Cecil!'

I give up, I thought.

My favourite story regarding the old guard took place at Chelsea one year when a member of the judging committee went back to a stand of conifers and said to the man running it, 'Do you know, if you'd had a bit more colour there you might have stood a chance.'

'What do you mean, colour?' said the bloke.

'I mean flowers, man, flowers!'

This chap almost lost it with him. He said, 'Would you mind walking away from my stand, please, before I say something I regret.'

'Well, if you're going to be like that!'

If he'd made some remarks about variegation, then fair enough. But flowers, on a conifer?

That's not to say that the judges of today don't get foxed every now and then, because believe me, we do. It doesn't matter if you have the knowledge of Roy Lancaster or Chris Brickell, there are going to be times when you have to stop and ask. Either that or you carry an encyclopaedia with you. Horticulture's a big old subject, you know.

I remember a couple of years ago walking past a stand at Chelsea, and as I did I saw a saxifrage I didn't recognize.

'Excuse me,' I said to the exhibitor. 'That saxifrage you've got there.'

'Ah ha!' he said with a great big grin. 'I thought that might catch you out, Jim.' And then he proceeded to tell me all about it: where it came from and what it liked, etc. Do you know, though, if I hadn't asked that question and had just taken a punt, I might have marked him unfairly. You take my word for it, when it comes to this sort of thing, pride most definitely comes before a fall.

Anyway, back to our first day as judges. Later on, at the start of the ratification meeting, the chairman stood up.

'Now then, everybody, we have two new committee members here today, Mr Jim Buttress and Mr Bob Wadey. One word of advice, gentlemen: as my mother used to say, children should be seen and not heard, and that also goes for junior members of the Floral Committee. The rules state that during your first year on the committee you should do nothing but listen.'

After a few mumbles of 'Hear, hear, Mr Chairman!' à la the House of Lords, we were all dismissed.

I said to Bob, 'You just watch. I'll give that old buzzard seen and not heard! If I'm going to do this I'm going to do it properly. I'm not having them knocking out medals to diseased plants. It's ridiculous.'

'Just you be careful, Jim,' said Bob. 'You can't change the rules.'

Anyway, during the next ratification meeting I asked the chairman if I could have the floor for a minute. He looked terrified! 'Well, if you must.'

'Look,' I said to them. 'I know it says in the rules that I'm not supposed to get involved, but if all I'm going to do is just sit there for a year and listen to you lot I'm afraid I'll have to offer you my resignation. It's not in my nature.'

I was fully expecting them to accept my resignation readily and then start cracking open the champagne, but I was in for a real shock.

'Do you know, Mr Buttress,' said the chairman. 'I actually rather agree with you. What you said last week during the walk around was of course right, and I'm afraid we were a little too proud and embarrassed to admit as much. From now on you'll be free to make your point. As will you, Mr Wadey.'

Now it takes a lot to shock me. I'm a Crystal Palace fan, remember, and I've also read one or two of Alan Titchmarsh's novels! But this had me gone and no mistake. I couldn't believe it.

From there it just kind of grew and grew, until eventually I was selected as Vice Chairman of what's known as the RHS Floral Committee A, which is the role I hold to this day. The RHS judging committees are split into sections, just like our duties were at Wisley, so you'll have a tree and shrub committee and then an alpine committee, and so on. The Floral Committee A covers herbaceous plants – sweet peas and gladioli, for example. Members of each committee are chosen by their suitability, so unless you know exactly what you're talking about you won't get in. It never used to be like that but these days it's run exactly how it should be.

This role, by the way, nearly always falls to a member of the RHS Council, as he or she can then report back, so how the hell I got it I've no idea. Anyway, from that day onward I've done every single RHS flower show literally dozens of times. I'm also on the committee that decides who becomes a judge, and I like to think – without wanting to blow my own trumpet – that this all happened because I've been honest with people and because they think I'm genuine. I've never tried to make a name for myself, and if they ever came to me and said, your time's up, I'll happily move on. If something's rubbish, I'll tell you. But if I'm rubbish, you've got to tell me.

Now, as I said before, everyone helps everyone in horticulture and I remember coming to the aid of a mate of mine once who owned his own nursery. Back when I started judging and exhibiting, the only thing the nurseries could sell at Chelsea was seeds, and for the majority of the companies who came to the show it was their biggest earner of the year. Think about it. It's the start of the season and you've got literally hundreds of thousands of mad keen gardeners wandering round, and all with a few quid in their pocket. It was their Christmas if you like. These days they're allowed to sell plants and the like but one thing that hasn't changed is that nurseries are exhibitors and not traders. They have to apply of course, so they can't just turn up, and if their design isn't up to scratch they won't get in, it's as simple as that. Do you know who the most decorated exhibitor at Chelsea is? Hillier Garden Centres, the company I mentioned earlier. In 2015 they secured their seventieth gold medal!

Anyway, one day, about three weeks before Chelsea was due to begin, I saw this mate of mine walking down the street, and the poor bloke could hardly walk.

'Bloody hell, Graham,' I said. 'What's the matter with you?'

'Oh, Jim,' he said. 'I've had a nightmare.'

He was limping and one of his arms was all bandaged up. It looked serious.

'I was down in Malvern at a show last week and just as I was coming out of a shop, having bought a new shirt for Chelsea, this old girl lost control of her car, went straight into one of those old wooden lamp posts and this is the result. My arm's completely shattered. I've got plates, pins and all kinds of rubbish in it. This is going to ruin me, Jim.'

'How do you mean, ruin you? You're still alive, aren't you?'

'Yeah, but I can't do Chelsea, can I? I mean, look at me. I could just about take the money all right, but what about the display? That was my biggest earner by a country mile. I'm a one-man band at Chelsea and I can't afford to pay anybody. I don't know what I'm going to do.'

Well, to me it was obvious.

'I'll do it for you,' I said.

'You're joking. Really, Jim?'

'Course I will. As long as I tell the powers that be that I can't judge you. I mean, why not?'

So that's what we did. Graham managed to get all his flowers down there and then once I'd got them unpacked I set to work with another chap, and he gave the instructions. You should have seen the look on Graham's face when I'd finished. It was a picture.

'That's fantastic, Jim,' he said. 'You really have saved my bacon, mate. What can I do to thank you?'

'Nothing,' I said. 'You'd do the same for me, wouldn't you? I'll tell you what: I'll let you buy me lunch.'

When we got back from having a sandwich there was a letter on Graham's display that we thought was from the judges. They'd been due to start the preliminary rounds and so we thought it must have been news of either a thumbs-up or a thumbs-down.

I opened the envelope and showed the contents to Graham.

'What does it say, mate? You should be the first to see.'

He just looked at it and started laughing.

'I think you'd better read it for yourself, Jim,' he said, and so I turned the piece of paper round and had a look.

'What a load of rubbish,' it read, and then underneath that, 'NO MEDAL!'

It wasn't from the judges at all. It was from all the other exhibitors. They must have heard I was helping Graham and so decided to give me a bit of my own medicine. They'd all been waiting for us to get back and so when we opened the envelope they were all in stitches. That's what Chelsea's like, though. It's a family.

I'll give you another example.

I told you about Perennial, the gardeners' charity? Well a few years ago they were left a legacy from a rich old lady who lived in Hackney. She was a spinster, a little bit eccentric, and there were only two things that mattered in her life: her best friend and her garden, which was huge. I remember seeing a photograph and it was full of flowers. Nothing else, just flowers. Floral diarrhoea, I called it. Anyway, when this old girl passed away it turned out she'd left half her money to St Joseph's Hospice in Hackney, who had looked after her best friend before she'd died, and half to Perennial. She had a family, apparently, who never visited her, and so rather than everything going straight to them she decided to do some good with it. Good for her.

In the end Perennial decided that in memory of this old girl and as a thank you for the legacy she left them they'd build a courtyard garden that would be assembled at Chelsea. Then, once that was over and done with it would be moved lock, stock and barrel over to the gardens at St Joseph's, where it would stay in perpetuity.

The three people charged with creating this garden were me, the head gardener at St Joseph's and a designer, and I have to say it wasn't easy. Working to somebody else's design never is really. That's not being big-headed, by the way. It's just natural. When there's no hierarchy in place everyone tries to push their own ideas forward.

Now I can't remember who it was but somebody decided that it would be a good idea to have three or four granite tombstones included in this garden, all carved with flowers. Bearing in mind where the garden was going once Chelsea had finished I thought it might have been in bad taste. I mean, come on; if you're sitting in God's waiting room the last thing you want to see when you're gazing out of the window is a reminder of what's coming to you. I argued about this until I was blue in the face but by the time I turned up at the job they'd already had the cranes in and so there they were. Given how small courtyard gardens are, once these monstrosities were in place it looked more like a private mausoleum than anything else. I thought, flaming hell. There's no way we were going to win gold with this.

Anyway, as I'd been asked to do the flowers in this garden I set to work doing the very best I could, and because it was being transported back to the hospice I decided to use plenty of grasses and permanent perennials. The only semi-perennial I used was something called *Verbena bonariensis*, which is a tall purple flower and that gave us a nice bit of height. The finished result wasn't what I'd have liked it to be, of course, but then, there we go; people have different ideas. I still thought we might snatch a silver, though, or if the panel were feeling charitable, maybe even a silver gilt.

Come judgement day, there we all were waiting for the decision, and just as I was handed our certificate the girl from the BBC approached me followed by her cameraman.

'You must be over the moon,' she beamed, as I pulled out confirmation of a bronze.

'You've got to be bloody joking!' I said.

I was devastated – not for me and the other two but for the charity. Getting a gold medal is worth more in publicity than you can imagine and they manage to turn a lot of that into donations.

Well, this girl from the BBC must have thought all her Christmases had come at once, and before I could say anything else she darted off back to her studio, cut it, and that was it. That picture of my face went on every single opening of Chelsea that week. Senior judge, Jim Buttress, with a face like thunder? That'll do.

All my mates at the show were gutted for us. I had Alan Titchmarsh, Carol Klein, Joe Swift and all the others down there, consoling us.

'Never mind, Jim,' they said. 'We'll give you a plug later on. You'll still get plenty of punters.'

Do you know, because of us only getting bronze and them using my ugly crestfallen mug on the opening credits of the TV coverage, we got more visitors than ever before.

'You looked so sad,' they all said. 'We just had to come and see you.'

When I saw the judges I didn't half rip into them. Some of it I couldn't argue with but I honestly thought they'd been unfair. But then I would, wouldn't I? That's one of the difficulties of being on both sides of the fence but, do you know, I wouldn't change it for the world.

Before we get back to the day job let me just bring you up to date re Chelsea because although I've now retired from exhibiting, my last four years were some of the happiest and most successful I've had. Best of all though, for three of those years I've been involved in something pretty special. Let me explain.

In 2012 I started exhibiting with Adam Frost, who is an extraordinarily talented garden designer; and on the strength of the first garden we did together (which won us a gold, by the way, as did the second we did in 2013) he managed to set up the Homebase Academy, which is the first of its kind anywhere in the country.

Basically it enables boys and girls from all over the country – people who would normally just be pushing Dutch trolleys round and stacking shelves – to take their

RHS Level II. This means that they get the training, the qualification, and at the end of it the chance to become an assistant manager at a Homebase Garden Centre. So instead of people going in there, asking something, and the staff just saying 'I don't know,' they can offer some proper advice. We started with six trainees and according to Adam we'll be up to forty by 2016. Homebase know that not every employee's going to use the qualification within the company but that's one of those things. What's important is that they're getting some young people on the horticultural ladder.

One thing I haven't told you about yet is how I started wearing my bowler hat. It's a question I'm often asked, so here goes. When I did that first exhibit at Chelsea with RHS Wisley I was fascinated by the fact that all the judges and head gardeners wore bowlers. Until then I thought that only people like Pop wore them – professional men who worked in the city – but I was wrong. Many years later I was at the Chelsea Flower Show with Roy Lancaster, Matt Biggs and Alan Titchmarsh and I said, 'Do you know what, next year we should bring the bowler back,' and they all said, 'What a good idea!' So I put the word round to the other judges and the following year I bought one and wore it to the show. The thing is, I was the only one. At first I felt like a bit of a berk but then after a while I forgot I was even wearing it. These days if I turn up to judge a show without it I'm in trouble!

One of the privileges of being a judge is that we can turn up at a show whenever we like, and as Chelsea opens its gates on a Monday I always make sure I'm there the Saturday and Sunday before. The first thing I do is walk the entire show, just to get a feel of it. Then, once I've done that, I'll visit every exhibit I'll be judging and I get my eye in. You can't just wait for the day and then decide. I suppose it's my homework and I always make plenty of notes.

There was a time when the exhibitors used to get a bit twitchy about judges doing this – I think it unnerved them a bit and they thought they were being spied on – but because I was also an exhibitor they knew they could trust me. The only thing I was interested in was making sure the best exhibit won and in order to do that I needed time.

What I also used to do, in fact I still do it sometimes, was look at some exhibits I'm not judging and then mark them. This is just for my own benefit as it enables me to see how close I am to the team actually judging them. Keeps me on my toes, I suppose.

Come Monday morning it's like another world, because in addition to having tens of thousands of visitors walking round you've got things like Caribbean bands and jazz bands; not to mention all the television cameras. The entire place comes to life really but from a judging point of view it's essential that you have that little bit of peace and quiet beforehand.

These days prejudging on the Saturday and Sunday is a prerequisite but when I first started judging Chelsea it was anything but. The majority of judges didn't bother coming in then (they didn't have to so it was fair enough), and because the judging took place after lunch some of them were, shall we say, a little bit merry. I'm certainly not suggesting that anyone turned up pie-eyed, but you're affecting people's livelihoods here and so you have to be as professional as they are. Today we judge at 8 a.m. on the Monday morning and that works perfectly.

Who you're judging with is also very important and that's always the first thing I want to know. I'll make a note on each exhibit as to who on my team is best qualified to comment first and that's how the discussion starts. Then, once everyone has had their say, we'll vote on it. Then after lunch

we'll go and see our friends the terminators – as I affection-
ately call the moderators – and the rest you will find out
later.

I could go on for days and days about the Chelsea Flower
Show and, who knows, one day I might even write a book
about it. I promise I'll try and squeeze a bit more in before
we finish, but for now let's get back to the Royal Parks,
because as well as writing a few words about the Queen and
the Queen Mum, there's life at Greenwich Park plus the
mother of all storms to tell you about.

12. Greenwich Royal Park

As I said earlier, because I used to be in charge of the Central Royal Parks I often get billed as the 'Queen's Gardener' but if truth be known I wasn't even the Queen's Gardener's governor. The position of head gardener was held by a lovely Sussex man called Fred Nutbeam (what a great name for a head gardener), and he answered to just one person: HM the Queen. As far as I know he'd been her head gardener since the 1950s and they were as thick as thieves. Back then Buckingham Palace was the Queen's official residence so she and the family were there all the time. It was their home then and so that was her back garden. Fred told me he used to push Charlie, Anne, Andrew and Edward around in the wheelbarrow when they weren't at school!

These days it's no longer her official residence and as far as I know it's not nearly as pretty as it was. Fred used to have this huge herbaceous border full of daffodils in the spring, followed by sweet peas and gladioli, but it's not there anymore. There also used to be pink flamingo in the lake, until the foxes got them about twenty years ago. It broke Her Majesty's heart that did. Do you know Fred used to have a greenhouse at Buckingham Palace where he had his own collection of orchids, and on the Queen's birthdays he used to take some up to the palace for her. He was totally devoted to the Queen and to those gardens. Anything she wanted, Fred would get. He used to run rings round the boss, for the simple reason that he knew he couldn't bear being the one to say no to the Queen, and so Fred knew that basically he'd get whatever he wanted. The times when his boss did refuse something Fred would say, 'It's your call but she's not going to like it.' The Queen didn't know anything about it of course, but Fred's boss didn't know that. He used to wink at me after the meeting and say, 'Works every time, Jim!' He was a shrewd old thing, was Fred.

My role with regards to Buckingham Palace was the same as with all the other parks and gardens: to liaise with those in charge (in this case Fred) and make sure everything ran smoothly, and I used to go down there every so often to say hello.

The first time I ever spoke to Fred was when he called the office one day, about a week after I started.

'I hear you're the new kid on the block,' he said. 'I think we should have a meeting.'

Now until I started there I'd never even been to a Royal Park. I mean why would I? I was too busy working or playing sport and so it was a completely new experience. Hyde Park, Kensington Park, St James's, Buck House. It was all fresh.

Going to Buckingham Palace was obviously a bit different from visiting any of the other parks or gardens, but even so the security involved was a lot different from how it is today. I remember pulling up round the back of Buckingham Palace that first time I met Fred. His entrance was opposite where the Coal Board used to be and when I rang the bell he came out and opened the gate. You couldn't do that these days.

'You must be Jim,' he said. 'Park over there, would you?'

He was a typical head gardener was Fred. He had a weathered, ruddy face and was quite jowly.

Once I'd parked up he took me into his house and I had

tea with him and his wife. 'Right then,' he said. 'Let's find out a bit about you, shall we?'

And then he started asking me questions.

'Who have you worked for?'

'Bob Corbin.'

'I know Bob Corbin. How is he?'

'He's well.'

'You've done a bit of horticulture then, Jim? Makes a change for somebody in the Royal Parks, I can tell you.'

Old Fred gave me a proper grilling and for a little while I felt like one of our apprentices. From what I could make out, when somebody became Superintendent of the Royal Parks they could often get a little bit above themselves and so Fred was obviously testing the water. Did I have my feet on the ground, or my head up my . . .

Anyway, after we'd had a good old chat he smiled, stood up and said, 'I think you'll be all right. Come on then, I'll take you for a tour.'

I remember him showing me round and me thinking, Jesus, I'm in Buckingham Palace! I felt like a schoolboy, to be honest; like I was on a trip or something. It got even better though because just as we were walking round the lake and then onto the lawn that backs onto the palace, the doors opened, a few corgis ran out, and then out came the Queen.

'Bloody hell, Fred,' I said. 'Is that her?'

'What, you nervous, Jim? Don't be, she's fine.'

I tried to look composed but I have a funny feeling that I probably failed miserably.

'Morning, Freddie,' said HM. 'How are you getting on?' Fred started talking to her – she ignored me.

'All fine thanks, Your Majesty. 'Ere look,' he said, pointing to me. 'I've got a new boss.'

'Have you really? You don't need a new boss, Freddie. You've got me.'

Because I thought Fred had now introduced me to Her Majesty I started bowing. The thing is I didn't stop! She must have thought I was a relative of Fred's who wasn't quite normal or something. I'm still trying to block that out.

So from then on every so often I'd get a call from Fred. 'Do you want to come down for a cuppa, Jim? The wife likes you so get yourself down. We'll have some tea and then I'll take you round.'

I never had to tell Fred what to do, of course. He just told me what he needed and I'd sort it. As I said, he only had one boss, and she was a lot higher up than I was.

Once I'd got to know Fred a bit better I asked him one day if I could bring old Pop round.

'Course you can,' he said. 'Just you tell me when and I'll make sure I give him the full tour.'

And that's what he did. My old dad was like a kid in a sweetshop that day. You should have seen his face. I'd never seen him so excited.

Now when it comes to the Queen Mother, it won't surprise you to learn that the story I want to tell you about takes place, not at Clarence House but at Cheltenham racecourse. Like the Queen she also had a gardener, a lady called Benny, and once again I just used to coordinate everything. The only difference was that whenever I saw the Queen Mother, instead of standing there and bowing like an idiot, I used to go inside for a drink. That was just the way she was. If you were in her house she wanted to know all about you – and about everyone you knew. The first thing she'd say to me whenever I went round there was, 'Now then, Jim. What's happening with all your staff?'

She wanted to know all the stories and gossip.

I'm not sure if I'm allowed to refer to a member of the royal family as a sweetie, but if I am, the Queen Mum was one. She just seemed to have a knack of making people feel comfortable. Anyway, once I had a drink in my hand we'd have a chat about racing or about what was going on in the Royal Parks. It was just a catch-up and a gossip really.

When it comes to Cheltenham I'm as mad keen as anyone and back then I'd say at least twenty per cent of my annual earnings used to go on that meeting. It was the high-light of my social calendar and I always used to go with about five or six mates. I remember one year I was walking round the back of the stand we were in when all of a sudden I saw one of the Queen Mum's security guards.

'What are you doing here, Jim?'

'What do you think I'm doing here? Having a good drink and a punt or two.'

He said, 'I'll tell you what. Pull up here after the third race and you can come upstairs. I know she'd love to see you.'

After the third race I said to my mates, 'In ten minutes' time, you look up towards the Royal Box. I might just have a surprise for you.' And then off I went.

'Come on then, Jim, follow me,' the security guard said, and so up we went to the Royal Box. Sure enough, sitting there at a table with a glass in her hand was the Queen Mum surrounded by some of her friends. I said to the guard, 'Before I go and say hello, would you mind if I just went and stood at the front of the box for a moment. I just want to see if I can see my mates.' He said, 'Of course not, so long as you're quick.'

I strolled to the front of the box, located my mates who were about fifty feet below, and then gave them a royal wave.

You should have seen the looks on their faces. It was a mixture of surprise and disgust, I think!

When I went back down they collared me straight away.

'How the bloody hell did you get up there?' they asked.

'I've got contacts.'

'Contacts? Bloody hell, Jim. You'd get where water wouldn't!'

'Yeah, probably.'

In 1982, after I'd been at the Central Royal Parks for about eight years, the position of Superintendent at Greenwich Park became available. I was touching forty now, and in addition to being tired of having to spread myself across so many different locations I fancied a change. I'd had great fun but at the end of the day eight years is a long time, and as such a move wasn't going to affect what I did at the Chelsea Flower Show – either exhibiting or judging – I thought I'd go for it. I'm not saying for a moment that I was a shoo-in for the job but I must have given a good interview because a few days later I was told I'd got it.

Greenwich Park is situated on top of a hill just overlooking Canary Wharf, the Thames and the City of London and contains the Prime Meridian line and Royal Observatory. It's also part of the Greenwich Maritime World Heritage Site, which is home to the National Maritime Museum and Old Royal Naval College. The most historic of all the Royal Parks, it dates back to Roman times and has been enclosed since 1427.

Now some of you will have been to Greenwich Park before and some of you won't, but just through the main gates on the right-hand side there's a beautiful 150-year-old lodge with a garden, reception room, dining room, four bedrooms, and God knows what else. Well, that was my pad! I have to admit it was definitely one of my more salubrious residences.

It was quite funny, because last thing at night, once the constable had locked the front gate, I'd call the dogs out and quite literally let them run wild. It's enclosed, you see, unlike Hyde Park, and so I knew that they wouldn't come to any danger. Not a bad garden for them, was it? The Arabs of London could sleep easy at last.

Anyway, the man I was taking over from at Greenwich was called Jack Murray, and he was, not to put too fine a point on it, a professional Scotsman. Now if you go back through the horticultural history books of the twentieth century you'll see that from the 1950s onwards there were an awful lot of head gardeners from Scotland and the north of England who came down to London looking for work. That was where the money was, I suppose. The Royal Parks were absolutely teeming with them for a time and when I took over at the Central Royal Parks I remember Ron Keating coming up to me and saying, 'At last, somebody who I can understand!' He was only joking, by the way.

So, as I said, this bloke who I was taking over from was a bit of a professional Scotsman; in fact I believe they used to call him the Laird of the Manor, and for very good reason. He'd actually organize shooting parties in Greenwich Park and even get one or two of the labourers to beat for him. They weren't shooting grouse, by the way. After all, this was a suburban park, not a moor. No, they were shooting things like rabbits and foxes. Do you know, he even had a crest on the front of his car. It had an Alsatian or something on it.

What stopped all this being just amusing was the way he used to treat the staff at Greenwich. Apparently Christmas was the worst time of year to be there because on

Christmas Eve, instead of letting everyone get away early, or as soon as the work was done, he'd keep them there until 5 p.m. He'd just sit there looking at his watch. When they eventually left to go home every single one of them had to pass his office and not once did either he or any of the staff ever wish each other a Merry Christmas. I mean, how horrible is that? I'm not saying for one minute that I was ever boss of the century but I couldn't bear the thought of any of my lads or lasses just walking out on Christmas Eve without me wishing them the compliments of the season. Apparently that was what old Murray did though.

I was also told that if his nibs was ever invited to an event at the Naval College he would insist on having a police escort home. This would be long after the park was closed, by the way, and so there was never anybody about. He even used to make the officer driving the police car turn the blue lights on! It was like the Prime Minister leaving Downing Street.

This used to have the staff in hysterics, apparently. Once they were ready for him (but not before, so as not to spoil the effect) Murray would march out of the Naval College with his nose in the air, complete with kilt, sporran and all the other paraphernalia. The only thing missing was a fanfare! His old wife, bless her, always used to follow him out about two minutes later. Once his majesty had ushered her into the back he'd then get into his great-crested car and bawl at the policeman.

'Right, start your engine!'

It can't have been more than about half a mile to the lodge and the only audience they ever had were rabbits and a couple of labourers.

Up until the 1970s the park police – or park keepers, as they were known – were more like security guards really, and although they had the uniforms and the cars, they didn't have the same powers as the normal police. They just nicked kids pinching conkers, really. It was the same in all the Royal Parks, apart from Hyde Park, which had the Met. Then, in 1974, it all changed and they created the Royal Parks Constabulary. Once again they weren't proper policemen and women but they did have more powers than the old lot and, my God, did some of them know it. The vast majority of these people were as good as gold but for every five or six diamonds you'd get a nasty little dictator or two. You know the kind: traffic wardens without the charm. Those boys were Murray's favourites of course, and he'd have them parading all over the place.

I was at war with these idiots from the day I moved in there until the day I moved out, because instead of them helping us deal with real day-to-day problems like vandalism, they used to stop people for having chipped windscreens and defective rear lights. They even set up a bloody roadblock one day, and there's only one road leading in and out! I have to say, I'm painting a pretty bizarre picture of Greenwich pre my appointment, but from the day I first drove through those gates as the governor I just got story after story.

Once I'd accepted the job I had to go and speak to the old duffer once or twice and, without any word of a lie, he was one of the saddest, bitterest people I think I've ever met. It was tragic.

The first time we had a chat he said, 'Do you know what? I've been working for the Royal Parks for well over twenty years and when I leave this place there won't be one person who'll come and say goodbye. They'll just cheer at the gate.'

What do you say to that? I couldn't agree with him, but at the same time I couldn't disagree with him. I just thought, sorry, mate, but at the end of the day you reap what you sow.

Do you know, on Christmas Day he used to go down to the nursery, which is situated to the rear of the deer enclosure, and why? Well, that was the only place he could get a bit of company. The bloke who ran the nursery, a lovely gentle Irishman called George Boyd, used to come in for an hour or so just to check the heating and what have you, and because Murray was so lonely he'd sometimes keep him there for three or four hours. George didn't have the heart to leave him, and all the time his family were waiting for him at home. George's wife, who also used to work at Greenwich, as did their son as a matter of fact, used to go absolutely ballistic, and who can blame her? George, though – he used to sit with Murray for hours and listen to his problems. That's real charity.

One Christmas, and as much as I feel sorry for Murray this was him all over, he ordered a constable to go and buy some mince pies for him and his wife. This was Christmas Day circa 1981, by the way. There were no garages open or corner shops. Anyway, the next day Murray went in to inspect the petrol book and this constable had written in 'ninety-five miles'.

'What the hell's this?' he shouted to the policeman.

'It was for those mince pies you sent me for, Mr Murray.'

It turns out it had taken this bloke almost three hours to find a shop that was open. He just kept on driving and driving and he too had a family waiting for him at home. Worse still though, Murray was all for putting him on a bloody charge because of the petrol!

From that first day that I sat with Murray I vowed that I wouldn't change a thing until I saw the furniture van leaving and him behind it. It would have broken his heart if I had. Yes, I know he was a first class whatsit, but at the end of the day nobody's born like that. Something had turned him sour and the only thing guaranteed now for the poor old boy was that he was going to die a very sad and lonely old man.

From a purely selfish point of view, the situation that Murray had created at Greenwich and was now about to leave was tailor-made for me, because I always insisted on treating staff like human beings. They all got the shock of their lives when I started there. I think some of them thought I was taking the 'you know what'.

Naturally I managed to seek out the ones who supported even worse football teams than I did and I let them have it! After that the banter started and the atmosphere began to change. It won't surprise you to know that I also began organizing the odd shindig or two, the first of which was the mother of all Christmas parties. Even though I hadn't moved in there yet, I decided to hold the party in the lodge where Murray had lived, just so they could all have a look round. You should have seen them. It was like they were going round some kind of chamber of horrors!

'I've had so many mouthfuls in this place, Jim,' one of them said to me. 'I keep thinking the old bastard's going to jump out!'

I got my catering mate from the police to do the grub and a mate of mine who owned a pub over in Banstead to sort out the booze. What a night we had. By the end of it the entire place was just awash with people doing impressions of Murray.

'I don't give a damn if it's Christmas Day and you've got a wife and four kids waiting for you at home. Get out there and find me some bloody mince pies, you Sassenach!'

Anyway, over the coming weeks, months and years, we set about creating one of the happiest working environments you can ever imagine. On Christmas Eve, the moment we'd finished whatever we needed to do, that was it – off. And for the poor beggars who did have to come in for an hour or two on Christmas Day – well, let's just say that the ones who weren't driving always left with a bit of a smile on their faces.

Because morale had been so low at Greenwich and because Murray's priorities had always lain elsewhere, from an aesthetic point of view the place was quite tired and so as soon as I was able I set about reminding these boys and girls what it was we all did for a living. We gave that place a complete facelift. We must have ripped out every single flower bed in the park and, as with Chelsea, I got some of the apprentices there to start chucking in a few ideas, and they didn't let me down. Within six months it looked absolutely stunning and the team there were just out of this world. We created island beds where the shrub beds had been and so instead of having one huge bed of shrubs thirty or forty feet wide you had some variety. People used to spend hours looking round them. When it came to the bedding schemes, instead of using begonias and petunias like they'd always done we started using feature plants, things like canna lilies, standard geraniums and fuchsias. Once they were in we'd plant other flowers around them.

That was the difference between looking after several parks and just the one. I couldn't really get that involved while I was at the Central Parks, for the simple reason that there was just too much to do. Now I was the king of just one castle and so I gave it my all. I promise you I loved every single man, woman, tree, shrub, flower and plant in that entire park. It was my El Dorado.

By the time I started at Greenwich I'd already begun carving out a second career doing talks, which is what takes up most of my time these days, and because I was so proud of the place I started putting the word about to my audiences that we might be willing to do a few guided tours. I did this thinking we might get the odd minibus every so often, but in no time at all we had coachfuls of people turning up and so eventually they became a regular fixture. I'd get calls almost every day.

'Mr Buttress? This is Mrs Noades from Chislehurst. You came and spoke at our annual lunch last Tuesday. I was wondering: would you mind if a few of us came to look round your nursery?'

And that was what it was like day after day. We never charged anything of course and, believe me, they would have willingly paid.

One of my charge hands, a brilliant young plantsman named Barry Last, became my partner in crime with regards to the tours and I even used to introduce him as the boss sometimes.

'Ladies and gentlemen, welcome to Greenwich Park. And now let me introduce you to the Superintendent of the Royal Parks, Mr Barry Last!'

Like me, Barry had the gift of the gab, and he'd spend hours with these old girls, taking them round the nursery and answering all their questions. He'd introduce them to every single flower and plant in that place and if there were any that they weren't familiar with, he'd give them chapter and verse. They loved him.

In 1989 old George Boyd retired from the nursery and we took on a new manager called Mark Wasilewski. Now back then, if you were an apprentice in horticulture there were three places where you could learn your trade: local parks, mental institutions or the very large NHS hospitals – the latter two being almost completely self-sufficient as they had farms on site and grew all their own veg. Now Mark had come up through a big NHS hospital down in Somerset and when we first met we hit it off immediately. He's the boss at Green Park and St James's now and I stay with him every year when I do Chelsea. He transformed that nursery at Greenwich and once he'd found his feet I never even went near the place. I didn't have to. Mark always said that coming to Greenwich from the hospital in Somerset, where he'd always been treated very well, was like going from one home to another, and because he felt so at home – and because I wasn't breathing down his neck all the time – he hit the ground running. I've always been the same: what's the point in telling a person how to do something if they already know what they're doing? It's the idiots you've got to chase. Give people with ability the respect they deserve and it pays dividends.

Mark used to say, 'Who? Jim Buttress? We never see him.'

As I said, they didn't have to. I had complete trust in Mark and anything I needed I knew he'd turn it round. Don't get me wrong, George Boyd was a wonderful man and I trusted him implicitly, but he was more than ready to retire by then, and what's more he'd earned the right to. Mark was young, enthusiastic and very talented and once he took charge that nursery became a hive of activity again. He even started to get involved with all the tours and some of the talks and things.

As I've said, the bedding displays under Murray had been awful. Year after year everything had stayed exactly the same and so the staff were working on autopilot. We'd changed all that, of course, but once Mark came on board he started growing a wider variety of plants and so it moved up to another level. I think the people who benefited from this most were the apprentices, because it doesn't matter what park you're based in, you're only ever as good as the people teaching you.

With Linda at Stockholm airport.
She's the brains of the outfit and I'd be lost without her.

Working with the Children's Flower Society, which encourages
schoolchildren to take an interest in horticulture.

Working to clear up after the devastating storm in 1987.
Keith Diplock, my assistant superintendent, is giving me a hand.

The governor of Greenwich. Taken in 1990, the National
Maritime Museum is in the background.

Winning a silver medal at Chelsea
with London in Bloom, 2002.

Looking good in a skirt.
Perth had won Britain in Bloom, and
I was there for the award ceremony,
which I co-hosted with my fellow
judge Mark Wasilewski.

Being awarded the Victoria Medal of Honour in 2006 by the RHS.
Penelope Keith was guest of honour.

Judging gentians at the Harrogate Spring Flower Show in 2011.

The World Garden at Lullingstone Castle as I found it
when Tom first showed me round – full of weeds!

And the garden today, a genuine horticultural attraction.

When Prince Charles and Camilla visited Lullingstone I made sure the entire team got in the shot. You can see the late Reg the Sioux from Dartford, and Tom Hart Dyke smiling behind Prince Charles.

With my fellow judges on the BBC's *Big Allotment Challenge*. From left to right, Fern Britton, me, Jonathan Moseley and Thane Prince.

I was asked to come out of retirement to judge for Britain in Bloom's fiftieth anniversary. This is part of Oldham's entry, with some children from St Anne's school and fellow judge Roger Burnett.

With award-winning designer Adam Frost at Chelsea in 2014.
I started exhibiting with him a couple of years earlier.

Anyway, all this experimentation in the flower beds was taken to rather ridiculous extremes on one occasion. I'd been out for the day, I forget where, and when I got back my secretary, a lovely lady who's no longer with us called Sylvia, started giggling.

'What's up with you?' I asked her.

'I think you'd better come and look, Jim,' she said. 'Some of the apprentices have made you a little present.'

Some present! They'd done out an entire flower bed in the colours of Millwall Football Club, complete with the letters MFC underneath.

I thought, *you little baskets!*

It was absolutely tremendous.

Every member of staff at Greenwich who had anything to do with the apprentices always went out of their way to make them feel as important as anyone else. I didn't have to tell them to do that, although I did play a part in creating the culture that led to it. It was the same with the staff. We had people there who couldn't read or write but that didn't matter one iota. They were as important as anyone else.

One of my favourite people at Greenwich was a lad called Derek, one of the kindest, gentlest people you could ever meet. He was one of the ones who couldn't read or write, and because he lived in a hostel he'd be in at 6 a.m. every morning, seven days a week, just so he could escape from all the thugs and lowlifes he had to live with.

Derek's job was picking up litter and emptying bins. That's all he did, day in, day out. The highlight of his week was going to the tip in the lorry and that's about all he had to look forward to. Not much of a life, is it? Anyway, despite the majority of us at Greenwich getting on like a house on fire, we still suffered from one or two coppers who liked to throw their weight about. There was one in particular, who shall obviously have to remain nameless, who used to love picking on people, especially those who couldn't defend themselves. We've all known people like that.

One morning Derek was emptying one of the bins when this idiot shouted over to him.

'Oi, dumbhead. Somebody's wiped dog dirt on the main gates. Get over here and clean it off, now.'

Now as I said, Derek was a gentle soul but he was also extremely nervous. Well, you would be sharing a room with half a dozen thugs. But because he was nervous he would only take orders from people he really trusted and so he told the copper that he would have to go through me.

The next thing I know I've got Sylvie on the phone.

'For Christ's sake, Jim, get over here. It's all kicked off.'

'What's happened?'

'It's Derek. They've arrested him and he's in a hell of a state. I think they're going to take him down to the nick.'

I shot over there as quick as I could and I confronted this prat.

'What's going on then?'

It turned out that when Derek refused to clean up the gate this copper had started bawling at him and Derek, who was scared stiff, had eventually gone for him.

'You release him now,' I said.

'I will not. He attacked me and I'm going to make sure he's charged.'

This prat was in his element. After speaking to Derek I went back to him.

'Right then,' I said. 'I've spoken to Derek.'

'And I suppose he tried to deny it?'

'Not at all,' I said. 'As a matter of fact he was very honest about it and, do you know what, if I'd been him I'd have done exactly the same thing. Now here's the deal. Either you release him now and you apologize to him, or I will move heaven and earth to make your life a misery. You might have a uniform and the power to lock up a vandal, but I know your boss; what's more I know a lot of people who'd bend over backwards to see you go down. That's what happens, you see, when you make a lot of enemies. They come back to haunt you. Now release him.'

You should have seen the state Derek was in when they let him out. He was absolutely terrified. They'd convinced him that in addition to getting charged with assault he'd also lose his job, and at the end of the day the poor boy had nothing else.

'I'm sorry, Mr B. I didn't mean it. Honestly I didn't, Mr B. Please don't sack me. You're not going to sack me, are you, Mr B?'

He was in such a state, bless him.

'Calm down, Derek,' I said. 'Nobody's going to get sacked, I promise. Now let's go back to my office and have a cup of tea, shall we?'

In the end Derek did clean the gates, once I'd asked him to, and I'll tell you something else, he got five hours' over-time for doing it!

Before I move on to my last story about Greenwich I just want to briefly tell you about another charity I'm involved in, and about a trick that was played on me while I was working at the park. The charity in question is called the London Gardens Society and we give out awards once a year for the best gardens in various categories. Prince Edward is the patron and I've been with the society now for about thirty years, much of that time as chairman.

Now when it comes to mumping, the police are probably up there with yours truly, and so come the end of the season at Greenwich we'd suddenly start getting a few extra visitors. They used to come from Deptford police station, Gerald Road and Peckham; and they'd all be scouting for plants, flowers and whatever they could get their hands on. This wasn't for their private gardens, by the way. It was because the London Gardens Society had a category for best police station and because it wasn't budgeted for they had to go mumping. We did what we could of course, but at the end of the day it was first come, first served and so some of them left happy, and some less so.

Anyway, one year, not long after the LGS awards had been given out, I received a telephone call in the office.

'Is that Mr James Buttress?'

Nobody calls me James so right from the off I was edgy.

'That's right,' I said. 'Who's this?'

'This is Inspector Brown from Scotland Yard,' said the voice. 'We understand from various sources that you've been supplying plants to several of our police stations, namely Gerald Road, Peckham and Deptford.'

I couldn't possibly tell you what I said to myself at the time but it definitely ended with the word 'hell'.

'We have had one or two policemen and women up here,' I pleaded. 'But I can assure you, constable, that no money ever changed hands. They were just taking whatever we had left over.'

'Inspector!'

'Sorry, inspector.'

'Don't give me that! You've had a racket going and what's

more you've been found out! We'll be speaking to the minister in charge of the Royal Park first thing tomorrow morning.'

By this time I was bricking it but before I could go on pleading, the voice on the other end of the phone just said, 'You bastard, Buttress!'

It wasn't Inspector Brown at all; it was the copper who did the hanging baskets up at Gerald Road. Gerald Road has been closed for a number of years now but back then they always put on a magnificent display, and more often than not they won an award. Not so Deptford. If Gerald Road was *Dixon of Dock Green*, Deptford was probably *The Sweeney*. It was rough. Anyway, that year they'd obviously had enough and so instead of settling for last place, which was normally the case, they were up to that nursery faster than you can say 'ello, 'ello, 'ello. Apparently the judges were amazed when they saw what they'd done.

'Where the hell did you get all this?' they asked.

'Oh, there's a little nursery we know. They look after us.'

Little nursery, my foot! They'd almost cleaned us out.

Anyway, that phone call was Gerald Road's revenge!

A few days after they won I got a call from one of the officers at Deptford and he was absolutely over the moon. It had done wonders for morale, apparently, and so to celebrate they'd decided to hold a big lunch with the mayor and what have you.

'We couldn't have done it without you and your boys, Jim. Would you all come to the lunch and help us celebrate?'

George Boyd was still in charge at the time and so me, him and my assistant, Dippy, all put our glad rags on and off we went to Deptford.

Dear old George. At the end of the day he was the reason they'd won, not me, and they made such a fuss of him. They were pouring whisky down his neck like there was no tomorrow. Eventually he went to the toilet and about half an hour later he still wasn't back.

I said to Dippy, 'Where the bloody hell's George? We've got to go in ten minutes.'

We went outside and there was George, flat on his back in one of the award-winning flower beds. He was completely Brahms and Liszt.

'Quick,' I said. 'Let's get him in the back of the van. His missus is going to go spare!'

And she did.

'What have you done to him?' she cried as we carried him through the door.

'It wasn't us, it was the police.'

'The POLICE!'

It was no use. In the end we just made our excuses, turned and fled. As we were leaving I heard her say, 'That's the last time you ever go out with that Jim Buttress! He's a bad influence.'

13. The Storm of '87

The most traumatic thing I've experienced in all my years on this earth is the great storm of 1987. It wasn't all that long ago so the majority of you reading this will probably remember it. What made it worse was that nobody in the country was expecting it, and especially not the weatherman Michael Fish. Do you remember what he said when that woman rang in? I do.

'Earlier on today a woman rang the BBC and said she'd heard there was a hurricane on the way. Well, if you're watching, don't worry. There isn't.'

Talk about dropping a clanger. We had no idea this thing was on its way. We were clueless.

The night it all began I'd been out to the pub, as is my wont, and I can't have been in bed more than a couple of hours when all of a sudden I was woken up by the sound of banging. What the bloody hell's that? I thought. It sounded like there was a thunderstorm going on in the next room and the dogs were going absolutely berserk. I got up and as I was going downstairs there was a knocking at the front door. When I opened it, it was Christine, one of the coppers on duty.

'Where's your partner in crime?' I asked her. 'There are supposed to be two of you on. And what the hell's happening?'

'It looks like a storm, Jim, or a hurricane. A branch has

come through one of his windows and so he's had to go home. His wife's terrified.'

I got Christine inside while I dressed and then we climbed in her police van and went for a quick drive through the park to get a proper look at what was happening. Well, we didn't have to drive very far. There were roof tiles, estate agents' boards and God knows what else flying around above our heads at about a hundred miles an hour, and in all directions. It was like the entire place was just blowing up in front of us.

'I've seen enough, Christine. Let's get back and get inside.'

On the way back I started to see cars being lifted up, and then trees. This thing was like a typhoon. Whatever got in its way was just destroyed.

When we got inside I made us a cup of tea and we sat there listening to it all unfold. It was horrific. Neither of us spoke. We just listened to the carnage outside.

Once it had all calmed down a bit and it had started getting light we managed to pluck up the courage to go outside and assess the damage. This in itself was terrifying because we honestly didn't know what to expect. Would there be dead bodies out there? We had no idea. In the end the storm did claim a total of twenty-two lives and it caused over two billion pounds' worth of damage.

From the moment we opened the front door we could see that it was serious. Basically, nothing was where it should have been. There were cars upside down in the middle of the road and abandoned buses. It was just chaos. The most important thing was that nobody had been hurt – or at least we didn't think so – but the park itself was in one hell of a mess. It was pure devastation. In all we lost over two hundred and fifty trees. Two hundred and fifty! What the hell am I going to do? I thought.

In the end I went back inside, picked up the phone and called Sid Ludlow. He was the only copper who lived on site and so even though he hadn't been on duty that night I was pretty sure he'd be around. Sure enough, he picked up the phone straight away.

'What the hell's happened, governor?'

'I don't know yet. Now look, whatever you do, don't open any of the gates, OK? Leave them all locked. I don't want any cars or pedestrians coming in.'

'Yes, guv.'

After that we went back outside and spent the next few hours trying to make a detailed assessment of what we'd lost. The first place I went was the flower garden – which was full of deer. Greenwich has one of the oldest enclosed deer herds in the country and the fence that normally kept them in had come down. Deer don't like wind and so once they started seeing trees coming down they naturally scarpered. Well, there weren't too many trees in the flower garden. What's more there was quite a lot to eat!

Now I've always said as a racing man that if you could train a deer to run in the National Hunt they'd win the Grand National easily. And therein lay the problem. Some of the fences along the road were only five or six feet high and so if something spooked them and they all scattered, half of them could be free and clear by lunchtime.

'Bloody hell, Christine,' I said. 'You can't round these things up like sheep. If they escape the chances are they'll be shot. There are too many to tranquillize.'

I ran back inside, picked up the phone and called ten of my best members of staff. I said, 'I don't care what you're doing. I need you in here NOW!' This would have been about 7 a.m. and despite there being no buses every single one of them turned up.

'Right, Dippy,' I said. 'Get on to the police and ask them if they can patrol the perimeter fence as best they can. As far as I'm concerned this is a crime scene and I don't want anybody in here.'

Don't forget, this wasn't just a park we were looking after. We had the Royal Observatory and the Naval College to attend to, not to mention the Maritime Museum. Greenwich Park is like a small historical town.

Fortunately the only damage any of the buildings suffered was superficial. It was the trees that bore the brunt – apart from the older ones that is. Some of the oaks and the sweet chestnuts in Greenwich must be four or five hundred years old yet as far as I could make out they hadn't moved an inch. Not one of them. Call that wind, mate? Never!

The only positive I could find from any of this, apart from the fact that none of the staff had been hurt, was that when the trees had been pulled up the roots had gone as well. This was because in the days leading up to the storm it had been raining almost constantly and so the ground was like a sponge.

Anyway, once I'd finished making a full assessment of the damage, I knew that the main job was going to be getting rid of these trees and so I set to work putting together a plan of action. Actually that's nonsense; there was no plan involved. I just winged it! They don't teach you how to deal with the aftermath of storms at Wisley.

The first thing I did was to get Paul, who worked in our stores department, to go out and buy exactly what I thought we'd need to complete the job. Once again this was going to be guesswork, but I figured that with all the other parks and gardens being in the same boat there might be a rush for one or two essentials and so the sooner he got up there the better.

'Right, Paul,' I said. 'I want you to go and get me four circular saws, protective clothing, spare blades and as much fuel as you can carry. OK?'

'Yes, governor.'

And so off he went.

Now I was allowed to approve purchases up to a certain value. Anything over that and I had to get permission from the Pope, the Archbishop of Canterbury and heaven knows who else. It was a red-tape nightmare.

Paul said, 'Are you sure this is going to be OK, governor? This takes you well over the limit.'

I said, 'Don't you worry about that, Paul. You just look lively and go and get the stuff before the rush starts.'

Fortunately Paul was one of the first at the door when the suppliers opened but by the time he was leaving the place it was packed.

'You were absolutely right, guv. If I'd gone there now we'd have been stuffed.'

Sure enough, come late morning, I was getting calls from all over the place asking if we had any fuel or any chainsaws going spare. Thank God for that, I thought.

It's times like this when the Old Pals act comes in to play. Do you know what that is? Well because I was on such good terms with all the nurseries and what have you, I started getting calls from them asking me if there was anything I wanted reserving before it went crazy. These weren't the big boys, by the way. These were the small places where I might spend the odd couple of hundred quid. Absolute diamonds they were.

Just as Paul and I were unloading the van, one of the blokes who worked on the tree team at Hyde Park turned up.

He couldn't get up there because of what had happened and he'd come to ask if he could help us instead.

'You what?' I said. 'Talk about a gift from God!'

I had him through those gates in about five seconds flat. What's more, I managed to keep hold of him for almost two weeks, much to the annoyance of my colleagues up the road. They said it was as good as kidnapping, and to be honest with you, I couldn't really argue with them. We didn't have a tree team at Greenwich and needs must. Even some of the coppers offered to help once they were sure the perimeter was secure. It was real Blitz spirit.

At about midday I got everyone into the mess room and told them what was what.

'Right then,' I said. 'This is the score. These trees need clearing and I'm not going to be opening the park until it's done. Nobody, regardless of rank or superiority, gets preferential treatment. I'll tell you what to do and when, but apart from that we're all equal. We're going to do it together. We're only going to have two breaks in the day, a morning break for breakfast and then one for lunch, and I'm shortening the first one to ten minutes and the second to half an hour. There'll be no afternoon break, we'll finish each day as usual at 5 p.m., and each one of you will receive two hours' overtime every day until we're finished. OK?'

'Yes, governor.'

After that I split them all up into teams, gave them their orders and away they went.

Come the early afternoon I started getting calls from all the TV companies asking if they could film the damage. Greenwich was by far the worst affected and so everyone was interested. Now I can't remember who told me or when, but sometime before that somebody had once mentioned to me that TV companies not only need to get permission if they want to film somewhere but that they should also pay a statutory fee. Anyway, for some reason this piece of knowledge had stayed with me and so when the TV people turned up I asked the question. Well, they weren't going to offer it, were they? Sure enough, when I mentioned the fee they nodded and it was duly paid – in cash. That money went straight into my safe and you'll never believe what I had planned for it. Or perhaps you will?

After that I started receiving telephone calls from wood carvers asking if we might be able to supply them. They usually used woods like laburnum and holly and because we'd lost some of each I said we could.

'Come back in a week,' I said. 'And I'll make sure we put some aside for you.'

That saved us a job of course, and at the same time it added a little bit to my kitty.

Right in the middle of this catastrophe I received the sad news that old Bill Fuller was on his way out. He'd been battling cancer for a good long while and unfortunately he'd reached the end. The matron at his nursing home called me one morning and when she told me he hadn't got long I went straight down there.

'He never stops talking about you, Jim, and I know he'd love to see you.'

And I him.

I think I said Percy Thrower was the first hero I ever had in life, and of course he was when I was seven or eight. But when it comes to real life and real heroes – well, top of the list alongside Pop would have to be Bill. He was responsible for virtually my entire education and on top of that he got me into Wisley, which, although I didn't exactly pass with flying colours, still taught me a great deal and was the catalyst for everything that's happened since. That's how important Bill was to me. I owe him the lot.

When I got down to the home I was shown into his room. The old boy was fast asleep at the time and, my God, he looked bad. He was just skin and bone really and when it came to colour there was nothing between him and the sheets he was lying on.

As I went to sit down I must have nudged his bed or something, because all of a sudden he woke up with a jolt.

'Jesus Christ, Jim! I thought you were the bloody under-taker.'

I sat there with him for about two hours, reminiscing about the old days, and if he'd been stronger and I hadn't just lost two hundred and fifty trees we could have done at least two more. I could tell he was proud of me, and, do you know, I was proud of him. Bill Fuller was one of the finest plantsmen I ever met and almost certainly the most knowl-edgeable. Old Pop might have been taught by the great E. A. Bowles, but I was taught by the great Bill Fuller, and in my eyes he's the greatest of the lot.

What really hurt me was that I wasn't able to make it to Bill's funeral. Not only did I have Greenwich to sort out, which was going to be a pretty monumental task in itself, but on the day it was due to take place I was also supposed to be hosting a big charity dinner up in London. This event was absolutely massive and was in aid of several children's chari-ties. They had Edmundo Ros and his Latin Rhythms lined up to play and were going to be auctioning trips to Barba-dos. I mean, how could I possibly let them down? Bill's funeral was going to be miles away and so the only way I could make it was to clear the entire day, and I just couldn't.

In the end my brother Pat went in my place and he said it was a lovely service. When they got to the crematorium, though, things became a bit comical because just as the coffin was passing through the curtains on its way to you know where, it suddenly stopped and the curtains started closing again, then opening, then closing. This went on for about ten minutes until they finally managed to fix it, by which time the entire chapel was in hysterics – vicar included. Old Bill would have absolutely loved it!

My band of merry men and women and I worked our backsides off for two whole weeks trying to make that park presentable again, but because I'd refused to open the gates while the work was going on we began incurring the wrath of some of the more vocal locals. Things had come to a head on the Sunday, about three days after the storm, when a large crowd gathered at the gates demanding to get in. One of these protesters – the ringleader – was about a hundred and fifty years old and had fought in every siege since Mafeking.

'Why can't I get in?' he asked the copper.

'Well, I don't know whether you've heard, sir, but there's been a terrible storm.'

'Storm? You don't know the meaning of the word. I served against the Japanese, mate, and I helped put Jerry to bed.'

Now the crowd were getting behind him.

'You tell him, granddad! It's a public park. We should be allowed in.'

'Don't have a go at me,' said the copper. 'It wasn't my decision.'

'Well, whose was it then?'

He didn't need asking twice. That policeman was straight

on his walkie-talkie and before I knew it I was on my way over there.

'I'm the park superintendent. Can I help you, sir?'

'Well hopefully. I want to come into this park, now!'

I said, 'Now, look. This is nothing personal, sir. I just don't want your death on my hands. It's still very dangerous in there but if you give us another week to ten days we'll have it all cleared and you'll be able to walk to your heart's content.'

As I was walking away he shouted, 'Perhaps if you'd planted them deep enough in the first place you might not be in this mess!'

There was no answer to that.

The next day I got another call from the same copper.

'We've got an old girl here, Jim. You know the one that comes to feed the geese?'

He didn't need to say another word. This old dear used to come into the park seven days a week to feed the Canada geese. She even had names for them.

'Gertie. Here, Gertie. Come along, Bertie. Don't you look a hungry boy?'

They were all she had in the world. Anyway, when I got there the poor old thing was in a right state.

'I'm so worried about my boys and girls,' she said. 'They haven't been fed for days and I want to make sure they're OK.'

I said, 'Look, my dear, it's still dangerous in there. Gertie, Bertie and all their friends are absolutely fine. Now you give me the bread and I'll make sure they get it with your compliments. We'll be open again in a week or so.'

'Oh would you? I'd be so very grateful. They rely on me, you know.'

'I'm sure they do. Now as I said, you just leave it with me.'

Sadly, Bertie and Gertie (at least I think it was them) were found dead under a tree and the rest of them had quite sensibly flown off to sunnier climes.

We had some real characters down at Greenwich. Lovely people but just a little bit eccentric. I remember one regular visitor used to push his Pekinese around in a pram. It is to this day one of the strangest sights I've ever seen in a park but to him it was perfectly normal. When it was hot he even had a little umbrella on the pram that used to keep the sun off them.

Another regular at the park was Terry Waite's wife. She used to come in every day with her spaniel, and even though we knew who she was and that her husband was being held captive we never once mentioned it. It was all dog talk. Then, when Terry was released in 1991, some of the staff put yellow ribbons round some of the trees where she walked.

One of the most interesting regulars we had was a man who was the chief executive of some massive corporate company. His chauffeur would drive him in each morning and take him straight to the statue of General Wolfe, which overlooks Canary Wharf. Once the chauffeur had let him out this bloke would stand at the foot of the statue for fifteen or twenty minutes. Apparently it used to galvanize him and prepare him for the stresses of the day ahead.

Anyway, the only problem we had left once we'd finished chopping up these two hundred and fifty trees was getting rid of the roots, and once again the method I chose for disposing of them was ever so slightly unorthodox.

This bloke came in to see me one day and he owned a breakdown company. I'm not talking the AA or the RAC, by the way, I'm talking cranes, chains and wagons the size of bloody oil tankers. He lived nearby and he'd obviously seen what we'd been up to.

'I hope you don't mind me asking,' he said, 'but how are you intending to shift all those roots. There must be getting on for a few hundred tons there.'

'Funny you should ask,' I said. 'I have absolutely no idea.'

We'd got rid of most of the timber just by burning it, but because the roots wouldn't burn they'd become a bit of an issue.

'Well, look,' he said, 'I own an industrial breakdown and removal company. I could shift that lot for you no problem. Business is a bit slack at the moment and so I'd be happy to do you a deal. It'd only take a day.'

Well, with no other ideas on the table I just went for it.

'Why not,' I said. 'It's the only worry I have left before we can open the gates again and so if you can solve it, brilliant. How much are we going to be looking at?'

'I've never priced a job like this before,' he said. 'Let me get rid of it all for you and we'll see how we go.'

The next day in they all came, and as I said before, they had cranes, chains, winches, trailers and all sorts of marvellous machinery. They even had bulldozers and flat-bedded artics. It was unbelievable.

Come five o'clock every single root had been removed and so we were clear to open up the following day.

Just before we opened the gates the next day, Dippy said to me, ''Ere, guv. Don't you think we should put a sign up just in case there are any swingers about?'

Now before you all start writing in and complaining, 'swingers' has a totally different meaning in the world of horticulture. Basically a swinger is a branch that has crashed into another tree and is just sitting there. More often than not nothing happens, but if the storm were to come back and we'd missed one we could be in trouble.

'Good idea, Dippy,' I said to him. 'I'll get one drawn up.'

So, by the time we opened the gates we had a big sign at the entrance that read

BEWARE
DANGEROUS TREES!

By the end of the day some wit had written underneath it *DO NOT FEED*.

A few days later the removal man came back in to see me about money, and when he told me the cost I almost died. Had I exceeded the limit? Only by about a hundred times! We were into lottery numbers. To be fair to the man, he'd written down everything: every man-hour and litre of fuel. It made no difference though. I was in trouble.

Dippy just looked at the figures and said, 'Nothing to do with me. You're the governor.'

Thanks very much!

I said to the bloke, 'Right. How are we going to get round this?' In the end I had to do a bit of creative accounting on the order front and, needless to say, when everything was totted up, I was hauled in front of a disciplinary. There were two charges: one, for exceeding the amount I was allowed to authorize, and two, for using a year's supply of dairy nuts in one day. That's something I haven't told you about yet. You see, in order to get those deer back into what's called The Wilderness, which is the area where they live, we ended up making three trails of dairy nuts about half a mile long. This is what we used to supplement their food with in the winter and it was the only way we could think of getting them to the other side of the fence so we could mend it.

Once we'd laid the trails, Fred, whose job it was to look after the deer, came over to me.

'Right then,' he said. 'I'll go to the other side of the fence and I'll start rattling the tin. That'll make them think it's dinner time.'

'OK. Now what do you want me to do?'

'Bugger off,' he said. 'If they see anyone else moving they'll get spooked, and if that happens, it'll be over. We'll only get one chance.'

So off he went to the other side of the fence and started rattling his tin. I'd done exactly as I was told, by the way, and had buggered off, but I made sure I could see everything. Sure enough, a minute or two later these deer started making their way towards the trails we'd laid. The one they were all watching was the big stag and the moment he started nibbling they all did. Almost there, I thought. Then, once they were all at it, Fred began moving slowly backwards and before we knew it they were all safely back where they belonged. It was a crude method, I grant you, but, my God, it was effective. We didn't lose one deer.

'Quick, lads,' I shouted, once the deer were all over the line. 'Get that bloody fence back up!'

So, in addition to Root-gate, which had put me firmly at the top of the Royal Parks' most-wanted list, I was also seen as being the mastermind behind Nut-gate, and it was now just a question of which job centre I was going to attend.

Years ago, old Pop had once said to me, 'If you've ever done wrong, boy, always have the decency to hold your hands up and admit it,' and so that's exactly what I did. I walked into that disciplinary and I said, 'Gentlemen, before we go any further, I have let the side down. What I did was a disgrace, as not only did I exceed my authority but I failed in my duty as a park superintendent. My only line of defence is that I love that park and those trees were my friends, but you're absolutely right, and I was completely out of order. I'm sorry.'

Now if I'd gone in there all guns blazing and said, 'Before you start, were any of you actually there when all this happened?' I'd have lost before I'd even begun. There was only one thing to do and that was to come clean. There was a reprimand put in the book but I think they must have appreciated my honesty.

In the end, though, we'd achieved exactly what we'd set out to do. The park had reopened quickly and, most important of all, nobody had been hurt. It was all done by the seat of our pants of course, but we were cleaning up after a storm for heaven's sake! Desperate times call for desperate measures. What an adventure, though. I'll tell you, they don't make them like that anymore.

A few days after my disciplinary I went into my safe and took out all the TV and wood money.

'What are you going to do with that?' asked Dippy.

'We're going to have a party, mate,' I said.

That afternoon I went down to the local working men's club, where some of my men drank, and I asked to speak to the owner.

I said, 'Right. Can you provide a disco?'

'Yes, no problem at all.'

'Can you do a buffet?'

'Well of course we can.'

'OK then. I think we're in business.' And so I gave them the date and away we went. Anything that was left over went behind the bar and we had one of the biggest celebrations in history. Think about what we'd all been through. I know it wasn't exactly the war but in a way this was our VE Day.

Now a few days after we'd opened the park again the BBC had rung and they'd asked if they could come down and speak to me.

'We'd like to know what the park means to you, Mr Buttress, and how you've all coped since the storm.'

Fair enough, I thought.

Anyway, down they came and I ended up giving the mother of all interviews. I paid tribute to every single person who'd been involved in that clear-up and I may even have shed a tear or two.

After the interview I asked the producer if I could have a copy.

'We're having a bit of a get-together next week,' I said. 'And it's really to celebrate the fact that we all got through it. Would there be any chance of you sending me a copy?'

'Of course,' he said. 'Not a problem.'

As I'd paid tribute to just about everyone who was going to be there that night, I'd planned to play this interview at the party. They had a video recorder there and so I thought, why not? It'll be a nice touch. Anyway, halfway through the night, when everyone had had a few, I sat them all down, put this thing on, and then waited for the tears and words of thanks. Words of thanks? Tears of laughter more like. It was the wrong programme. They'd sent me a show about bloody squirrels!

In 1996 the opportunity to take early retirement arose, and after a little bit of toing and froing I decided to take it. Life since the storm had been steady enough and I'd spent a lot of that time helping redesign parts of the park. More open vistas were what we decided upon, and we even ended up cutting down a few more trees! I think it worked though, and when I eventually left the park it looked absolutely amazing.

It seemed like the right time to leave Greenwich for two reasons really: first, because of the amount of time I was now spending doing talks and judging, which was something I was keen to build on, and second, because things were changing at the Royal Parks and, to be honest, I was starting to clash with one or two of the new guard. Had I been twenty years younger I might have stayed and fought my corner a bit more, but at fifty-one I was of the opinion that life was too short. What would be the point of getting into rucks with certain individuals when all the time I could be out there judging shows, doing talks and meeting people? It was a complete no-brainer.

Before we move on I just want to tell you one little story about my retirement, and don't worry, it doesn't involve alcohol, discos or squirrels!

I could be a real stickler for detail when I was a superintendent, and on an evening while I was out with the dogs I'd have a good look round, and occasionally I'd spot things and then write them down: litter bin needs replacing, post needs straightening, dead branch in flower bed. Then, when I got back inside I'd write it all on Post-it notes and then go over to the office and put them on the relevant foreman's desk. They used to hate me for it! It was attention to detail, though. You remember that huge display I told you about in Croydon; the one with the errant bamboo cane? Well that's where it started to rub off on me.

Anyway, come my retirement bash one of the foremen stood up and said, 'We've got several presents for you, governor, but probably the most important is this. You've spent years giving them to us so we thought you should have some back.' And he held up this bloody great big box of Post-it notes. There must have been thousands of them. The entire room was in hysterics. I've still got some at home but, as Linda keeps telling me, the only person who needs reminding these days is me!

14. Buttress in Bloom

In hindsight, leaving the Royal Parks when I did was probably one of the best decisions I ever made. Talk about a new lease of life. The only appointments I now had written in my diary were things I really looked forward to; none more so than my schedule for judging Britain in Bloom.

This competition has given me more joy over the years than just about anything else I've been involved in. You see Britain in Bloom's got everything: goodies, baddies, amazing characters, success, failure, and triumph over adversity. It's like a very long-running horticultural soap opera. Think *The Archers*, but with flowers instead of sheep.

I served my apprenticeship for Britain in Bloom while I was at Hyde Park, judging first of all London in Bloom, and then South East in Bloom. Every region runs its own 'In Bloom' competition, whether that be the North East, North West, Scotland or wherever, and the number of categories entered within the region determines the number of entries you can have in Britain in Bloom. Does that make sense? The categories are small village, village, large village, small town, town, large town, small city, city and large city. Then you have a few others, like coastal resorts, urban communities and business districts, and each category winner from each region goes through to Britain in Bloom.

Britain in Bloom, for those who don't know, was started by a horticultural journalist called Roy Hay way back in 1964. He'd been on holiday in France during the Fleurissement de

France, which is their version of Bloom, and he'd been amazed by how beautiful it all looked. He was so impressed, in fact, that when he got home he approached the British Tourist Authority about setting up a British version and the rest, as they say, is history. Today over 200,000 people give up their time for Britain in Bloom and when the judging takes place each August you can almost smell the excitement and anticipation.

Funnily enough, one of the reasons I was invited to join the committee at Britain in Bloom was because it was suffering from the same cliquishness that had been hampering the RHS, and fortunately somebody within the organization plucked up the courage to demand some fresh blood. Once again there had been very little contact between the entrants and the judges and so feedback was almost non-existent. Each entrant was supposed to receive a report after they'd been judged, outlining what they did right and wrong and how they could improve, but from what I could gather these rarely arrived. It was a shambles.

My first assignment for Britain in Bloom was at a town on the south coast. Two senior judges would go round and mark the town first, and then I'd follow and do my own scores. As long as they tallied, or thereabout, I should be OK.

As the train from Greenwich left at about 5 a.m. I had to be up dead early and when I eventually arrived at the Town Hall the only person there was the mayor. She was a big cheerful woman, kind of like Hattie Jacques, and she made me feel very welcome.

'Good morning! You must be our trainee judge.'

'That's right,' I said. 'And judging by the jewellery, you must be the mayor?'

'I am indeed. Very pleased to meet you. I have to admit

I'm actually quite nervous. We didn't do terribly well last year.'

'Well we're in the same boat then, Your Worship, because this is my first time. Don't worry though, we'll look after each other.'

That seemed to put her at ease a bit.

Eventually the two senior judges turned up. They had arrived the night before and they weren't happy.

'Our hotel was not up to scratch,' one of them said. 'The food was ordinary at best and as for the wine list. Anyway, I suppose we'd better get on.'

There were no 'good mornings' to either me or the mayor. They just walked on. After a few hundred yards one of them stopped.

'Did you receive a report last year?'

'Not so much a report,' said the mayor. 'More a list really, telling us what we'd done wrong.'

'Well, you obviously didn't take any notice.'

Honestly, the behaviour of these two people was absolutely appalling. I was so embarrassed. As for the poor mayor, she was shaking.

'Take no notice,' I said to her. 'Once all this has finished we'll sit down with your committee and have a chat about how you can improve. OK?'

'That would be very kind of you. I have to say I'm not enjoying this at all.'

She wasn't the only one.

At the top of the high street, outside the public conveniences, there was a brass band waiting and as the judging party approached they revved up and started playing a tune or two. 'Summer in the City' was one of them and I thought it was a really nice touch. Not surprisingly, the two senior judges didn't even acknowledge the band and just walked straight past but as there was a little crowd gathering the mayor suggested we stop for a bit.

'They're very good, you know. They've been playing together for years.'

'It's not a very salubrious place to ask them to play, though,' I said.

'You have seen the age of the band, Mr Buttress?' asked the mayor.

'Ah!' I said. 'I see what you mean.'

They were even older than the Rolling Stones!

After we'd finished judging there was a little get-together in the Town Hall and once again the senior judges made a point of keeping themselves very much to themselves. I, on the other hand, was new to all this and so I thought, sod you. I'm going to get to know these people. You can act like a couple of pompous idiots if you want but it doesn't mean I have to. These people had made such an effort yet Hinge & Bracket insisted on treating them with contempt. What's the point?

In the end they couldn't get me a taxi back to the station and so they took me in the mayor's car! It was the first time I'd ever been driven by a uniformed chauffeur.

The following day I had to go and do the same thing at Reading, and this time the senior judges were Mark Mattock, the famous rose-grower, and David Welch, who was my last boss at the Royal Parks. What a difference! It was like chalk and cheese.

The day we judged Reading coincided with the first day of the Reading Festival, which is a very famous rock festival (apparently), and you should have seen some of the sights. There were people with blue hair, green hair; people with studs in their heads and chains through their ears. Some of the women were virtually naked. Talk about Britain in Bloom!

David Welch looked at me. 'I've never seen anything like it, Jim. This is fantastic!'

A couple of minutes later the welcome party arrived at the station to pick us up, but when I looked round to tell David he'd disappeared.

'Where's Welchy?' I said to Mark. 'He was here a minute ago.'

We looked round and there, sitting on the station steps, was David Welch surrounded by a load of hippies. I have no idea what they were singing but he seemed to know the words. That was him, though.

David Welch was a legend in the world of horticulture and he did more good in the Royal Parks than the previous five Chief Execs put together. Before that he'd literally transformed Aberdeen, turning it from what was known as the 'granite city' into the 'floral city', and by the time he left there to join the Royal Parks in 1992 the gardens boasted more than two million rose bushes! That was typical David: completely over the top. According to one of his obituaries he once described himself as 'an advocate of floral vulgarity and swaggering excesses of colour'. That's a perfect description.

The Winter Gardens in Aberdeen are named after David and when he died in 2000 he was buried there, but it's the effect he had on the Royal Parks that still brings a lump to my throat. For a start he planted literally millions of daffodil bulbs along The Mall and brought it completely back to life. After that he pedestrianized the area in front of Buckingham Palace, repaired the Serpentine Lido, instigated the Regent's Park Flower Show and replanted the Rose Garden in Hyde Park. He also came up with the idea of building a playground in Kensington Gardens in memory of Princess Diana. David's goal at the Royal Parks was simple: to make them as accessible and enjoyable as humanly possible, and he succeeded with flying colours. He even insisted on getting rid of all the Keep Off The Grass signs!

Anyway, when we were about halfway around Reading, one of the mayor's party said, 'I'm so sorry but we seem to have lost one of your judges.'

'Oh God,' said Mark. 'Where the hell's he gone now?'

We looked everywhere for Welchy and in the end he was found in an estate agent's somewhere, talking to the staff about property prices. He'd stop and talk to anyone and everyone would David. He was the benchmark.

A few days later I was told that the marks I'd given had been almost the same as the four senior judges and so as far as they were concerned I was in.

After four or five years, in about 1988, the chairman of the judges at Britain in Bloom, a chap called Bob Sweet, decided to retire and he handed the reins on to me. This meant I'd gone from trainee judge to chairman in double quick time and I absolutely loved it. Along came the first week of August and off we went. You ask Linda, I was like a kid on Christmas morning when Bloom came round. We went everywhere: the Isle of Man, Jersey, Scotland, Cornwall, Northern Ireland.

The first time I went to Northern Ireland was right in the middle of the Troubles and we were driven round in an armoured vehicle, and even had to have armed guards with us. For Britain in Bloom! I'm sitting there with my clipboard and I'm thinking, holy crap, what have we let ourselves in for?

I got talking to the bloke taking us round and said, 'Look mate, I'm a Catholic.' And he said, 'No problem, I'm a Proddy. We're not going to have a fight, are we?'

'I don't think so,' I replied.

'Well that's the trouble,' he said. 'The real people in this country don't want to. And do you know the only thing that's going to solve all this. It's when they put all the aggro-merchants into one room and let them punch the crap out of each other. Get 'em in there and let them get it out of their system.'

He wasn't mincing his words.

'Now you see those two blokes over there: one watering the plants and the other driving the tractor? Well the one driving the tractor's a Catholic and the other one's a Proddy. Their only argument is if he goes too fast or if he doesn't water properly.'

'Fair enough,' I said. 'Now it all makes sense.'

Do you know, the more I went round that place the more I fell in love with it, but especially the people. I remember one year we went to Ballymena, which was an absolute tinderbox of a town. Everyone was fighting everyone else. When we got there, the guide said, 'I'll tell you what, once you've finished judging let me show you the other side of Ballymena. The parts you're judging are perfectly normal but, mark my words, there's a very ugly side to it.'

He wasn't lying. Once we'd done he gave us a quick tour of one of the local council estates and I'd never seen anything like it. It was like a rainy Beirut. There was bomb damage everywhere, and the graffiti? It was just wall-to-wall sectarianism. Pure hatred.

'Bloody hell,' I said to him. 'This is worse than I imagined.'

The following year when we went back to Ballymena we had the same guide.

'Jim,' he said. 'We've had a breakthrough.'

'Really?'

He said, 'You remember the place I showed you last time after the judging?'

'How could I forget it?'

He said, 'Right, come on. I'm going to show you.'

Once Britain in Bloom had taken off in Ballymena the people from this estate had gone to the council to ask why they couldn't have something similar, and the council had basically replied that if they couldn't look after what they'd already got, why should the council bother? It was nothing to do with religion or politics. They were just being honest.

When we got there, it was a transformation. I didn't remember seeing one single flower the last time and now the place was awash with them. Every garden was immaculate. The green, which according to our guide was only ever used for bonfires, had been returfed and was now like a bowling green.

'I don't believe it,' I said to him. 'And all this has happened within a year?'

'It's all down to Britain in Bloom, Jim.'

It was too.

That's the power of Britain in Bloom and is what sets it apart from every other competition in the world. I mean, how many events do you know that can basically change the face of a community, and not just aesthetically? According to our guide the mood of the place was about as unrecognizable as the flower beds. There were still tussles and disagreements, of course, I mean you're not going to untangle several hundred years of antagonism with a few daffs and a rose bush. The point is that people were smiling again and, what's more, they were taking a pride in where they lived.

*

Now I, like many of you reading this book, was brought up in the steam train era. When Pop and I used to have the allotment at Haywards Heath, some of the time I'd go and stand on the bridge and watch the trains coming out of the station on their way to Brighton and every now and again I might get a wave from the driver or, if I was lucky, a toot, toot. Then, as the train went through the tunnel, all the smoke would come up and just for a moment I'd be completely engulfed by it. I used to love it!

Anyway, one day we were judging this little town in Northern Ireland (I'm sorry but I can't for the life of me remember its name), and while we were walking round I suddenly heard a toot, toot!

'My God!' I said to the guide. 'Was that a steam train I just heard?'

'That? Oh, that's the local steam club. They've got an old engine and once a month they'll drive it up and down for a couple of miles just to make sure it works.'

I said to this bloke, 'If there's one thing in this world I love as much as a nice garden it's a steam train.'

Quick as a flash he shouted, 'The judge likes steam! For Christ's sake get that engine back up here NOW!'

A few seconds later – toot, toot – and there it was in all its glory, and it was a cracker. The driver let me stoke it and, just for a few yards, he even let me drive it. Talk about a dream come true. This had no influence on the marks I gave, by the way.

Another Britain in Bloom success story I'd like to tell you about is Cleethorpes. Back then, all these seaside towns like Yarmouth, Blackpool and Skegness were heading to ruin, and because the days of funfairs and summer seasons were now over they had to change tack. Cleethorpes was probably one of the quickest off the mark and so, before things could get any worse, they got together with the council and they formed Cleethorpes in Bloom. Now my role initially was to go up there and bang the drum for them and it was something I was more than happy to do. When I say bang the drum, I mean to motivate people and try and get more of them involved. I was more than aware of the effect Bloom could have on a community and so with Cleethorpes needing a bit of a push, up I went.

They always said to me, 'Jim, you can't hide your enthusiasm, can you?' and I said, 'I don't have to. This is genuine. I love this competition and I'm aware of what it can do. Let's get out there and bang that drum!'

Eventually Cleethorpes went on to become the overall Britain in Bloom champions, and they did that from a standing start because their town really was virtually on its knees.

Not long after they won I went back up there and, once again, word must have got around about my love of steam trains because, you know those little trains they have at seaside resorts, the ones that often run along the seafront? Well, the moment I got up there they had me sitting in one of these things and before I knew it I had a cap and there were cameras going off everywhere. Talk about a good atmosphere. That place was buzzing!

Another time I remember actually judging somewhere from the back of a horse and cart, and it was pretty obvious from the moment we set off that the last thing Dobbin wanted to do was carry me and my partners in crime around. He just went slower and slower and slower. It was only supposed to take an hour and a half but when that was up we'd only done half the village. In the end I said, 'Look, I'm not being funny, but I think Dobbin needs a rest. Couldn't we just walk the rest of the route?' The bloke in charge was dead relieved. He said, 'I'm glad you said that, Jim. He's not normally like this, I promise you. It must be you!'

That's Britain in Bloom, you see. Real stories featuring real people – and animals!

Another great example of the power of Britain in Bloom is Guernsey. Now the Channel Islands used to produce some of the best cut-flowers and tomatoes anywhere in the world but eventually that market was usurped by the Dutch and the islands struggled a bit after that. Once again, rather than sitting around and just wallowing the people of Guernsey got in touch and asked if I'd come out there and help them set up Guernsey in Bloom. 'No problem!' I said. So out I flew and we got to work. Now they're called parishes out there, not boroughs like in the rest of Britain, so they have the Parish of St Peter Port and the Parish of Le Bordage, and what have you. It's a stunning little island. So around I went with the Jimmy Buttress bandwagon, banging the drum for Guernsey in Bloom and, do you know what, they've never looked back. What a fantastic job they've done. Once again, I'm not saying that it's solved all their problems, but it's certainly helped bolster the tourism industry and it's improved morale. They've never forgotten me for it, and the next time I went back there they presented me with a beautiful little milk churn to say thanks. Have you ever tried Guernsey milk? It's astonishing. Like nothing you've ever tasted before. Every time I go back there now I'm treated like a king, but the icing on the cake is that they've won one or two gold medals along the way, and deservedly so. Great place, great people.

Even though I always tried to be as laid-back and as approachable as I could, people still sometimes dreaded the visit. It means so much to them, you see. I remember going to judge a place in Scotland one year and when I arrived I was collared by a very worried-looking lady.

'Oh, Mr Buttress! Could I have a word with you, please, before you begin.'

'Of course you can, my dear. What can I do for you?'

'Well, we're in the middle of installing a new flood-prevention scheme which means there's a tremendous amount of work going on. You won't be too hard on us, Mr Buttress, will you?'

She was right regarding the work. There were cranes, bulldozers and pile drivers absolutely everywhere.

I said, 'Look, my dear, this is a working community and I'm just here to see what you've done florally. I'm not going to mark you down because you're trying to prevent a flood! So what, if there's a bit of mud on the road and a few bulldozers about. Makes no difference to me and it'll make no difference to your marks.'

'Do you really mean that?'

I said, 'Of course I do. I wouldn't have said it if I didn't mean it. Now come on, just you calm down and let's go and see what you've done. And don't worry!'

My co-judge at this place was Mark Mattock, and as we were walking towards the bridge where most of the work was going on all of a sudden we heard a load of honking and hooting. We looked up and there in front of us was this enormous bloody crane, and as it turned away from us, there, on the jib of the crane were two hard hats covered in flowers. All the workers started cheering and one of them said, 'What do you reckon to that then, gentlemen? Going to win, is it?'

I think I must have told that story at every talk I've given since then. It's one of my absolute favourites.

Not long after this, Mark Mattock and I managed to

reduce the entire arrivals hall at Heathrow, Terminal what-ever-it-was, to floods of tears; or rather the man on the tannoy did. We'd caught a flight down to Heathrow from Scotland and when we arrived we were told to wait in the arrivals hall for an announcement about whoever was picking us up.

Anyway, after about fifteen minutes the tannoy went 'bing bong', and a gentleman with a heavy Indian accent said, 'Ladies and gentlemen, would Messrs Buttock and Mattress please come to the information desk. That's Messrs *Buttock and Mattress.* Thank you.'

I went to another place once with a judge called Doug Stacey. When we were on duty we always wore a green jacket. That was our uniform. Anyway, Doug and I had stopped at a motorway service on our way to wherever it was and I said to him, 'I've just got to go to the toilet, mate. I'll be back in a minute.' Before I had gone two steps this bloke came up and said, 'I'm sorry, gentlemen, but you're in the wrong place. Would you care to follow me, please?' And he took us off into this lounge. Well, we were offered tea, coffee, sandwiches and buns. It was great hospitality! I said to Doug, 'What the hell's going on?'

It turned out they thought we were coach drivers! All the coach drivers wore coloured jackets back then and were fed and watered in their own special room, so it was just a case of mistaken identity, albeit a very welcome one.

When I first came on the scene as a national judge for Britain in Bloom we were able to give out discretionary awards. These were for things like Best Park, Best Pub, Cleanest Town, Best Tourist Attraction, so the town, village or city would be the main entry, and everything else discretionary. Our job, as we went round, was to collect as much information as possible about what was going on. Ask questions, make notes and even take the odd photograph. It was a real reconnaissance mission if you like, and we'd come back from these places with dozens of leaflets and handouts. I even used to tell the tourist information people there to keep me up to date with what they had going on, and I'll tell you what, it didn't matter where I'd been I always managed to find an entry for every single category. The way I looked at it was, the more people you had getting involved in all this the more chances you had of winning, and at the end of the day, success breeds success.

Bloom holds a lot of sway when it comes to tourism, and the moment somewhere wins an award it goes everywhere: on the headed notepaper and on the website. Once I began to really appreciate that there was no stopping me.

When it came to submitting entrants for these discretionary awards I always ended up winning. I had to sell them to the panel, you see, and because I'd done my homework on all of them I could give chapter and verse. I was like a walking, talking tourist authority for every town, village or city I visited. I used to get so carried away with it all but the effect it had was just infectious.

Once I became chairman of the judges I got Mark Wasilewski on board. I think I've already said that Mark's a clever boy, and once he saw how competitive I was with these discretionary awards he could appreciate what I was trying to do and so he got involved. Before I knew where I was everyone was at it and so we were no longer just judges, we were advocates. People banging the drum!

The only thing I wasn't keen on when I first started with Bloom was the fact that there was only one award per category, so it was either first or nothing. Now if you add this to the fact that hardly anybody received any feedback it was just ludicrous. Apart from the winner all anybody else knew was that they'd failed. Feedback is essential of course, but so is a system where you have gold, silver gilt, silver, bronze, as not only does it let the entrants know exactly where they stand but it gives them an attainable goal. It's not rocket science.

In 2002 when the RHS took over as the organizing body of Britain in Bloom they called us judges in and said, 'Right then. What changes do you want to make?' And because they knew us all and trusted us they went with many of our recommendations, one being the changes to the awards structure, so these days you can win gold, silver gilt, silver or bronze. Job done!

Now as Bloom started to expand, some of the main protagonists like Durham, Perth and Coventry started expressing an interest in hosting a ceremony to give out the awards. This was something new to us as before that we hadn't had a ceremony as such. Nevertheless we thought it would be a terrific idea.

One of the first award ceremonies for Britain in Bloom took place at Durham Cathedral and what a night that was. It was like Carry on Bloom!

Now one of the companies up for an award in the commercial category that year was a factory I'd judged down in a place called Thurrock in Essex. I think they made things like washing-up detergents. Their factory was based in an old quarry and I have to admit we feared the worst when we got there, as from a distance it was all chimneys, smoke and noise.

As we drove through the gates I got the shock of my life. Just in front of the main doors to the factory was a great big garden that would have been worthy of the Royal Parks. Honestly! They had established silver birches, rose beds and even a couple of statues. Then, along the front of the factory were about a hundred beautiful hanging baskets. They were perfect. I said to my fellow judge, 'That's going to take some beating, that is. Have you ever seen anything like it?' Well, he hadn't and neither had I. Now this was a discretionary award that I'd have to pitch for and so I set about taking as many photos as possible, after which I began finding out the story behind it.

The people who owned this factory were three brothers, and their personal secretary, who had been looking after them for donkey's years, told them one day that she was fed up with working in a crap hole and that she wanted to do something about it. To cut a long story short, they gave her permission to tidy it up, so she went out and got it landscaped. And then the boys saw the bill. They had a fit apparently. The secretary was unrepentant though, and everybody who came there loved it. It didn't take them long to come round. They were the talk of industrial Essex.

Anyway, these three boys and their secretary had been invited up to Durham to the ceremony although they didn't know the result. All they'd been told was that they'd been nominated.

When they arrived the secretary came straight up to me and said, 'If nothing else, Jim, this award nomination has given me the most restful journey I've ever had with these three. Normally about five minutes after we set off somewhere they're at it: arguing about who beat who at golf, or about some business decision. Today, though, they're as nervous as kittens!'

Once everyone sat down the ceremony got under way.

'Ladies and gentlemen,' said the compere. 'Please be upstanding for the Bishop of Durham.'

And then up stood the bishop, all robed-up with his mitre and his crook, to give us the official welcome.

'Welcome to our wonderful cathedral, ladies and gentlemen. God is the gardener's friend! Now please would you
welcome the director general of the Tidy Britain Group,
Professor Graham Ashworth.'

Tidy Britain were the original organizing body of Britain
in Bloom before the RHS, and Professor Ashworth, who
was a lovely old boy, was also quite a religious gentleman.
Anyway, when he got up into the pulpit after being introduced by the bishop he all but delivered a sermon, and you
should have seen the bishop's face. He did not look happy!

All through the ceremony I kept looking over at the secretary and her three Essex boys and she was right, they were
nervous. They were like three fidgeting schoolboys.

Eventually we got to their category.

'Now we move on to the commercial award,' said the
compere. First he read out bronze; not them. Then silver.
Still not them. Silver gilt? Nope. You should have seen them
now. They were about five inches off their pew.

'And the winner is . . .'

When he announced that the boys from Thurrock had
won, they leapt out of their pew, punched the air and
shouted, 'GET IN THERE!' It reminded me of what happens when a horse comes in at twenty to one. They were
cock-a-hoop!

When they got home they ended up taking over the three
roundabouts leading up to the factory. They had them landscaped – the lot. Isn't that a great story?

Britain in Bloom is the largest community charity in the
world and I'm telling you now, it changes lives. There must
be hundreds of thousands of people involved in Britain
in Bloom and they come from all walks of life. I've seen
ninety-year-olds painting lamp posts, vicars watering hanging

baskets outside pubs, and five-year-olds weeding paths; and why do they do it? Because they want to make the place in which they live, work and play better for them and for anyone else who comes to visit.

I'll tell you what though, it's not all sweetness and light, because in addition to being called one or two choice names over the years I've even had people squaring up to me and asking me outside. That last one was completely ridiculous, because when he had a go we already were outside! The person who squared up to me had taken umbrage because I'd awarded his village a bronze and he was all for knocking my lights out. I mean, fancy having a pop at a Britain in Bloom judge. Sad isn't it?

Funnily enough once he'd been pulled off me and carted away, a member of his committee came up to me and said, 'Thank God for that, Jim. Perhaps he'll resign now so we can get on with some of the things you've told us to.'

I remember we once awarded a certain town, village or city – I can't say which – a silver gilt award and when the representative walked passed me to go and collect it she growled, 'You horrible bastard.' That's just the way it goes, though.

This kind of thing happens in every situation, by the way, whether it's Britain in Bloom, Chelsea, Hampton Court or an independent show. It's inevitable. You can't have winners without losers, and vice versa. The vast majority of exhibitors take it on the chin and try and learn from the experience – and, as I've already said, we'll do whatever we can to help – but you always get one or two who take it personally; or at least that's what they claim.

They might say something like, 'You've always had it in for me, Buttress,' when what they really mean is, 'I just can't stand losing.'

The worst experience I've ever had took place at an independent show about five or six years ago. I can't go into too much detail for obvious reasons; suffice to say that the opinions of myself and the exhibitor in question differed somewhat. We'd already had a few words at a previous show when they hadn't got what they wanted and I'd told them exactly where they'd gone wrong.

Anyway, the moment the certificates were handed out they were on to me.

'Typical! You only give gold to your mates, Buttress. The whole thing's a fix.'

I said, 'Do you really think that? I mean *really*? I gave you a lot of feedback last year yet you've made exactly the same mistakes. I can't see what more I can do.'

In the absence of any reasonable argument the exhibitor then began shouting and swearing at me. This was right in the middle of the show, by the way.

I said, 'Look, not only are you embarrassing yourself but you're upsetting and offending other members of the public. The RHS would not appreciate this and so before it goes any further I'm going to walk away.' They still didn't stop, though, in fact if anything it got worse.

As I walked away two other exhibitors came over. 'Are you OK, Jim?' they asked. 'We saw and heard everything. If you want witnesses just you say the word.'

I was doing a talk that night but I was so shaken up by what had happened that when I got to the end of the road I had to pull into a lay-by. Luckily there was a mobile cafe there and so I went and bought myself a cup of tea. Trouble is I could hardly hold the cup I was shaking so much. I was in a right state.

'Right Jim,' I said to myself. 'Pull yourself together. You've got to be professional about this.'

The next morning I called Bob Sweet, who was Head of Judging at the RHS. 'Jim,' he said. 'You're the third judge who's complained today. Rest assured it will be dealt with.'

I said, 'I just wanted you to know, Bob, because if I'd been a first-time judge I'd have jacked it in there and then.'

A few weeks later I received a letter, not from the exhibitor but from their other half, basically saying that although they agreed with their spouse they admitted that he didn't deal with it very well. As apologies go it wasn't even worthy of a bronze and I was told that if I wanted to take it further I could, but what would have been the point? They're the ones with the problem, not me. Let 'em stew.

Anyway, let's get back to the good stuff, shall we?

Because Britain in Bloom means so much to so many you often hear rumours about sabotage and the like, but to be honest with you I think it's a load of rubbish. There's plenty of competition of course, not to mention some good-humoured banter, but in my opinion that's all it is – banter.

There was one story I thought might have been true. I'm not going to say where it was for reasons that will soon become apparent, but it's an absolute corker. What's more it's got a happy ending.

This particular village had gone to great lengths to do well in Bloom one year and had got virtually the entire population involved. There were hanging baskets outside every door and apparently the bedding around the village green was something to behold. They couldn't wait for us to arrive! Anyway, a day or two before the judging took place disaster struck, when one morning they woke to find every plant in every basket or flower bed had died. The previous evening everything had been OK, so what could have happened? Well, there was only one answer, wasn't there – sabotage!

Within minutes of everyone seeing the carnage, fingers

were being pointed and accusations thrown. It was mayhem! You can understand why they started accusing other villages, can't you? I mean nobody's going to sabotage their own display.

To cut a long story short, the person responsible for watering the baskets and bedding realized that someone had sneakily put acid in the water bowser. Twenty-four hours later and it was all dead.

Instead of sitting back and having a good laugh like I'm sure most people did, do you know what the nearby villagers did, the ones that had been accused of sabotage? They rallied round and they replaced all the flowers for them. How about that, eh? *That's* what Britain in Bloom is all about.

While the vast majority of towns and villages get prepared well in advance for Britain in Bloom you do get the odd committee who like to leave things to the last minute. There have even been times when they've been planting as we've been judging. Seriously! Many's the time we've been judging one end of a village while volunteers have been planting the other. I always know when it happened for two reasons: A) everyone's in a right fluster and B) the soil looked freshly turned. I always used to pull a plant out, give them a knowing look and say, 'You want to make sure they're firmed in properly, otherwise they won't last five minutes.' There were always a few scarlet faces when that happened.

My favourite story when it comes to planting by the seat of your pants happened when we turned up at a train station one day. My fellow judge and I both had our green jackets on, not to mention all the badges, and when we walked out of the beautifully decorated station with all its pots and hanging baskets a taxi driver called us over.

'Oi,' he said. 'Are you one of them Britain in Bloom judges?'

I said, 'Yes, that's right.'

'Well I'll tell you what, none of this was here last night!'

To be fair it wasn't a bad effort.

When it comes to Britain in Bloom I've been the subject of one or two headlines over the years. I was judging the town of Battle in Kent one year and the only thing that let it down was the state of the abbey. Everything else, the market place, the park and so on, looked absolutely amazing but the abbey just looked – well, shabby. English Heritage owns the building and so when I wrote my report I mentioned them by name and I said that it was a pity they hadn't made the same effort as the townspeople. The papers got hold of this and the headline was: 'BRITAIN IN BLOOM JUDGE GOES TO BATTLE WITH ENGLISH HERITAGE'.

Not bad, eh? That's one of my favourites.

As opposed to getting the hump about this, English Heritage simply took the feedback on the chin and tidied up the front of the abbey. Job done!

Now because of my talent for talking, which I'm going to go into more in a bit, I ended up co-hosting quite a few of these big award ceremonies for Britain in Bloom and there are two in particular that I'd like to tell you about. Both have a slight footballing theme and the first takes place up at Perth in Scotland and the second in Coventry. Perth has won Britain in Bloom almost as many times as Palace have won the European Cup. Sorry, I meant the Second Division play-offs. They're one of the competition's big hitters, last winning a gold medal in 2014, and if you ever visit Perth you'll see exactly why. They've got enough volunteers to fill Hampden Park twice over and in addition to being an aesthetically magnificent city, it's pristine. The charity that runs what is basically Perth in Bloom is called Beautiful Perth, and never has an organization been more aptly named.

So a few years ago I was due to go up there with Mark Wasilewski for this ceremony and shortly before we went he said, 'Do you know, Jim, I'm going to order a kilt.'

'Well if you want to wear a skirt you're quite welcome to,' I said.

'I just thought it would be respectful. Won't you wear one too?'

'You must be joking! It took me over twenty years to save up to buy a dinner jacket and I fully intend to get my money's worth.'

He tried and he tried to persuade me to wear one at the ceremony but I'm afraid I just wasn't having it.

Anyway, unbeknownst to Mark, by the time we arrived in Scotland I'd actually warmed to the idea – more because of the potential comedy value than respect for tradition – and so as soon as he was out of the way I had a word with one of the organizers.

''Ere, Caroline. I know it's a bit late in the day but would there be any chance of you getting hold of a kilt for me for tonight?'

She said, 'I don't see why not, Jim. There are plenty of places that hire them out.'

'Marvellous,' I said. 'There's just one thing. Do you know if there are any clans whose tartan bears the colours claret and blue?'

'Yes, I'm pretty sure there are one or two. Is that what you're after?'

'Yes please, love. There's just one more thing. Would your old man mind helping me get into it? It'll have to be just before I go on because I don't want anyone to know.'

'No problem.'

So, about five minutes before I'm introduced on stage along comes Caroline's husband and, *voilà!* One Jim Mc-Buttress. When I walked on, the reception I received was hilarious. I got wolf whistles and cries of 'Look at the legs on that!' Mark was the most vociferous.

'You cheeky old bugger!' he said. 'All that talk about not wearing a skirt. I have to say though, it suits you!'

'Ladies and gentlemen,' I said. 'Thank you for that marvellous reception. It's always nice to have a warm welcome on your entrance. I bet you didn't know that the world's greatest football team had their own tartan. Well you do now!'

What a great night we had. I can't think of anything I'd rather celebrate more than people and communities coming together.

The last time I judged Britain in Bloom, apart from 2014 when I was coaxed out of retirement for a one-off, was in 2007 and the awards ceremony took place at the beautiful Coventry Cathedral. I'd done about twenty-five years by then and because of the amount of travelling involved I thought it was time to give somebody else a chance. Never outstay your welcome if you can help it, that's what I always say.

While I was sitting at my table waiting to be introduced on stage I noticed the woman sitting next to me was playing with her phone.

'You're not still working, are you?' I said to her.

'No, no. It's a message from my husband. Coventry City are playing away at Manchester United this evening and we're one-nil up!'

A minute or so later I was introduced onto the stage along with the very beautiful Susan Hampshire, who was my co-presenter. The boys were champing at the bit to get on stage and shake her hand. What a lady!

'Good evening, ladies and gentlemen,' I said. 'And welcome to the beautiful city of Coventry. You've obviously got a tremendous history here which I'm sure you're all very proud of, but I'll tell you what, it's about to get even better. Get this ladies and gentlemen, Manchester United, nil – Coventry City, one!'

They were all looking at me as if to say, how the bloody hell did he know that?

Any rate, this lady with the phone, who was actually Chief Executive of Coventry City Council, kept mouthing to me what was happening in the game. '*Coventry have hit the post!*' she'd mouth. And as soon as I understood I'd put my hand to my ear and say, 'We've got some more news coming through, ladies and gentlemen, direct from Old Trafford. Is it another goal? Hang on . . . Hang on a minute . . . NO! Coventry have just hit the post. More news as we have it.'

People didn't have internet on their phones in those days so this was news to everyone and I kept the commentary going all through the night. Even during the meal people kept looking over to me and mouthing, '*Any more news, Jim?*' In the end Coventry won two-nil and when I called the final score it got the biggest cheer of the night!

The reason I was invited back in 2014 was because it was the fiftieth anniversary of Britain in Bloom and when the chairman asked me, I couldn't say no, could I? Even if I had said no, Sue Biggs, who is the Director General of the RHS, had other ideas. 'There are no ifs or buts, Jim. You're coming back.' Well, you don't argue with the DG at the RHS. Or at least I don't. After all, she's the boss.

And where was the last place I judged for them? Aberdeen. Let me tell you, that city – the floral city – was absolutely rocking. The bedding, the parks, the herbaceous borders – everything about it was just screaming *Come on, give me gold and best in show!* And who was the guy who had looked after it all for nine years? David Welch.

When we'd finished the round I went to where his grave is and I said, 'Well, Welchy. This lot have done well, mate. I reckon it's going to be gold for them.'

And it was. He'd have been so, so proud of them. David Welch, the laird of the floral city.

15. Here Comes the Judge

Before I bring things right up to date with Lullingstone Castle and the Big Allotment Challenge, I want to concentrate a bit more on the judging process with the RHS, because over the past eight or nine years they've made changes which in my opinion puts the standard of judging higher than it's ever been.

First of all, let me give you the basics as to how we go about marking.

Well, it's all done using a card system and on each card you'll see:

— Excellent
— Very Good
— Good
— Satisfactory
— Poor

Each judge has their own card, of course, and will mark them as he or she sees fit. After judging takes place we'll all get together and I'll say, 'Right then. Let's do the first category, shall we, which is flowers.'

What's important here is that the judges aren't swayed by one another's decisions, and so rather than letting them have a chat before we record everything I always make sure they deliver their results without conferring and all at the same time. As chairman I'm only ever interested in honest opinions and so that's the way it's got to be.

It could be five against one, four against two or three against three – in which case I get the casting vote. We do that over three sections and then at the end of it I'll say to them all, 'Right then. Are you all happy?' And if they are we'll move on, but if they're not, we'll go back. 'I think we got it wrong with number six,' one of them might say, and so we'll go back and vote again. After all that's done we go straight in to see the terminators and between us all we'll allocate the awards.

'You ready to go, Jim?' they'll say.

'I am indeed. Right then, Evening Primrose Ltd – gold medal.'

Then a moderator might say, 'Are we all OK with that?' and then we'll go round the table. As long as everyone's in agreement, we'll rubber-stamp it.

'Right then, let's move on. Garlic Flower Ltd, silver gilt.'

'Sorry, Jim,' the moderators might say, 'we thought this was silver,' and so when that happens we'll re-vote, and so it goes on. Sometimes I win it, and sometimes I don't. The point is that the exhibitor is being judged as fairly as possible. As I said though, this has all happened in the last nine or ten years. Before that the exhibitors' meetings, which take place right at the end of a show, were basically just bickering sessions. 'Why did I get this when so-and-so got that?' or 'That judge isn't up to it in my opinion.' They weren't nasty about it like those other idiots I told you about and a lot of their concerns *were* perfectly legitimate. Nowadays we don't have that problem.

But the most important task from the RHS's point of view is making sure they have the right judges in place and that's something they take very, very seriously. Just the other week I was up there all day evaluating judges' performances. We'll talk about what shows they've done, what kind of marks they've given, and anything else that we think is relevant. Then, once that's finished, we'll talk about who stays and who goes.

'OK, Jim,' they'll say. 'Which of your judges should go back on the waiting list?'

'Well, there are three who I think should go straight back on the waiting list, for the simple reason they were indecisive and a little bit woolly. The exhibitors could sense it.'

'OK, Jim. Right then, any judges who might have potential for chairmanship?'

'I can give you three. There you go.'

'OK, and how about newcomers? Anyone you'd like to recommend?'

These days the judging committees on which I serve are allowed to nominate designate judges (whereas before they had to be nominated by the RHS Council), which is what Bob and I were when we were first invited on. Incidentally, the RHS Council is like the Cabinet, if you like, and comprises the President, Treasurer and fifteen members – all of whom are elected by the RHS membership.

The difference these days, then, is that judges are actually encouraged to offer opinions right from the off, which obviously allows us to get the measure of them. They're not allowed to vote, which I think is correct, but the sooner we can find out how they think, the better.

So that's how it works with the judges. It's like the weather really – constantly changing, and that's the way it's got to be. And there can be no favouritism, by the way. It doesn't matter how well you know or like a judge, if they're not performing, they've got to go. You owe it not just to yourself, but to every exhibitor out there.

The RHS has provided me with a lot over the years, not least one or two pretty marvellous jobs, but in addition to all the friendships, fun and opportunity, it has also bestowed upon me three honours which make me so proud that I still have to pinch myself occasionally. The first is making me chairman of one of the committees – the first non-council member (or commoner!) ever to be asked, and the second is awarding me the Associate of Honour, which the RHS did back in 1997. But it's the third and most recent distinction that still makes me grin, because in 2006, not long before I retired from judging Britain in Bloom, the Royal Horticul-tural Society awarded me the Victoria Medal of Honour, the highest honour the Society can bestow. There can only ever be sixty-three recipients in the world at any one time, which was the length in years of Queen Victoria's reign, and so when I peg it, they'll bring somebody else on board. It wasn't awarded in 2015 which means it was a good year for the recipients but a bad one for the Grim Reaper! Long may that continue.

When I opened the letter informing me that they were awarding me the VMH I just burst into tears. You know what I'm like by now. I could blub for England.

'Not another speeding ticket?' said Linda.

'Not this time, Linda. They're giving me the VMH!'

'They're what?!'

Penelope Keith, who, as many of you will know, is a mad keen gardener, presented me with the Associate of Honour back in 1997 and the VMH was presented to me by the President of the RHS. That ceremony took place at Hamp-ton Court, and my word did I celebrate! Just two years before that my old mate Alan Titchmarsh had been awarded the VMH and so I knew that I was in very, very good company. Funnily enough, two years *after* I was awarded the medal I presented Alan with a Vice Presidency of the RHS. What would old Frank Knight have said, eh, about me winning the Society's two top awards? Actually, I think he'd have had a bit of a chuckle!

Despite me being dead proud of my medals I've never really been one to wear them when I'm out; that is until Mr Titchmarsh got hold of me. We were at a show one day, I think it was Chelsea, and all of a sudden he came up to me, and he wasn't happy.

'What's wrong, Alan?' I asked him.

'You're not wearing your medals, Jim.'

'Well I don't usually bother.'

'You should bother, Jim. They've been earned. Wear them!'

He didn't mean it in a nasty way but I'll tell you what, you don't argue with Mr Titchmarsh.

Nowadays I do wear them at official events or on special occasions and I don't mind admitting that it puts a bit of a spring in my step. Thanks, Titch.

When you get the letter through to say you're the recipient of an RHS award you're not really supposed to tell another living soul, but at the time the letter arrived about the Associate Medal in 1996 old Pop was dying of cancer and so it left me in a bit of a real quandary. 'You've got to tell him,' Linda said. 'Come on, he'll be over the moon.'

She was right, and besides, who was he going to tell? So I went down to see the old boy at his bungalow.

'Dad,' I said. 'I wanted you to be the first to know after Linda. They're awarding me the Associate Medal of Honour.'

'Good God, boy,' he said. 'You've finally done something useful just before I die!'

'Thanks, Dad!'

He was so proud though, bless him. As you know, Pop

was gardening through and through and so if I hadn't told him and he'd died I'd never have forgiven myself.

Now before I go on to one of my favourite RHS stories, which involves them sending me to Bahrain and leads nicely into my work at Lullingstone Castle, I just want to tell you what happened to Mum and Pop. They meant everything to me and, do you know what, it just wouldn't feel right covering it in a couple of sentences. It's a nice little story though.

When the old boy eventually retired from the insurance industry Mum started trying to persuade him to move down to Worthing. The poor thing had been itching to go back there ever since she and Pop left for Glasgow, and so in the end he said, 'OK, let's go.' You see Pop didn't care where he lived really. So long as he had his garden and a church nearby, a telly to watch the football on, he was happy.

In the end they moved into this beautiful little bungalow in a place called East Preston, which is just outside Worthing, and one of the reasons they chose East Preston was because on the one corner there was a Catholic church, and just round the other corner was a betting shop – which you could say was Mum's church. They knew what they liked, Mum and Pop.

Unfortunately it wasn't what Mum was expecting. You see she had this romantic notion that once they moved back she'd be straight back in touch with all her old friends again, but of course they'd all either passed away or moved. Mum wanted Worthing circa 1940, not circa 1980. It was a very different town now and the poor old girl was so disappointed. Actually she was devastated.

About a year later Mum went to hospital just for a minor operation, but when she woke up from the anaesthetic she wasn't the same person. From then on she just gradually deteriorated and eventually ended up bedridden. She couldn't walk, talk or do anything for herself. It was horrendous. Caroline, Pat and I are convinced she had a mini stroke while she was under the anaesthetic, and in a way that was when we lost our mum.

There was talk of her going into an old people's home but Pop was having none of it.

'She's my wife,' he said. 'I love her and I want to look after her. It's my duty.'

And that's what he did. Nine years he looked after Mum and not once did I hear him complain. She didn't know what day of the week it was, bless her, but despite her being in her own little world I still managed to extract the occasional reaction.

'You won't believe it, Mum,' I'd say. 'Piggott had three winners yesterday.'

That always got a flicker. Not a smile as such, but I could tell she was in there somewhere. Then sometimes if she hadn't heard my voice for a while she would crack a small smile when I turned up, and for a second – just for a second – it was like having her back.

Pop used to ask me to sit with her because half the time he didn't know what to do. He was such an active person he found just sitting down with her quite hard going. In the end he moved her bed next to the back window so he could spend all day in the garden but still keep his eye on her and she could see him. And the garden they had in East Preston was exactly the same as the ones he'd had in Haywards Heath and Purley. There was a big lawn, which he reduced by half to create a vegetable patch, a few flower beds, a shed and a greenhouse.

When Mum did eventually pass away it was a blessing for all concerned. Pop got to enjoy what time he had left and as for Mum . . . Well, that wasn't living. I knew what she was like and, you mark my words, she would have hated being in that state for so long.

Once Mum passed away I rather stupidly assumed Pop might need looking after a bit and when Christmas approached – his first Christmas without her – I made the suggestion that I could come down and spend it with him in East Preston.

'Why?' he said. 'There are three hundred and sixty-four other days in the year. Why do you want to come then?'

'Well, it's your first Christmas without Mum, Dad. I don't want you to be on your own.'

'And who says I'm going to be on my own?'

At the time I didn't quite know what he was getting at but when I went to see him next I got to know exactly what he meant. Now, being a religious man, Dad used to send out dozens and dozens of Christmas cards and subsequently he got a lot in return. While he was making the tea I had a flick through some of them: 'Dear Cuddy, So looking forward to seeing you for drinks on Christmas morning, Love, Mary'; 'Dear Cuddy, Really pleased you're coming to lunch, Love, Doris'.

I said to him, 'No wonder you don't want me around on Christmas Day. You wouldn't be able to fit me in!'

These were all the old widows he'd befriended down at the church and he'd planned out the entire day: drinks with Mary, lunch with Doris, tea with blah blah and then supper with the Widow Twankee. Perfect!

Pop was always a big churchgoer, as you already know, but once Mum passed away it became his life. He tended the grounds and the gardens and he helped organize all the different social activities. Do you know that when the old boy eventually died we could have filled the church four or five times over.

Now like most people from that generation Pop was always very smartly turned out, no matter what he was doing. He was ex-navy, of course. Then one day, about six months before he died, Caroline took me to one side.

'I'm a bit worried about Dad, Jim,' she said. 'He hasn't shaved this morning and that just isn't like him. Something's just not right.'

Now you show me a man who enjoys going to either the doctor or a hospital and I'll show you a gardener who wants to lay crazy paving over his or her lawn. They just don't exist. So I knew what kind of reaction I was going to get when I broached the subject, but I couldn't leave it any longer.

'Dad,' I said to him one morning. 'Look, Dad, something's up, isn't it? Now are you going to tell me what it is?'

Surprisingly enough he came straight out with it.

'Having a bit of trouble downstairs, boy, if you know what I mean. Bound to happen at my age, boy, bound to happen.'

'Well they can do marvellous things these days, Dad. Why don't I book you an—'

'Don't be so daft, boy! I don't want to waste anybody's time.'

Here we go, I thought. Ding, ding, round one! To cut a long story short, Caroline and I eventually managed to get him down to see the doctor and as you can imagine he was far from being the model patient.

'I don't want any flannel, Doc, all right? Just tell me how long I've got.'

'Mmm,' said the doctor after he'd finished examining him. 'I'm afraid I'm going to have to send you to see a specialist.'

'There, boy, I told you! Bloody useless. A complete waste of time.'

'Shh, Dad!'

We couldn't get him out of that surgery fast enough.

His behaviour when we went to see the specialist was even better – or worse, whichever way you look at it. For a start this bloke was about fifty years younger than Pop and you should have seen the look on his face when he first saw him.

'You do realize that I'm probably old enough to be your grandfather,' began the reluctant patient.

'I'd have said great grandfather,' replied the, by now, equally reluctant specialist.

'What a cheek!'

He's met his match here, I thought.

In the end Pop gave it to him straight.

'Now look, son. Before I leave here I want to know exactly what's wrong with me and whether you can do anything, and if you can't, I want to know how long I've got. I'm not afraid to die. I've had a good crack so if that's it, fine. Just tell me.'

Well, the look on this doctor's face. He must have felt like he was in the army.

Pop had already had some scans and so after the examination the doctor sat him down in a chair and then sat on the edge of his desk.

'Right then, Mr Buttress,' he said. 'Do you have any hobbies?'

'Hobbies? Yes, of course I've got hobbies. I like gardening and I like football – watching, not playing.'

'Well I'll tell you what, Mr Buttress, I'm going to give you a yellow card and I'm afraid that the red one is only about six months away.'

It was prostate cancer, by the way, and that was it. Pop stood up, shook the bloke warmly by the hand and said,

'Thanks very much. That's all I needed to know.' And then he turned to me.

'Right, come on, boy. We've got things to do!'

It was as if he'd been given orders direct from the Admiralty.

'What do you want to do, Dad?' I asked.

'Well, I'll be dead in six months. There's a lot to sort out.'

He was like a whirling dervish.

'This is a lot to take in, Dad,' I said. 'Would you mind if we had a quick drink?'

'Well, it'll have to be a half. We've got things to do, boy! I've got a funeral to arrange.'

Talk about gallows humour. It wasn't funny at the time, I suppose, but looking back it's just hilarious. People obviously deal with news like that in different ways and Pop's way of dealing with it was to be very matter of fact. But he was always a very well-organized man. When a bill dropped through the door Pop would have a cheque written out within minutes, whereas Mum would always wait for the red ones. Even then she'd always argue the toss over whether they were right or not. Honestly, the number of times I saw her charging into the bank or the post office. Always on the war path! Old Pop, though, he was just the absolute opposite and this side of his character went into overdrive once he'd been shown a yellow.

I remember ringing up Caroline after we'd seen the specialist and asking her what we were going to do. You see, as we'd left the hospital Pop had stopped me suddenly.

'Boy,' he said. 'Whatever happens, promise me you won't put me in a home. I want to stay in the bungalow for as long as I possibly can.'

'OK, Dad, I promise.'

After talking it over with Caroline we decided that I'd do

the end of the week and the weekend and she would do the rest. Patrick not only had a very young family at the time but he also lived a long way away and so it would have been impossible for him to commit to any kind of rota. He helped whenever he could, though.

I used to go down every Thursday night and then on Monday lunchtime Caroline would turn up and take over. She had young kids at the time so how she managed I'll never know. She was fantastic. In the end we managed to take the old boy right to the wire and it was only at the very, very end of his life that he had to be taken into the local hospice. While he was at home we also had the help of some marvellous Macmillan nurses. They were absolutely terrific with Pop and they even complimented us on the job we'd done looking after him. That meant the absolute world to us because all we wanted to do was make sure he was comfortable.

I'd go and sit with him sometimes while he was asleep and then as soon as he woke up he'd say, 'Here, boy. Am I dead yet?'

'Well no, of course you're not dead, Dad, you're talking to me.'

'Good point, boy!'

And then he'd go back to sleep.

I remember one night he woke and shouted, 'For God's sake, Peter, open the bloody gates!' It was one of the only times I ever heard him swear.

A week or two before he went they fitted him with this machine that used to administer the morphine and one day I was outside in the garden having a fag when I suddenly heard Caroline shout, 'Jim, Jim! I need you back in here.'

When I arrived back in the room Pop was wrestling with

this bloody machine and trying to get it off him. There were arms and legs everywhere.

'I don't need drugs,' he shouted. 'All I want to do is die.'

The poor old boy was absolutely out of his mind.

My brother-in-law Bob and I eventually managed to get him back into bed but just when we thought he was quietening down a bit he sat up, lashed out and caught me right on the bloody chin. What a punch!

After that Caroline and I decided that we really had done as much as we could. We had to let the professionals take over now. I remember ringing the doctor and asking her what to do. I think we wanted her to take the responsibility for making the final decision away from us, which is just about what she did.

'I'm afraid it has to be your choice,' said the doctor. 'But I think I know what I'd do.'

That was the closest Caroline and I were going to get to an actual instruction and so very reluctantly – although with a definite sense of relief, if that makes sense – we arranged for Pop to be taken into the local hospice.

By the time the ambulance men turned up, Pop was falling in and out of consciousness and they had to be careful that he didn't click what was happening.

'Keep him talking,' they said when they were moving him.

'Where are we going, boy?' he asked.

'We're going to Fontwell, Dad,' I said, which was one of his favourite racecourses.

'Fontwell, boy? Well done.'

And that was the last thing my father said to me. They got him to the hospice and he died there about ten hours later. When the three of us went in to see him after he'd died one of the nurses had put a posy of flowers in his hand. That was such a sweet thing to do and so appropriate.

When it came to the funeral Pop had been true to his word. It was all organized, as were his affairs, and so really myself, Caroline and Pat didn't have to do a great deal.

On the morning of the funeral I remember standing outside the front of the bungalow when the dustmen turned up. Now Pop being Pop, he used to stand outside and watch the dustmen when they came down his street. It wasn't that he didn't trust them or anything, he just used to enjoy watching them work. Over the years they got to know the old boy well. He used to give them tomato plants and presents for the kids and what have you. They were friends of his. Anyway, along came the dustmen on the morning of Pop's funeral and when they saw me they asked where the old boy was.

'Haven't seen the Foreman, have you? We haven't seen him for a while.'

'I'm afraid he's gone,' I said.

'Oh no, you're joking. Did you hear that, Bob? The Foreman's gone.'

Bless them, they all looked absolutely gutted.

'When's the funeral?' one of them asked.

'Well it's today.'

'At his church?'

'That's right.'

'What time?'

'11 a.m.'

'Right, we'll be there.'

Before they carried on we had a really good chat about the old boy.

'We knew he used to watch to make sure we didn't drop anything!' one of them said. 'We'll miss that old boy. He was one of the best.'

Well, I wanted to laugh and cry all at the same time. I couldn't have been any prouder.

Now on the other side of the coin, Pop had also become friends with a daughter of the old Duke of Norfolk. You remember the old boy I'd seen in the beer tent when I was a kid?

Well she and Pop, through the church of course, used to help organize trips over to Lourdes. What it must have looked like I don't know. I mean Pop was into his eighties at the time and used a stick. And he was one of the helpers! But it was through these trips to Lourdes that she and Pop became really good friends and according to him she even used to visit him at the bungalow sometimes. Now the old duke had three daughters, but for the life of me I can't remember which one it was. She used to pitch up with a couple of dogs in tow apparently, and after Pop had made the tea they'd gossip for hours.

When Pop died we received a note from her asking when the funeral was and whether we'd have any objection to her attending. Well of course we had no objection, but by the day of the funeral I'd forgotten all about it.

Being a bit of a big mouth, and because nobody else wanted to, I volunteered to do the eulogy at the funeral and right towards the very end, just as I was about to finish, I looked down the church and I saw the three dustmen standing against a wall behind the pew where the duke's daughter was sitting.

I said, 'Do you know what, there's only one way I can sum up my old dad. It didn't matter whether you were a dustman or a duchess; he loved 'em all.'

With that I walked back to my pew. Talk about being fed a line! There was clapping and cheering. It was just perfect.

I had tears streaming down my face after that. I think everyone did.

Over the years the RHS has sent me all over the world judging and banging the horticultural drum. I've been to America, Canada, France and Germany. But by far the most interesting mission took place just a few years ago when they asked me to go out to Bahrain to help set up the Bahrain Garden Club's fortieth Annual Amateur Flower and Vegetable Show. They sent me over with a man called Stephen Bennett, who was Director of Shows at the RHS, and when we got there it was as though we'd travelled into the future. You know the Gardeners' World Show at the NEC? Well the venue made that look like a jamboree in a Boy Scouts' hut. This place was like fifteen aeroplane hangars all rolled into one. It must have been a mile long.

'Where's the show then?' I asked the woman who was looking after us. I was expecting something big.

'It's just over there,' she said, pointing towards the far end. And there, right in the far corner of this bloody great big building, was a little sign that read: 'Bahrain Garden Club Annual Amateur Flower and Vegetable Show'.

'Really?' I said to her. I'd been expecting at least fifty gi-normous tents, trestle tables half a mile long and a golf cart to take me round.

As it turned out, the BGC Annual Flower and Vegetable Show was really the equivalent of a smallish town show in the UK, with about a thousand or so entries, and so they brought along the lot: flowers, vegetables, preserves, cakes, cuddly toys. The committee were a lovely bunch of people too, a mixture of very enthusiastic locals and expatriates, and so once I'd got them all together I started dishing out the jobs. This was the day before the show opened, by the way.

'Right then, madam, you and I will split the flowers and veg into their correct classes. OK?'

'Absolutely, Mr Buttress!'

'Call me Jim.

'Madam, would you and your friend there kindly set up a table for the flower arranging?'

'Yes, of course.'

'Thank you very much. Right then, now who's on cake duty?'

After about ten minutes the entire place was an absolute hive of activity. We had people bustling about shifting plants, laying on tablecloths and preparing signs. Anyone reading this who has helped set up a show like this will know exactly what I mean.

'Right then,' I said once we'd finished the veg. 'What time do the judges arrive?'

'You're here,' said my helper.

'Beg pardon?'

'Well, we were hoping you'd do it, Mr Buttress.'

'What, all of it?'

'Yes. Is that OK?'

'Of course it is. I'd be delighted.' And so I did the lot: buns, cuddly toys, even jewellery. Can you imagine me, a ruddy-faced sports-mad gardener who likes a fag and a pint or two, walking round the Bahraini Exhibition Centre judging necklaces, brooches and rings? You couldn't make it up.

Come mid-afternoon they were ready to ask me another favour. Apparently the Queen Consort of Bahrain would be coming the following day and would I mind escorting her round the show and explaining what I'd done.

'Of course not,' I said. 'I'd be absolutely delighted.'

So at about three o'clock the following day the Queen Consort arrived and we started to make our way round the show. It was packed by the way. Half of Bahrain must have been there. She was only really interested in the fruit, veg and flower arranging and so I suggested that we start with the fruit.

'This way please, Your Highness. I think we'll start with the strawberries and raspberries if that's OK. They're definitely one of the highlights of the show.'

Well they were. By the time we got to the table there wasn't a single strawberry or raspberry left. Only stalks.

'Where have they gone?' I whispered to my helper.

'The kids must have eaten them. This is what happened last year.'

'Oh, brilliant!'

But they didn't just gobble up the fruits of the forest. They had the lot! Every table we went to had either half-eaten fruit on it or no fruit at all.

'Hungry lot you've got here!'

'It appears so.'

Fortunately the youth of Bahrain were far less fond of veg than they were of fruit and so that went without a hitch. Thank heavens she wasn't into cakes, though, because those tables had suffered even more than the fruit. They were completely wiped out!

One of the flower-arranging classes had built a seascape and to make it more realistic they'd put the arrangement in a vase that was half-filled with water and had goldfish, shells, seaweed and even a little shipwreck inside. I have to say it looked absolutely marvellous and the Queen Consort was dead impressed.

There was, however, one tiny problem. The oasis on

which this arrangement had been assembled sat in the middle of the vase and rose a good few inches above sea level. This meant that it gradually began sucking all of the oxygen out of the water and so when I arrived back there the following morning all the goldfish were dead. Before anyone else arrived I got a bucket, picked them all out, flushed them down the toilet and then filled it up again. They probably thought the kids had eaten them too!

On the evening of the last day of the show a banquet was held, to which Stephen and I were invited, and in addition to the Queen Consort and various Bahraini VIPs there was in attendance a very elegant lady. She'd been given the dubious honour of sitting next to yours truly but instead of all the usual pre-dinner platitudes she began proceedings with a short lesson in honesty.

'I'm so sorry,' she said, 'but I have absolutely no idea who you are.'

'I'm Jim Buttress.'

'Buttress, now let me see . . . No, sorry. I've completely drawn a blank. Should I know who you are?'

'No, I don't suppose so,' I said. 'I've been sent over by the RHS. I'm one of the chairmen of the judging committees.'

'Oh, now I know! How splendid. Yes, of course, Buttress. I judge myself you know, at the trial grounds.'

The moment I mentioned I was a judge she started chatting away like an old friend. I got the lot! Her father had been the British ambassador to Bahrain when they started the Bahrain Garden Club and because it was the fortieth anniversary she'd been invited back.

'So who's on your committee these days?' she asked. 'I'm sure I must know at least one of them.'

'Well, I don't know if you know Lady Boyd?'

'Old Boydy?' she said. 'I've known her for years!'

Everyone I knew, she knew. Once again though, that's horticulture. It might be big business these days but it's still set in a pretty small village.

A bit later on in the evening my new friend said to me, 'I wonder if you've read about a nephew of mine, Mr Buttress. His name's Tom Hart Dyke. He's been gallivanting all over South America studying orchids, don't you know. Almost got himself killed, the silly boy.'

Well as a matter of fact I had read about Tom, and just in case any of you haven't, allow me to enlighten you.

As well as being a horticulturalist Tom Hart Dyke is what's called a plant hunter, which is basically somebody who risks life and limb looking for new species of plant. The clue's in the name I suppose. Anyway, he'd gone hunting rare orchids in a place called the Darien Gap, which is a swathe of jungle on the Panama and Colombia border. He'd won a scholarship from somewhere, I think, and so had set off out there. Now apart from a few rare species of orchid, not to mention several hundredweight of venomous snakes, the Darien Gap is also home to the Revolutionary Armed Forces of Colombia, one of the most dangerous and feared guerrilla groups in the whole of Central America. These people used the lot – machetes, Kalashnikovs and rocket launchers – and to them life was cheap. Especially the life of an English orchid fancier!

Sure enough, after just a couple of days in the Darien Gap, Tom and his unfortunate travelling companion (somebody he'd only met a couple of days before and who had absolutely no interest in plants!) got surrounded by these guerrillas, beaten up and then kidnapped.

Now just as an aside, if I'd known then that I was going to end up working with this bloke for the best part of ten years I'd never have left Bahrain. As it was, it was a good story and once I told Tom's auntie as much as I knew she started to fill in all the gaps.

'They were held captive by these people for over nine months, Mr Buttress, and in a tiny hut with virtually no light. What's more they were only fed every two or three days, and even then only scraps. As I said, though, it was his own silly fault. I mean fancy running off into a dangerous jungle chasing orchids.'

'So how did they get through it?' I asked her.

'With great difficulty I should imagine!' she said. 'Well in actual fact, Mr Buttress, my nephew isn't quite as daft as I make him out to be, because do you know what kept him going through those long months? Planning a World Garden.'

'I beg your pardon.'

'A World Garden! You see, instead of letting boredom and lethargy get the better of him, whenever he began to lose hope he'd send himself off to a certain country and then write down the plants he'd include within a garden representing that particular country. He went all over the world while he was in that little hut and because they let him keep his biro and notebook he managed to record it all.'

I later found out that Tom also used his horticultural imaginary travelogue to keep his travelling companion from going under. This chap became ill after not very long and so to keep his spirits up Tom vocalized his thoughts and he took this boy with him on his travels.

In the end, Tom actually befriended one of these guerrillas (a young lady) and persuaded her to help him plan this garden on some sand outside the hut. She used to let him out for a few minutes every day and so with the help of a few twigs and stones he set to work. It had to be destroyed at the end of each day and so it was all in his mind really, but without it he'd have gone completely barmy.

In the end they let them go, and because of Tom's now legendary sense of direction they ended up back at the guerrilla camp within a couple of hours! The boss of these rebels was so sick of the sight of Tom and his mate that he dragged the two of them through a clearing or two and towards civilization. How the hell they didn't get killed I'll never know.

A few months after that somebody managed to interview a couple of these guerrillas and sure enough the only reason they spared them and let them go was that A) they were fed up with hearing about his bloody World Garden, and B) he seemed so passionate about it they decided to let him go and build it. Tom's imaginary World Garden saved their bloody lives!

Not long after I got back home from Bahrain my aristocratic friend got in touch with me and asked if I'd pop down and see Tom and perhaps give him some advice. After what she'd told me I just had to meet him, and so a few days later I went to see him at Lullingstone Castle in Kent, which is the family home, or seat, as these posh folk often say.

Well, just as I suspected, Tom Hart Dyke was a bit of an eccentric.

'Jimus!' he cried when I got out of my car. He's never, ever called me anything else, by the way. 'My aunt has told me all about you. Come and have a cup of tea, then I'll show you round.'

Since getting back from the jungle Tom had wasted no time at all building his World Garden and as soon as I'd finished my tea the grand tour began. Well, we may as well have been in the Darien Gap. It was awful. He had no money, bless him (that had all gone on his orchid hunt), and so he'd tried to wing it. Basically it was just two acres of solid weed.

When we got about halfway round he said, 'What do you reckon, Jimus?'

'Utterly amazing,' I said. 'I never knew couch grass grew in so many different countries.'

That went over his head.

Believe it or not, Tom had already opened his World Weed Garden to the public and later that day I watched him as he led some visitors round. He was like the Pied Piper.

'OK, ladies and gents, here we are in Northern Australia where you'll find tall grasses and low eucalyptus.'

Really? More like Scottish thistle and dandelion. They were going for it, though, and that's what impressed me. He wasn't showing them a World Garden; he was sharing a vision with them. It was a lesson in salesmanship.

When I got back home Linda asked me how it had gone.

'The garden itself is atrocious, Linda, but there's potential. And there's something about Tom. I've never seen confidence like it.'

'What are you going to do then?' she asked.

'I'm going to help him! I can't have him showing members of the public a field full of weeds. I'd never forgive myself.'

Over the past ten years or so Tom, myself and other volunteers and members of staff have worked tirelessly to bring this vision of his to life, and between us I think we've done one heck of a job. Every spare hour, day or week any of us have had has gone into creating the Lullingstone Castle World Plant Garden and as far as I know there's nothing else like it anywhere in the world.

A television company even made two six-part television series about it that went out on BBC2: *Save Lullingstone Castle* and *Return to Lullingstone Castle*. The producers must have thought all their Christmases had come at once. You had scatty Tom, the recently departed Red Indian Reg, a full-time member of staff who was a third-generation Sioux, and Tom's granny, who was his inspiration. She was a wonderful old girl and just as eccentric as him. Instead of using a Zimmer frame Granny used to push a bicycle round and in the basket on the front she'd have a pair of secateurs, a trowel, a kneeling mat and a book. She used to spend her entire life pottering round the gardens and he adored the old girl. In addition to Tom, Reg and Granny you also had me and Tom's parents, and so from the point of view of making a fly-on-the-wall documentary it was gold dust. Nothing at all was rehearsed, they simply followed us all around, and we pulled in millions of viewers. It was a horticultural *EastEnders* really. 'Will Tom finally be locked up?' 'Will Jim and Reg kill Tom?' 'Will Granny make it to the next episode?' Each week it was left on a bit of a cliffhanger and each week more and more people tuned in, probably out of curiosity more than anything else.

Before that first series went out they must have had about five hundred visitors a year at Lullingstone, and some of those were only there by mistake. Now they were starting to get hundreds every week and because they brought in a bit of money we were able to finish off and refine the World Garden, build a nursery and start sorting out the rest of the land. Today Lullingstone gets visitors from all over the world and it's become a genuine horticultural attraction. Not a bad story, is it?

People often ask me what my role is there and that's a difficult one. There are so many sides to it. One minute I'm a sounding board, the next an agony aunt and then finally I'm a gardener! It's a two-way thing, though, because in addition to all the wonderful friendships I've made there I've also learned a heck of a lot about plants I'd never even heard of. But to have been part of something like that almost from the off has been an absolute joy and I'm proud of young Tom. As I said earlier, his confidence and enthusiasm are infectious and he's got a heart of pure gold. People like that don't come along very often and so if you ever come across a Tom Hart Dyke take my advice: jump on and see where the ride takes you. I'm glad I did.

16. Allotmently Challenged

Before I bring this book of mine right up to date with the *Big Allotment Challenge* I want to talk about two of the other strings on my current bow: talking and broadcasting. I've been doing both for God knows how long, but as they play a bigger part in my life now than they've ever done before I thought this would be the perfect time to tell you about them.

I think I mentioned earlier that I was related to Fred Emney, the old stage and film actor. According to my younger brother Pat, we're also direct descendants of a very famous stage actor called Arthur Williams. Well, he was famous, back in the Victorian and Edwardian era. He appeared in over a thousand plays apparently, both in the West End and on Broadway. The point I'm trying to get across of course is that when it comes to using your mouth to make a living, my clan have got form.

Just to give you some idea of how much of my time I spend giving talks, in 2015 I did over a hundred and fifty up and down the country and to audiences ranging from fifty to over a thousand. Before I retired from the Royal Parks I might have done one or two a week but since then, and especially since the *Big Allotment Challenge* started, I'm rarely off the road.

Actually, while I'm finalizing this chapter let me just tell you what I've got on over the next few days. Tomorrow I'm in Broxbourne doing a talk and then the day after I'm hosting a big awards ceremony at Ruxley Manor in Kent. The following day I'm doing a talk in Edenbridge and after that I'm straight up to Malvern, where I'll be judging a show and then doing a talk. It's a live theatre event in Parham the day after that, followed by talks in Sittingbourne, Biggin Hill and then Westerham. That's just a week's worth! I'll tell you what though, it certainly beats working. No two days are ever the same doing talks, and there's usually an incident of some kind.

I remember one of the first talks I did after I retired. There was a woman in the front row and she slept from the moment I got up until the moment I sat down again. They must have given her Valium or something because throughout the entire talk she never batted an eyelid. I thought, I'm certainly on form today!

At the end of the talk the chairwoman got up and said, 'That's one of the best talks we've had for some time and I'll now call on Sybil for the vote of thanks,' and then she pointed at Sleeping Beauty.

'Well,' began Sybil. 'I have to say that in all my years as a gardener I've never heard such an entertaining talk, don't you agree, ladies?'

She'd never listened to a bloody word! I thought, you cheeky old mare.

But in addition to curing insomnia I'm also a pretty good deterrent, if truth be known. I'll give you two examples. I was asked to do a talk in a church hall somewhere but every time a member of the audience tried to ask a question this old girl at the front shouted out the answer, or should I say *an* answer. After ten minutes or so the natives began getting very restless indeed and so before it all kicked off I stood up, put on my jacket and said to this woman, 'As you know all the answers, why don't you come up here and take my place? No skin off my nose, I'll just go to the pub.' You should have seen the look on her face. It was like thunder! She was up and out of that hall faster than you could say aspidistra.

Before we started taking questions again this old boy came up to me and started shaking me by the hand. 'Thank you so much!' he said. 'We've been trying to get rid of her for years.'

Not long after that I was delivering a talk to a local society and, as is my wont, I started off proceedings with a joke or two, just to break the ice. After about the third joke this bloke stood up and stopped me.

'Now look here,' he said. 'I thought I'd come to watch you deliver a lecture, not a comedy routine.'

So I just carried on telling gags until he upped and left, then once he was gone, I did the rest of the talk.

Once again, after I'd finished about three people came flying up to me. 'Thank God you carried on with the jokes, Mr Buttress. That man's an absolute pain!'

There you are, you see. I'm like a talking nicotine shred. I get rid of all kinds of irritants.

Now some people will charge many thousands of pounds to go and speak to a group of people but that's something that's never sat well with me. If you charge an organization thousands of pounds that puts a ridiculous amount of pressure on them financially and in my experience strips all the enjoyment away. It just makes them nervous. I usually take a few quid to cover my expenses and then if funds allow a bit more as a fee. I'm happy, they're happy, and, as long as I perform, the audience are too. Job done!

Believe it or not, people still try and pull the wool. I remember once receiving a telephone call from the treasurer of a society and she wanted to book me for a talk.

'Before we look at dates, Mr Buttress, can we just talk about your fee, and please bear in mind that we have very little in the kitty.'

They were about forty miles away and so I suggested £50.

'No, no, no, we couldn't possibly afford that. I think we could just about manage half.'

'Oh, all right then,' I said. 'That'll just about cover the petrol.'

Anyway, when I got there it turned out she'd booked me as the speaker at their AGM. *Marvellous,* I thought. You see, because there's usually so much else going on at these meetings the audiences can often be somewhat distracted and so I wasn't exactly looking forward to it.

The big eye-opener for me was when the treasurer, who was the woman who booked me, got up to say her piece.

'Well, ladies and gentlemen,' she said. 'I'm happy to report we've had one of our best years ever and have in the bank a total of £7,461.'

When I got up to speak I said, 'I'm not surprised you've got so much in the bank if you only pay your speakers £25,' and I looked over at the treasurer. She just winked at me, the wily old thing. She'd got me all right, hook, line and sinker.

Another treasurer gave me one of my more memorable introductions. I was expecting a nice little build-up, to be honest. He'd been friendly enough and once again I wasn't charging the earth, but no!

'Ladies and gentlemen,' he said. 'Before I introduce our main speaker to the stage I would just like to take this opportunity to record my displeasure about the disgraceful cost of speakers these days. Half of them don't know what they're talking about and the other half are either incoherent or can't work a slide machine properly. We've had three this year that turned up late and when one of them was asked if he'd pose for a photograph he flatly refused. I'm telling you, this type of speaker is a scourge on our society!'

I'm pretty sure he was referring to their gardening society as opposed to society in general, but even so – talk about whipping the crowd into a frenzy! By the time he was ready to introduce me about half the audience had fallen asleep and the other half were baying for my blood.

'Ladies and gentlemen,' he said, turning to me. 'Our speaker this afternoon was very, very cheap; in fact we've paid little more than his expenses. Will you please put your hands together for Mr Jim Buttress.'

Redeemed at the last minute!

I later found out that the treasurer had indeed had his hands burnt once or twice by a couple of speakers who'd charged him thousands but delivered naff all and it had indeed left the society financially embarrassed. That's why they went for me, I think. I was all they could afford.

My favourite financial mix-up with regards to my talks involves a train fare and a couple of committee members who probably squeak when they walk. I'd been booked to speak at a lunch one day and the price we'd agreed on was my train fare, which was about £30 and would be sent to me in advance, and a further £40 for my trouble. It was a full day out including travel and so I thought that was about fair.

Anyway, after the lunch one of the aforementioned committee members came up to me brandishing an envelope.

'Here you are, Mr Buttress. We absolutely hate owing people and so I thought I'd hand you your cheque straight away.'

Naturally I was expecting to find a cheque for £40 when I opened the envelope, but instead I found one made out for the price of the train fare, which I'd already been paid. I thought to myself, well, I'm only ten quid down so I may as well leave it. No chance. About a week later I received an invoice from the people who'd hired me asking for their £30 back. No mention of my £40 fee! In the end I sent the invoice back with the cheque and put it down to experience.

About a year ago a gentleman booked me to speak at a lunch, and a week before it was due to take place I received an email from him informing me that they hadn't budgeted for my meal and would I mind waiting outside while they ate. Once they'd finished coffee somebody would introduce me and then away we'd go. This was a little bit much, I'm afraid. I mean I was only charging them £25 to speak. In the end I replied to the chap and told him that if it wasn't in the budget I'd be happy to pay for the meal myself.

'Good heavens no,' he replied. 'That would set a precedent. And besides, I don't think we have room for you.'

I know I've said it before but you really couldn't make it up, could you?

Now don't get me wrong, I enjoy every single one of these talks and over the years I've met some truly inspirational people. I've made a lot of friends too. But it's the kinds of experiences I'm telling you about that really make it for me. Never mind Tom Hart Dyke, I actually think we're a nation of eccentrics and we have among our number some truly wonderful characters. Horticulture in particular is absolutely full of them.

One of my favourite speaking jobs is hosting the theatre at Gardeners' World Live. Many of you will have been to the show, of course, and some of you may even have been daft enough to watch me ply my trade, but with that job it doesn't matter who I'm talking to, there's always a terrific atmosphere. Take Monty Don for instance. He loves me like a better-looking brother, does Monty, and from the moment I introduce him we're having fun. I'll start by saying, 'You know who's up next, girls, don't you? That's right; it's him, the Don. Now calm down, girls, calm down. He'll be here soon enough. Look at her over there. Her heart's almost beating out of her blouse!' Old Monty absolutely loves it and we always try and make sure we get three or four sessions together.

Now I don't know if you watch Monty's show but I always say that the only star of that programme is his dog, Nigel. Or, as Monty likes to call him, 'That bloody dog!'

We once devoted an entire interview to Nigel at the Gardeners' World theatre and it turned out that he started life as Rupert.

'That was his first name,' said Monty. 'Then the kids decided they didn't like Rupert and so after much deliberation we changed it to Nigel.'

See what I mean about a nation of eccentrics?

Now because Monty never trained as a gardener or did any kind of apprenticeship there's always been quite a bit of animosity shown towards him from various members of the horticultural establishment. Well, do you know what, I think that's absolute codswallop. Monty Don may well have been a late starter but, you mark my words, he's as passionate about horticulture as anyone else I know, and what's more, he knows what he's talking about. OK, so he never got his diploma. He's not the only one! Live and let live, that's what I say. Good luck to you, Monty.

My career as a broadcaster first started in the mid-1990s when I was asked to appear on a show called *Weekend Matters* on the radio station LBC. Basically this was a two-hour phone-in that went out on Saturday lunchtime and I was the gardening expert. A lovely girl called Therese Birch presented the show and I answered questions from Doris in East Finchley or Harry from Clapham. It was my voice that seemed to hook them in, in fact they went mad for it.

'Ooh, you sound just like treacle, you do,' the old dears used to say to me.

Anyway, after a good few years on *Weekend Matters* LBC got taken over by somebody and they decided to change the format; and do you know who they replaced me with? Boy George! There's not a lot you can say about that. That's the media for you, though. In one minute, out the next.

So about five years ago a very dear friend of mine at BBC Radio Kent said, 'Jim, the BBC is desperately looking for a new voice for a gardening show they do called *Dig It*. It goes out across two stations – BBC Radio Sussex and Surrey – every Sunday morning from 9 a.m. until noon. Would you mind if I put you forward?' I said, 'Of course not. I'd be very grateful.'

I'd been quite disappointed when LBC pulled the plug on *Weekend Matters*, for the simple reason that I was no longer having a laugh with the likes of Doris from East Finchley, and so when *Dig It* came along and I got the job, I was as pleased as Punch. They have five gardening experts in all and we each take it in turns to do the show.

The man who presents *Dig It* is called Joe Talbot and from the very first show I did with him we had a rapport going. That first show was absolute chaos by the way and for the first half-hour I didn't answer a single gardening question.

'Our first caller this morning is Roger from Esher. You're live with Jim Buttress, Roger. What's your question?'

'That's not Jim Buttress,' he said. 'I'd recognize that voice anywhere. It's George Baker. I love that Inspector Wexford thing you do. I had no idea you were a gardener, though.'

Joe Talbot was laughing his head off.

'No, Roger, I can assure you it's not George Baker, it's definitely Jim Buttress.'

'Don't believe you.'

Anyway, after Roger hung up Joe introduced the next caller.

'Morning, Joe,' he said. 'That last bloke's got it all wrong. That's not George Baker. It's Ray Winstone. You're my daughter's favourite actor, Ray.'

As I said, this must have gone on for about half an hour and the last caller we had before I finally got to answer a question on gardening said, 'It takes a woman to get it right. I'd know that voice anywhere and he's one of my favourite actors of all time. Morning, Bob!' She thought I was Bob Hoskins.

We now have a bit of a reputation, Joe and I, and it has to be said that he spends the majority of the three hours taking the rise out of me; and I him! It's just constant, good-humoured banter.

When I started on the *Big Allotment Challenge* he became a flaming nightmare.

'Good morning, ladies and gentlemen, and welcome to this Sunday's edition of *Dig It*. Our guest this morning is the now internationally renowned television personality, Mr Jim Buttress. He's far too famous to speak to us personally, ladies and gentlemen, and so he's asked us to forward this week's questions on to his personal secretary.' Honestly, he was relentless!

As is often the way, I first found out about the *Big Allotment Challenge* through appearing on *Dig It*. Every week when Joe and I aren't taking the rise out of each other they'll run a separate item on the show just to break things up a bit. This might be a piece about a certain plant or a new garden that's opening. Anyway, one week, not long after I started, the piece they had was all about a new programme the BBC were launching called the *Big Allotment Challenge*. I think they had a producer on there or something and Joe was interviewing her about the show. I must admit I wasn't impressed when I first heard about it and I remember telling Joe as much once the interview was over. I said, 'How can you run an allotment once a week? That's just ridiculous.'

The following day I was due down at Lullingstone to help Tom, and as I was getting out of the car he came running over.

'Jimus! I'm so sorry,' he said. 'I was meant to have given you this email the last time you were here and I forgot.'

Now because of judging commitments and what have you I hadn't been to Tom's in a while and it turned out the original email had been sent weeks ago. It read something like:

> Dear Mr Hart Dyke,
>
> My production company are making a programme for the BBC called the *Big Allotment Challenge*. We've been trying to contact your head gardener for some time now but without success. We understand he doesn't have an agent so if you could kindly put us in touch with him we'd be most grateful. We'd like to speak with him on a matter of some urgency.

To cut a long story short, these people wanted to audition me for the programme I thought was absolutely ridiculous!

So I turned up at their offices on Tottenham Court Road and they asked if they could film me judging some fruit and veg. 'Sure, no problem,' I said. And so to make it as

authentic as possible one of their production people darted
down to Tesco or wherever and came back with some potatoes and onions. Ten minutes later I'm standing there going,
'Well, what you've got to watch out for with onions is a soft
bottom or a soft top. OK? Now normally you'd have them
tied up with a nice piece of raffia but more important than
that is how you present the exterior of the onion. Don't take
too much of the skin off because that'll give too many clues
to the judge . . .' I just pretended I was at East Grinstead
Horticultural Show or somewhere and I went through the
entire process.

'Very interesting, Jim,' they kept on saying.

After they'd finished with me I went on my way and just
forgot about it. I wasn't expecting to hear back from them
anyway. About five weeks later I got a call from this company
asking if they could audition me again. 'Not a problem,' I
said.

'What we'd like to do this time, Mr Buttress, is take you
down to the site where we'll be filming the show. We've
already appointed the flower judge and we've also appointed
a preserve judge.' That last bit foxed me a little, but this was
television and so it was all new to me.

Once we got down there I started looking round these
allotments they were building and straight away I began telling them what I thought was wrong. 'Well, for a start you've
got to get rid of these weeds,' I said. 'If these are all going to
be on TV they've got to be perfect.' I don't know if this was
what they were hoping for but a week or so later I got a call
saying they were offering me the job. I still wasn't really sure
about it, to be honest, but as it was something I'd never done
before I thought, why not?

Once everything was in place the production company
organized a night out for the entire cast and crew. It was a

bit of a 'getting to know you' session really. The person I hit it off with most was the flower judge, Jonathan Moseley. He was in the same situation as me really – i.e. he didn't know what the bloody hell he was doing – and so we stuck together and looked out for each other.

Right towards the end of the night one of the production assistants came up to me. 'Mr Buttress,' she said. 'I'm from the wardrobe department. I wonder if I could have a chat with you about your wardrobe.'

I said, 'It'll be a quick chat, love. It's brown, about six feet high and from memory was bought from MFI.'

'I actually meant your clothes, Mr Buttress. The head of wardrobe will need to come round and have a look at what you've got.'

Linda couldn't bear to be there when this person turned up and so she made herself scarce.

'I just don't want to see the look on their face when you open your wardrobe door,' she said.

She had a point. You didn't so much get to Narnia if you stepped into my wardrobe as 1970s Woolwich.

When this wardrobe mistress, who it has to be said was an absolute sweetheart, eventually turned up I took her upstairs so that she could witness the full horror of my crimes against clothing. Unbelievably she didn't wince once and we even managed to find something to wear on the show, namely, my wellies!

I'm not trying to make out that doing talks, judging shows and working with the likes of Tom is in any way roughing it, but once we started filming *Allotment Challenge* it was like another world. There were Winnebagos, make-up artists, hair stylists, costume people, personal assistants and chefs. It wasn't quite what I was used to but I certainly wasn't complaining.

Now as to what the contestants produced, that was obviously decided weeks before we started filming. I mean, I could hardly say, 'Today I'd like you to grow five perfect cabbages and five straight carrots,' could I? And do you know the question people ask me most about *Allotment Challenge*? 'Who grew the vegetables?' And I always tell them, it was the contestants. They all arrived at the allotments sometime in March and we didn't start filming until July. Once they'd planted out they spent as much time there as they possibly could and the production company filmed about three days of it. They dealt with all the pests and the disease and the damage. The only thing the production company did was have somebody water them occasionally. That's it, you see. It's not like the *Great British Bake Off*, where all you need are a few ingredients and an oven. Growing vegetables takes months of care and attention. Some of the contestants didn't live that far away from the allotments and so were able to pop in all the time, but as I said, apart from some watering, they did it all themselves.

We filmed at Mapledurham, an Elizabethan mansion in Oxfordshire that has also been used for things like *Midsomer Murders* and *Miss Marple*. At the back of the mansion there was a ramshackle and overgrown walled garden and when the researcher first saw it they must have thought, *perfect!* Nothing there had been touched for decades and it was just the right size for about nine plots. The owners of the property must have been chuffed to bits as not only would they be getting a fee, I should imagine, but they'd be getting their entire walled garden renovated free of charge. Everyone's a winner!

The main criticism we received from viewers when the show first started was that the allotments we had were far too manicured, but that's television. The truth is that if we'd started with something similar to what old Larry has up in Manchester for instance, we'd have spent the first two episodes weeding. This show was all about the produce, and so we had to use just a little bit of poetic licence.

As much as I appreciated the way the production company looked after us all I have to admit that I didn't always agree with their methods and ideas. You see I think they were just trying to create a gardening version of the *Great British Bake Off* – full of goodies, baddies and drama – and because of this the show was never allowed to develop its own identity. I'm not Paul Hollywood, Jonathan certainly isn't Mary Berry (she's far prettier) and Fern isn't Mel or Sue. More importantly though, as I've already mentioned, making a cake is very different from growing vegetables.

The first thing the producers tried to do was create a 'them and us' dynamic between the judges and the contestants. This I found out very early on one day when I was outside having a fag. I saw some of the contestants so I said 'Good morning', but instead of saying good morning back they just looked embarrassed. When I asked them what was up they said they'd been told by the producers that the only time they could ever speak to the judges was when they were on set and the cameras were rolling. In other words, speak when you're spoken to. It sounds like my old granddad.

Well, as you know, that's not me at all and so that regulation went out of the window immediately. Do they impose that on *Bake Off*? I doubt it.

The next morning I was called into the production office. They were all there, the director and the producers, and I thought, what the hell have I done wrong?

'Jim,' they said, 'we're not being funny but we're trying to create a "them and us" scenario here so we can't have any fraternization with the contestants. After all, you are Judge Dread.'

I said, 'Now wait a minute. I never gave you that title. That was a joke somebody made during Britain in Bloom. I'm anything but Judge Dread.'

'That leads us on to the other matter,' they said. 'We'd like you to beef things up a bit if you would.'

'How do you mean?'

'Less of the "never mind, I'm sure you'll do better next time" and more of the "that carrot wouldn't win bronze in a village show" type thing.'

'You can stop right there,' I said. 'If you want somebody to play a character for you there are literally thousands of out of work actors out there. I'll tell you what, I'll pull out of the show now and you can go and find one, OK?'

'There's no need to take it so personally, Jim.'

I had to disagree. The power and responsibility you have as a judge is enormous, whether that's on the *Big Allotment Challenge*, at the Chelsea Flower Show or at a little village somewhere, and in my opinion the most important thing you need to have is integrity. If you haven't got that you have no right to judge anybody on anything. They wanted me to compromise my integrity for the sake of entertainment but I just couldn't do it.

Look, I understand why they asked me. After all, in their business it's all about viewing figures and so they have to create a show that's going to appeal to as many people as possible. Perhaps I'm just a bit old-fashioned.

Anyway, let's lighten the mood a bit, shall we. Do you know, for the second series of the *Big Allotment Challenge* we had a 9 p.m. watershed – for a gardening show? And do you know why we had a 9 p.m. watershed? Innuendo.

During series one there'd been a couple of comments

such as, 'What I'm really looking for is a stiff and erect stem,' and the powers that be at the BBC thought it was a bit too much. I have to admit that when the first series was being aired I got ribbed every time I went into my local.

'Evening, Jimbo. Got your hands on anything ripe and juicy this week?'

Once again it was like a Carry On film.

Do you know the best thing to come out of the *Big Allotment Challenge*? My relationship with Jonathan Moseley. Jonathan never, ever stops smiling and we've been asked to appear at all kinds of shows together. It's a double-act, like me and Joe Talbot. We do Question Time sessions together and all sorts of things. He's a big talent.

But the thing that changes most when you're on TV is that people occasionally recognize you, and because this leads into one of my favourite and most recent stories I think it's the perfect way to finish the book.

At the end of the 2014 season at Lullingstone Castle Tom held his annual plant and craft fair. The purpose of this was to give us one last opportunity to make a few quid, after which Tom could go and spend it all getting lost and looking for orchids. Only joking! Seriously though, if you've never been to Lullingstone Castle, go.

Now as you know I love young Tom to bits, but when it comes to things like organization he's about as much use as a bag of black carrots. Not a clue. Now bearing in mind we were expecting at least twenty-five to thirty stallholders on the morning of the fair, not to mention hundreds of cars later on, you might have thought Tom would have marked out the plots, allocated them and then arranged parking. Don't be daft. When we strolled down there after breakfast I said to him, 'Where are the stallholders going, Tom?'

'Well, I thought we could just let them sort it out for themselves.'

I said, 'You are joking? If you do that it will be absolute chaos.'

'Oh God,' he said. 'What are we going to do?'

'Right,' I said. 'Pass me that high-visibility jacket over there and go and get me a pen, a clipboard and some paper. They're going to be here soon.'

Fortunately by the time the stallholders started arriving I'd made a plan of where each one could go and so generally things went without a hitch. As they were all trundling through the gates one of them went up to Tom.

'Excuse me,' she said, pointing over to me. 'That car park attendant over there. The one with the high-visibility jacket. Isn't he one of the judges from the *Big Allotment Challenge*?'

'That's right, madam, yes he is.'

'Oh dear,' she said. 'Look at the poor old thing. Like most actors I suppose he's out of work at the moment.'